"There has long been need of a broad interpretation of American Catholicism, which would place its major men and movements in the context of both the United States and Roman Catholicism . . . THE CATHOLIC EXPERIENCE is a provocative and illuminating study of American Catholicism from the late Colonial period to the present . . . Here then is a lucid swift-moving account of how contemporary American Catholicism 'got that way.' "   Chicago *Sun-Times*

"Father Andrew M. Greeley's THE CATHOLIC EXPERIENCE is an important book—fascinating, provocative, and, to borrow a word from Bishop James Shannon's Foreword, 'disturbing.' Not a scholarly treatise which will earn a prominent place in permanent libraries, nor a study which could pass without question by some adversely cited, it is a challenging survey which could well be a catalyst for today's American Catholic community. As such, THE CATHOLIC EXPERIENCE should take high priority on anyone's list of books to be read."
The Tablet

"The interpretation is valuable because it brings the insights of a liberal of the present to the men and events of the American Catholic past, and also because it is a pioneer attempt in the interpretation of American Catholic history . . . All in all, Greeley has produced an informative introduction to American Catholic history for beginners and a thought-provoking interpretation for those with more background."   *America*

"Any book that tells something more of 'the story of American Catholicism,' to use Maynard's phrase, is something to be welcomed . . . Altogether, if this is not exactly the book you wanted, you can be excited, informed, and inspired by the book you have. It will leave its mark."   *The Pilot*

Other Books by Andrew M. Greeley

AND YOUNG MEN SHALL SEE VISIONS
THE CHANGING CATHOLIC COLLEGE
THE CHURCH AND THE SUBURBS
A FUTURE TO HOPE IN
THE HESITANT PILGRIM*
LETTERS TO NANCY*
RELIGION AND CAREER
STRANGERS IN THE HOUSE*
THE UNCERTAIN TRUMPET
THE EDUCATION OF CATHOLIC AMERICANS**
(with Peter H. Rossi)

* Available in Image Books
** Available in Anchor Books

THE
CATHOLIC
EXPERIENCE

AN INTERPRETATION OF
THE HISTORY OF AMERICAN CATHOLICISM

Andrew M. Greeley

IMAGE BOOKS

A DIVISION OF DOUBLEDAY & COMPANY, INC.
GARDEN CITY, NEW YORK

Image Books edition 1969
by special arrangement with Doubleday & Company, Inc.

Image Books edition published March 1969

For the Caseys
—Jim and Snarf—
and their future in the Catholic Experience
in the United States

CONTENTS

FOREWORD

The Catholic Church in the United States is a complex phenomenon. Its ethnic variety, its European heritage, its frontier mutations, and its regional variations have eluded or exceeded the analytical powers of many of its chroniclers.

European Catholics, often hankering for a return of the monarchy and the bliss of being the sole "established" church, have regularly contended that the church in the United States is too American, or too democratic, or too pluralistic, and not sufficiently Catholic. Proponents of this view enjoyed their finest hour in 1898 when their alarms persuaded Pope Leo XIII to condemn the phantom "Heresy of Americanism" in his carefully worded letter *Testem benevolentiae*. The passage of time and the vigor of American Catholicism have done much to allay these fears.

At the other end of the spectrum the Catholic Church in the United States has regularly defended itself at home against precisely the opposite charge, namely, the vague Protestant suspicion that it is too Catholic and too Roman and not sufficiently American. John F. Kennedy and a welcome new ecumenical spirit have gone far to lay these dark fears to rest.

Within the field marked by these conflicting opinions Father Andrew M. Greeley has written this sociological interpretation of American Catholic thought and growth. His large organizing hypothesis holds that from the earliest days of this republic the progressive "Americanizers" (John Carroll, John England, John Ireland, John Keane, John Spalding, John Kennedy, John Egan, and John XXIII) have won the verbal and intellectual battles and lost the real wars of power and control to the conservative "anti-Americanizers."

Father Greeley feels that the story of American Catholicism has been told by professional historians in bits and pieces but not in large terms which give these parts their meaning and proper relationship. The hypothesis of this book offers one large meaningful pattern for organizing and understanding a variety of currents, often conflicting, in American Catholic history.

It is a most readable book, refreshing in its candor and directness. Father Greeley makes no attempt to be the disinterested chronicler. His sharply phrased and frequently free-swinging opinions brighten every chapter.

It is a good book. If the author burns strong incense to Chicago's "Whiz Kids" he is not the only one in the American Church to do so. But it is a stimulating and helpful book as it proposes a new way of looking at the church in America. The deep concern of its author for the church today shows on every page.

It is a disturbing book. It conclusions are ominous. I predict that it will make a significant contribution to the current wideranging discussion of renewal in the church. A book like this helps focus a discussion which is currently in danger of becoming polemical and prejudiced rather than reasonable and open to new evidence and fresh insights. It is a welcome and serious scholarly work by a competent and professional sociologist.

✠JAMES P. SHANNON
Auxiliary Bishop of St. Paul-Minneapolis

INTRODUCTION

The present volume is to be considered an essay toward the sociological interpretation of the history of the Catholic Church in the United States. The principal reason for attempting such a mammoth task is that it needs to be done. As I have tried in recent years to understand and interpret the present condition of the American Church, it has become increasingly obvious to me that the present cannot be understood without knowing the past. Even if one chooses to reject the past as meaningless and a mistake (after some commentators on contemporary American Catholicism), it is still necessary to have a clear notion of precisely what one is rejecting. As I started to delve into the rather meager literature on the history of the American Church, two points became obvious: (1) While there are some excellent monographs in American Catholic history, there does not exist any single volume which attempts to tie the themes and threads of the last two hundred years of the Church in this country together into a unified interpretation. (2) Far from lacking impressive traditions, the American Catholic Church has a history filled with great men and profound ideas. Much of what the church universal has come to accept in the renewal of the Second Vatican Council was anticipated for at least one hundred years in the lives and teaching of the giants of the American Church.

Then it occurred to me that the general ignorance of this

history both on the part of rank-and-file Catholics and on the part of those claiming to be intellectuals is astonishing. Only a handful of scholars are engaged in attempting to analyze the history of American Catholicism and a good number of these are saddled with heavy administrative responsibilities. No more than four or five American Catholic universities have a chair of American Church history. If those who wish to destroy most of the structure of the American Church and rebuild it along a Dutch or French or German model can ignore the greatness of the American Catholic tradition, it is largely because the tradition has been ignored by the Church itself.

The absence of self-consciousness in American Catholicism, in itself a social and historical phenomenon, was probably occasioned by the pall cast on American Catholicism by the Americanism and Modernism controversies of the turn of the century. It is time the pall be lifted.

It is therefore indispensable that we begin to attempt to understand the American Catholic experience and that some Catholic scholars turn their talents to social historical interpretation. If one is convinced that such a work must be done and sees no one doing it, one is strongly tempted to begin oneself. As this book will make clear, I have not resisted the temptation.

I am under no illusion that the present volume represents anything more than a beginning, but it does seem to me that someone must begin, someone must attempt to organize around a series of themes the phenomena which make up the history of the American Church—themes which will give coherence and systematic meaning to the varied past out of which we come. It is more than just the expected modesty from the author which leads me to say that I am quite sure that more refined and polished interpretations will be necessary as the years go on. But such interpretations will not appear unless relatively unrefined interpretations appear first. In an age of dialogue, I would claim that this volume begins the dialogue on the meaning of the American Catholic phenomenon.

As the first paragraph of this chapter indicated, the present volume is an attempt at a *sociological* interpretation of the

American Church. Social interpretations need not, of course, be done by sociologists, but this particular one is in fact being done by someone with sociological training. The perspective of my own training will be that from which I view the American Catholic phenomenon. The development of the American Church will be seen primarily as an acculturation process and the major themes of American Catholic history will be described as a working out of a conscious conflict over the nature and pace of this acculturation, as a battle between two groups that I will call for want of better names the Americanizers and the anti-Americanizers.

It should be noted that this volume is not and does not pretend to be a comprehensive history of the American Church. It is rather a systematic treatment of major themes, a presentation of "the big picture" with the necessary elimination of much detail. I can claim to be nothing more than an amateur historian. I have read the literature of American Catholic history but have done no original research. I trust that there are few inaccuracies or misunderstandings in the text of the work. But if historians find me in error on matters of detail, I will cheerfully admit their correction. I will have to be persuaded, however, that my errors of detail are immense before I will be prepared to change my interpretation of the phenomenon I am attempting to describe.

Any *interpretation,* if it is an honest one, acknowledges that it proceeds from the point of view of its author and that its validity as an interpretation depends on the utility of the point of view for providing systematic explanations of that which is being described. It should be obvious that others can and will interpret American Catholicism differently than I have. I can only plead that my interpretation must ultimately be judged not on any individual judgments I may make (for example, while sharing his great admiration for Cardinal Gibbons, I find myself disagreeing with Monsignor John Tracy Ellis on the Gibbons personality; thus I think his failure to support his friends Keane and O'Connell and his failure to react more vigorously to the phony condemnation of the phony Americanism heresy did great harm to the American Church), but rather on the utility of the whole model for understanding and ordering the many complex elements which make up American Catholic history and on the usefulness of this interpretation to stir up others to similar and more refined works of interpretation.

I shall not hesitate to make my own point of view explicit nor will I attempt to conceal my sympathy with the Americanizers in their two-century battle against the anti-Americanizers, nor will I hesitate to offer my opinion on controversial matters; thus I will make it perfectly clear that the Americanism controversy and the condemnation of a heresy which did not exist by the unfortunate encyclical of Leo XIII was disaster both for American Catholicism and for the whole Church. I surely expect that people will disagree with my opinions, but an interpretation is a work of opinion and must be judged on whether as a system of opinions it's useful as a model to examine reality.

The sociologist who attempts to fashion an interpretation of the phenomena of American Catholic history labors under a number of serious disadvantages. Since his raw material must come from the publications of historians, he is limited by both the quality and the quantity of historical material available. There is much quantity in American Catholic history but rather less quality. Many of the publications are "official" and edifying but hardly very informative. Among those that have been produced by competent scholars there remains a tendency to be gentle with the hierarchy of the past and even on occasion to obscure controversial material (as we will note in the chapter on the Americanists, the full story on Lancaster Spalding has yet to be told).

In addition, most of the better works are concerned with the Church as structure; diocesan histories and biographies of hierarchs abound, but histories of the ministry of the Church to its people are virtually nonexistent. Hence the sociological interpreter is forced in the present state of the data to limit his efforts to a consideration of the Church as official structure and can say very little about the development of American Catholics as a branch of the Church as "people of God." He is also virtually forced to weave his interpretative essays around the major personalities of the various eras of Catholic history in the United States since the available data are so closely tied to biographies of these great figures (a necessity which from the viewpoint of reader interest may not be so unfortunate). It is therefore extremely difficult to search out major historic movements which transcend the personalities that grew out of these movements.

Nor have I found myself able to say much in the present essays about the religious orders. I have no doubt that they have made an extremely important contribution to the American Catholic experience but this contribution is simply not recorded in comprehensive scholarly works—save for an occasional impressive volume such as Colman Barry's history of St. John's Abbey. Most biographies of the religious founders in his country may be excellent hagiography (though I doubt it) but they are of no help to the sociological interpreter of history.

Finally, for all practical purposes the written history of the American Church comes to an end with the death of Gibbons. Contemporary ecclesiastical history is almost nonexistent—for a number of reasons, not the least of which is the lack of historians, particularly those who are brave enough to venture into the thorny controversies which have raged in more recent years. Hence the last three essays in this volume are forced to deal with material much different from those used in the first five.

It is surely not my intention to criticize the little band of historians of American Catholicism; they have done first-rate work under very adverse circumstances. I simply lament that there have not been more of them. Perhaps as American Catholicism grows more self-conscious there will emerge new historians who will do battle with the huge amounts of source materials which must abound. The Catholic Church in the United States has a fascinating history and one is forced to suspect that much of the story remains to be told. Until it is told, however, the sociological interpreter must make do with what material he has available since it is only the secondary sources of the historians that can provide him with his primary sources. Some readers may object to the absence of the *apparatus* of footnotes and to the popular style of the essays in this volume. They are of course perfectly free to object. But they should not conclude that the interpretation presented is not meant seriously. The standard histories provide all the bibliographic references that are required and there seems no reason to duplicate them.

The book was prepared in odd hours of "free time" when I was on the staff of the National Opinion Research Center at the University of Chicago. I am grateful to the two directors of the Center, Peter Rossi and Norman Bradburn, for encouraging it. I am also especially grateful to Daniel Herr for suggesting the idea of the book and pushing the suggestion with his usual gentle charm. Various parts have been read by Philip Gleason, Eugene Kennedy, Michael Schiltz, John Hotchkin, John Egan, and William Quinn, whose suggestions have proved quite helpful. I am also grateful to Bishop James Shannon for consenting to write the foreword.

ANDREW M. GREELEY

Chicago
March 12, 1967

THE
CATHOLIC
EXPERIENCE

I

BASIC THEMES

The overwhelming fact about American Catholicism is that like all other Christian religions in the United States, it is a religion of immigrants. However, the Catholic immigration reached its flood tide after the establishment of the American republic as a basically Anglo-Saxon Protestant society. Thus, Catholicism was not only an immigrant religion but an immigrant religion coming into a culture which, for a number of historical reasons, was antipathetic to Catholicism. Therefore, this particular immigrant religion was faced with the dilemma of becoming American enough to survive in the new society and remaining Catholic enough to maintain its allegiance to the world-wide Roman Catholic faith.

The basic theme of this work will be that American Catholicism has been for two centuries caught in an ambivalence about the society of which it has become a part. One strong strain of thought, dating all the way back to John Carroll, the first bishop of the United States, has argued that far from having to fear American society and American culture, the Catholic Church ought rather to rejoice in it because American institutions provide a situation in which Catholicism can grow and flourish as it has nowhere else in the world. From this point of view, there are no dangers in dialogue with American democracy but only opportunity. The Catholic Church need not fear to become as American as possible and to adapt

American democratic institutions and mentality to its own ecclesiastical structure. In such a viewpoint Catholicism in the United States must become as completely American as it can as quickly as it possibly can and then proclaim the benefits of cooperation with a society believing in human freedom and political democracy to the rest of the Catholic Church.

The anti-Americanizing tradition is much less sanguine about American society and culture. It is conscious that Catholicism is a minority group in a country which is unfriendly to it. It is aware of the immensity of non-Catholic religious bigotry and the threat to the faith of Catholics, particularly Catholic immigrants, in this unfriendly society. Catholicism must be viewed as a subculture having values which are distinctively different from the values of the larger society and it must be wary of permitting its values to be corrupted by the materialism, secularism, paganism of the society in which it finds itself. The good will and sincerity of non-Catholics is not to be presumed until it is established. And the Church's role in American life is not to become thoroughly integrated into it but rather to stand apart from it and condemn those evils which it sees all around it (without any attempt to engage in dialogue with those who seem to be practicing the evils). Only such vigorous and forthright denunciation of the evils of American culture will protect the faith of Catholics from being corrupted by the immorality of the world in which they live. While the Americanizers do not see the possibility that by becoming thoroughly American the Church would become any less Catholic, the anti-Americanizers are conscious of this problem and fearful that the more the Church compromises with American institutions and American culture the less Catholic it will become.

In theory, the Americanizers have carried the day. Insofar as American Catholicism has any heroes at all, these heroes (Carroll, England, and Gibbons) are surely Americanizers. Just as historians in the United States point out that the liberal tradition in this country is the older tradition and that authentic conservatism consists essentially of conserving this liberal tradition, so the Americanizing tradition within the Church has on its side both seniority and the approbation of being the "official" position. But while the Americanizers have carried the day in theory and there are few if any American Catholics today who would explicitly espouse the anti-Americanizing position, in practice the victory of the Americanizers has been anything but complete. Ecclesiastical policy as distinguished from ecclesiastical theory has frequently been of the anti-Americanizing variety.

Thus the battle between the Americanizers and the anti-Americanizers continues to rage, though as we shall suggest in the chapter on John Kennedy, the question has become largely academic as far as the lay Catholic population goes. Indeed, if the clergy and the hierarchy of the United States do not finally and definitively end the dialogue in favor of the Americanizers, it would seem to the present author that American Catholicism is in for difficult times in the years to come. But it should be noted that during the years of great immigration much could be said for the anti-Americanizing position. The relative success of the truculent Archbishop John Hughes in defending his flock from nativist violence as opposed to the abject failure of the gentle and open-minded Archbishop Francis Patrick Kenrick would indicate that at least on pragmatic grounds the anti-Americanizing strategy may have been the necessary one under some circumstances and at some times. However, as we will conclude at the end of this volume, even on pragmatic grounds it no longer has much to be said for it.

The distinction between the Americanizers and the anti-Americanizers in some instances is hard to make. Thus Archbishop Ambrose Maréchal was the legitimate heir of the aristocratic tradition of the native American Church begun by John Carroll; and Maréchal's constant foe, John England, was a migrant from Ireland who did not hesitate to pontificate on the American situation with little regard for the niceties of the Carroll tradition. Yet we will contend that Carroll and England were Americanizers and Maréchal was not. Similarly, the hot-tempered Bernard McQuaid of Rochester was one of the "liberals" at the First Vatican Council, but history has deservedly ranked him as one of the "conservative" villains of the Americanism controversy. (McQuaid was a difficult man, given on occasion to saying very nasty and vindictive things, but there was a certain violent integrity about him which makes him far more admirable than some of his contemporaries, including his friend and metropolitan, Archbishop Michael Corrigan of New York.)

Furthermore, John Hughes of New York was by no one's standards a moderate, and hardly an exemplar of ecumenical attitudes, but his loyalty to the United States was above question and his willingness to serve as an emissary abroad for President Lincoln leaves no doubt as to the sincerity of his Americanism. Hughes's attitudes and behavior indicated an accommodation that would become typical in the years that followed. Churchmen could follow a rather narrow and anti-Americanizing policy both in the internal organization of the Church and in day-to-day contact with non-Catholics while at the same time they would be fervently loyal to the American government and to the American democratic processes as long as these processes were at work outside the Church and not inside it.

But while it may be difficult at times to say exactly who was an Americanizer and who was not, the struggle over which of these two options ought to be followed has been the single most important theme of American Catholic history.

It should be noted too that in many respects the anti-Americanizing theme reflected the style and the posture of the universal church during the eighteenth, nineteenth, and twentieth centuries much more accurately than did the style and the posture of the Americanizers. Catholicism was still in the midst of the deep freeze of the Counter Reformation, fighting for its life and feeling acutely suspicious of the contemporary world and all its pomps and works. A narrow, suspicious, defensive, and reactionary mentality was far more typical of the churchmen during these years than was the opposite. We can well imagine the shock to European Catholicism when John Ireland with his fiery rhetoric and imperious manner appeared on the scene announcing that the rest of the Catholic world ought to look to America for guidance in solving its problems—which often seems to have meant that the universal church should look to John Ireland for guidance. (For all his faults, they could have done worse.)

Ireland and the other Americanizing missionaries to Europe were ahead of their time, but the good spirit of John Ireland must have smiled (and given his personality, it may have been a none too gentle smile) when Pope John condemned the prophets of doom at the opening of the Vatican Council and predicted a new era for the Church of friendly dialogue with the modern world. John Ireland would have enjoyed Vatican II immensely.

Within this overriding theme of conflict between the Americanizers and the anti-Americanizers, certain other themes must be identified. First of all, American Catholicism was consistently and conscientiously loyal to Rome. Even under the most severe provocations there was never any reason for the slightest doubt about the orthodoxy and the fidelity of the American Church (which is not to say that Roman officials did not doubt). The most liberal of the liberals, Carroll, England, and John Keane, were, when the chips were down, the most loyal and obedient sons that the Roman Church could possibly have asked for. But along with this loyalty there was both an insistence on the legitimate independence of the American Church and an impatience with the lack of sympathy and understanding so often encountered in Rome. American Catholicism was ready to do what it was told but only after it had made its own position as clear as it possibly could, and often with grave dissatisfaction over the way Rome had reacted to a problem. Thus John Carroll insisted on the need for full episcopal powers if he was to govern the new Church in a proper fashion, and was most displeased when severe limitations were imposed on these powers. It probably did not help Carroll's peace of mind—though it certainly improved his administrative position—when these limitations were removed and it was explained to him that the limitations resulted not from any intent on Rome's part but rather from a transcribing mistake made by a clerk in the Roman Curia.

These misunderstandings and confusions continued at least until after the First World War when Bishops Joseph Schrembs and Peter Muldoon had to fight desperately to

preserve their National Catholic Welfare Conference from
Roman interdiction because the Curia feared that the NCWC
would be the first step in some sort of separate American
Church (a suspicion which surely seems laughable at the
present time). One suspects that the spirits of Schrembs and
Muldoon are also amused at the emphasis on the establish-
ment of national hierarchies in the documents of the Second
Vatican Council.

It is difficult to be an American Catholic and not grow angry as one reads of the constant mistakes and misunderstandings of the Roman Curia in dealing with the American
Church. (We are told that the United States occupied a file
in the offices of the Congregation for the Propagation of the
Faith jointly with the Canary Islands.) But such impatience
would not in the final analysis be justified. Given the organizational structure of the Catholic Church in the century before
the Second Vatican Council, such misunderstandings were inevitable. Roman officials simply could not be expected to understand the nature of the American phenomenon, and its
peculiarities must have been a constant trial and torment to
them. Americans might be highly incensed when Bishop John
Keane was advised by Roman officials to be careful in his
public statements lest he offend European Catholic sensibilities.
But on the other hand, if we attempt to see things from the
viewpoint of the Roman officials, Keane must have seemed a
strange, peculiar, and quite possibly dangerous man with his
flashing personality and his fiery rhetoric.[1]

One does not know for certain whether these tensions
came to an end in 1920; but since there are virtually no historical documents covering the relationships of the American
hierarchy with Rome since 1920, it is very difficult for the
scholar to describe the relationships since the founding of the
NCWC. But certainly there is a widespread popular impression that neither has the loyalty of the American Church

[1] This is not to say that the way Rome treated Keane was just or
charitable or Christian; even given the justifications for the lack of
understanding, Keane deserved much better treatment than he received, as we shall note in the chapter on the Americanist controversy.

faltered nor have the misunderstandings and frictions been eliminated.

Secondly, American Catholicism has almost never wavered in its loyalty to the American government. From John Carroll trying vainly to persuade the French Canadians to join the revolutionary cause to Cardinal Spellman preaching victory in Vietnam, there is a completely unbroken history of intense and quite explicit patriotism. At times this patriotism has seemed too intense and too unquestioning to the minds of critics both inside and outside the Church. The reason for the unquestioned patriotism probably was that the most serious attack that the nativists launched against American Catholicism argued that it was impossible to simultaneously be a good Catholic and a good American. Patriotism and at times superpatriotism were an almost inevitable reaction to these charges.[2] Even those bishops who would be the most un-American in their own personal governmental styles never doubted in the slightest the rightness of American political democracy as a governmental system. In this context, one can understand the peculiar ambivalence of the American Church about political involvement of the clergy and hierarchy. Only one priest, Father Gabriel Richard of Detroit, ever sat in the United States Congress. Clergy do not seek public offices and are forbidden to endorse candidates *from*

[2] Dorothy Dohen has recently interpreted the Americanism of the hierarchy as an unquestioning nationalism which was blind to all faults of American foreign policy. Such an interpretation is hard to reconcile with some historical data, but even if it were completely true it would not be the whole truth. Miss Dohen refuses persistently to see that the patriotism of the Church leaders of the nineteenth century was part of their conviction that the freedom and democracy of the American republic constituted not only the most impressive polity that man had ever put together but also provided an atmosphere for the Church more favorable than any it had ever known. Given the circumstances of the nineteenth century, it is not surprising that this conviction could lead to attitudes toward foreign policy that might seem naïve in our day. But the nationalism of the American Church cannot be understood except as part of what at least to the present writer seems a legitimate admiration of American democracy. See Dorothy Dohen, *Nationalism and American Catholicism* (New York: Sheed & Ward, 1967).

the pulpit (unlike many Protestant ministers who feel no compunctions about partisan politicking on Sunday morning). Early bishops such as John Hughes even thought it was inappropriate for them to vote in an election since this might be interpreted as a form of political activity unbecoming a cleric. But while direct intervention in party politics has happened only very rarely (and almost always unsuccessfully), it would be less than true to say that the clergy, particularly the Irish clergy, stayed out of politics. They frequently sought political office for their friends and did not bother to keep secret their close friendships for certain political leaders. John Ireland, for example, made no secret of his friendship with the Republican party and particularly with Theodore Roosevelt. Cardinal Gibbons was a confidant of a whole string of Presidents even though his own political preferences were a closely guarded secret. On the local level some of this informal alliance between ecclesiastical leaders and political leaders could be attributed to common ancestry and common religion and common concern for protecting the rights of Catholic immigrants. From the viewpoint of the political leaders, of course, the churchmen were important civic personages whose help and assistance were imperative in accomplishing civic goals. It is difficult to see how church leaders could have possibly avoided some sort of political involvement, though not all the involvement was either wise or beneficial to the long-run good of the Church.

The Catholic Church has officially stayed out of politics, but unofficially there are a number of churchmen who have been up to their necks in politics. Obviously such involvement is not merely limited to Catholic clerics; given the rather unusual nature of American society, in which no religion is established but all religions are unofficially if not officially encouraged, such involvements are probably inevitable. In any case, to say that Catholicism was not established in the United States is surely true but it is not the whole truth. While it was not the established Church, neither was it a Church without influence or power. Liberals and conservatives might disagree on exactly how the power was to be used but there is little

trace in the history of American Catholicism of explicit refusal to have anything to do with the political order, refusal
which at least in theory might have been more appropriate.
John Carroll showed the way for this paradox as he did for so
many other developments in American Catholicism. While he
observed to the Continental Congress that there were many
good reasons why a man of religion should not become involved in political activity, he nonetheless did go on the Congress's mission to Quebec.

Thirdly, it is extremely important to emphasize that American Catholicism was at no time after 1820 an aristocratic
religion. The early native American Church of John Carroll
and his successors was governed by the colonial aristocracy of
Maryland, which was thoroughly American and thoroughly
part of the early American establishment. While by European
standards, the Carrolls may not have been aristocrats, by
American standards they were. However, the vast majority of
the bishops and priests of later years were men of the people.
There was a caste distinction between clergy and laity, but
this distinction was not re-enforced—as it was so often in
Europe—by a social class distinction. Whatever conflicts and
friction may have developed between clergy and laity did not
assume the terrifying dimensions of the social class struggle in
Europe, where the clergy readily became identified with the
ancien régime.

Hence, American Catholicism has been free until very recently from the doctrinaire anticlericalism which has plagued
the Church in Europe, and has been able to avoid substantial
loss among its working-class membership. On the other hand,
it would be a mistake to exaggerate the matter of the closeness
between the clergy and people. Priests and bishops were men
of the people, but only within their own ethnic groups, and
there was considerable conflict across ethnic lines when the
clergy or hierarchy represented one ethnic group and the laity
in a given parish or diocese represented another group. This
ethnic conflict between clergy and laity has not led to any
major apostasy in the American Church though it has given
rise to a considerable number of schisms, some of which still

persist (of which the most prominent is the Polish-American National Church). Catholicism has been something less than skillful in resolving the problem of ethnic conflict among its members, and the strong trend toward Americanization pushed by the liberal wing of the Church has only served to exacerbate the ethnic difficulties. Nor have these difficulties vanished even at the present time.

Fourthly, American Catholicism has benefited considerably from the general religious atmosphere of American society. It would be beyond the scope of the present volume to delve deeply into the question of why organized religion has prospered so much more in the United States than it has in other Western industrial countries. The absence of an established church, the lack of conflict between an aristocratic church and an industrial working class, and the voluntary approach to non-public organizations in American society surely have all contributed their part to the maintenance of organized religion in a society which is officially neutral toward specific religions and indeed toward religion in general (up to a point). In addition, religion has been most useful as a means of social identification both for "old stock" Protestants as well as for the newer ethnic immigrant groups. An immigrant would identify himself as an Irish Catholic or a Swedish Lutheran because he needed some sort of identification in the new society and because the new society persisted in defining him in such fashion. American discrimination against religious ethnic groups was strong enough to forge a bond of unity within these groups and yet not strong enough to impose serious disadvantages on members of the group which would lead them to apostatize in order to achieve social mobility. Hence, there is every reason to suppose that the bitter anti-Catholicism of the various nativistic movements of the nineteenth and twentieth centuries actually reinforced the strength of the Catholic Church in American society rather than weakened it. If Catholics were denounced by devout American Protestants, they would respond by being devout American Catholics and eventually by proving to the Protestants that they were better Americans than the Protestants were. In an avowedly and consciously religious society, the prejudices and discriminations which Catholics experienced provided a cement which held the American Church together.

Fifthly, American Catholicism has set great store in its educational systems. Education was important to all Americans, and Catholics were no different from other Americans in viewing education as a solution to most social and religious ills. In addition, however, to the normal American faith in education, Catholics had a faith of their own, particularly those Catholics of Irish origin who viewed the state-supported schools in Ireland as an attempt on the part of the British government to weaken and destroy the Roman Catholic faith in young people. The Irish clergy and hierarchy that came to this country took it for granted that the faith of young Catholics would be in serious danger unless it was protected in an explicitly Catholic school system. Just as their ancestors in Ireland had been forced to establish "hedge schools" to resist Protestant influence in the state-supported schools, so the Irish-American clergy and people would form their own separate school system to protect the faith of their children and to deepen the religious fervor of the immigrants as they became part of American society. John Carroll, who had to go abroad to get a Catholic education, himself founded a college, a seminary, and an academy for girls, and virtually every bishop who has succeeded him has put Catholic education near the top of the list of priorities for his administration. There would be attempts on the part of some episcopal leaders to work out an accommodation with the public school system. John Hughes's notion of accommodation was state support for Catholic schools, but nativist sentiment in New York in the 1840s would not hear of such an arrangement. A half century later, John Ireland in the Faribault plan attempted to turn several Catholic schools over to the state on an experimental basis with religion being taught in the schools after the regular class hours. After a bitter battle, Ireland won Rome's toleration for the Faribault plan, but nothing could win the toleration of the nativist opponents of such an experiment and the Faribault plan was eventually abandoned not because of Roman but because of American Protestant opposition. Just as most Catholic bishops and priests

(and lay people too, for that matter) assumed as almost unquestionable the notion that a separate Catholic school system
was essential for the survival of the faith in the United States,
so American Protestants viewed the separate school system as
the worst offense (along with clerical celibacy) of the alien
Church which had come into its midst. Hence the schools not
only have been an important part of American Catholicism
from the very beginning, they have also been an important
subject of controversy between American Catholics and non-
Catholics. Furthermore, there have always been a number of
American Catholics, lay and clerical, who have had grave
reservations about whether a separate school system was a
necessary or prudent adaptation to American problems.

Sixthly, there has been a long tradition of "collegiality"
among the American bishops and priests, even though the
word was not used until after the Second Vatican Council.
Carroll summoned a meeting of his fellow priests in the
country even before the establishment of the American hierarchy to devise ways of arranging the legal ownership for
Jesuit property after the suppression of the Society of Jesus.
The provincial and plenary councils of Baltimore in the nineteenth century represent an unbroken tradition of group government within the American Church which cannot be
matched anywhere in the world. John England in the 1820s
insisted most vehemently (without impressing Ambrose
Maréchal one whit) that the problems of the American
Church required the bishops to live up to Rome's injunctions
for triennial meetings. When Maréchal wouldn't listen to his
suggestions, England applied pressure in Rome to see that
these meetings took place and was rewarded for his troubles
by having all his suggestions politely ignored when the bishops
did assemble. Later on in the century, after the Third Council
of Baltimore, the American archbishops and later the whole
American hierarchy met on a yearly basis; and with the
foundation of a National Catholic Welfare Conference after
the First World War, the annual bishops' meeting became an
integral part of the NCWC organization. Hence the recent
establishment of a canonical national hierarchy (and a con-
sequent revision of the NCWC into the U. S. Catholic Con-

ference) as a result of the Second Vatican Council represents but one new step in a long tradition of consensual government by American bishops.

Seventhly, there is also a tradition in the American Church of election of bishops. Carroll himself was elected (at his own insistence) by his fellow priests, and his two coadjutors, Lawrence Graessl and Leonard Neale, were also elected. In later years, Rome's choice of bishops was usually based on recommendations made by elections of the bishops of the province or the archbishops of the country. However, the leaders of the American Church were frequently concerned with bringing more grass-roots participation into the selection of episcopal nominees. Martin John Spalding was particularly interested in this subject but it was only under Gibbons' leadership at the Third Council of Baltimore that irremovable directors and diocesan consultors of a diocese were given the right to submit a "terna," a list of three names, to Rome when a see fell vacant, a "terna" which was matched by that of the bishops of the province or the archbishops of the country (the latter if the vacant see was an archepiscopacy). This privilege was abrogated in 1916, apparently because of the difficulty of keeping the results of the diocesan election secret. However, at their first national meeting, the newly reorganized national hierarchy of the United States in 1966 set up a commission to investigate ways to provide both the priests and laity of the diocese with a share in the nomination of new bishops. While the tradition of popular participation in the selection of bishops has frequently been a muted one in the United States, the tradition is still there and it seems very likely—to the present writer, at least—that it will grow much stronger and more insistent in the years immediately to come.

Eighthly, the American Church, as befits a church in a "land of plenty," has always been optimistic and expansionist. Although there is a long history of financial mistakes and in the years since the Depression considerable evidence of financial conservatism in certain quarters in the American Church, optimism about the future and expectation of rapid expansion has been a hallmark both of the conservative and liberal traditions in American Catholicism. (The conservatives do not doubt expansion; they simply are a little bit more cautious in their expectations of how rapidly it will occur.) It was not long after the establishment of the first diocese in Baltimore that Carroll began to think of the division of his diocese into yet other dioceses; and the growth of bishoprics, parishes, schools, hospitals, universities, and every other conceivable kind of church structure has proceeded at a frantic pace ever since. In some cases, the expansion may have been too rapid (as, for example, the rather premature establishment of an archdiocese in Oregon City in the first half of the nineteenth century). Financial and personal risks may have been taken which even the most optimistic would find hard to justify. Nonetheless, the faith in growth and expansion was typical of American society, and by and large did not betray the American Church. Much of the growth was pragmatic and little of it was based either on theory or careful planning. As a matter of fact, the American Church has eschewed research and planning long after other institutions in the United States have become convinced that research and planning are absolutely essential before organizational expansion is attempted. The lack of any theory around which to organize and focus growth has been a handicap to American Catholicism and it becomes more of a handicap with each passing year. On the other hand, the blatant pragmatism which has characterized much of the American Church since the beginning, has left that church open to experimentation and flexibility. While very few innovations can be credited to carefully-thought-out theories, neither have there been very many experiments vetoed on the ground that they were opposed to ecclesiastical traditions. The leaders of the American Church have apparently made most of the decisions after asking two questions: Do we need this particular development? and Will it work if we try it? Hence, like Topsy, American Catholicism "just grew." If it has been generally open and experimental in its approach, it has also been completely lacking in self-consciousness (although the Americanists of the last part of the nineteenth century tried mightily to develop some self-consciousness before they were unceremoniously slapped down by their American enemies, and, to put the matter charitably, by uninformed Roman officials).

Another somewhat negative element in the pragmatic and flexible approach to the American Church is that it has been infected by the American notion that new buildings and new organizations more or less automatically will produce qualitative improvements in human life. The American Church has been a building church and it has dotted the landscape with more buildings than any other national manifestation of Catholicism in the world. Construction does not necessarily impede the growth and development of the human spirit and the religious fervor, but it does not necessarily guarantee them either; and it is to be feared that at times at least during its history American Catholicism seemed to act on the assumption that construction of buildings and development of the faith were virtually one and the same thing.

Finally, there has been a general conviction through two hundred years of American Catholic history that the American environment was good for the Catholic Church. Even the conservatives who felt that it was necessary constantly to be on guard against the corrupting influences of this environment and that there was a considerable danger in becoming too Americanized, nevertheless were prepared to admit that if sufficient care was maintained the religious freedom in American society provided an extremely healthy environment for the prosperous development of the faith. While some of the Americanists at the close of the nineteenth century argued that such religious freedom was a good thing in theory as well as in practice, and while most American Catholics have always believed this, it was not until the writings of John Courtney Murray began to appear in the 1940s and 1950s that American Catholic theologians seriously argued in favor of religious freedom. And even Father Murray encountered vigorous and at times violent opposition from members of the faculty of the Catholic University of America for this "novel" notion. Murray was even forbidden to attend the first session of the Vatican Council because of his "advanced" thinking on the subject (or as he himself put it, he was "disinvited" from the first session). Fortunately, American bishops insisted that Murray come to the later sessions of the council, where he became one of the grand architects of the conciliar document on religious freedom. Even the most conservative of the anti-Americanizing faction of the American hierarchy could cheerfully vote for such a document. But, as we have noted, the anti-Americanizers have in recent years been anti-Americanizers in practice but rarely in theory.

It should be noted in conclusion that "Americanization" frequently meant rather different things. For John Carroll it involved organizing the Church along lines that he thought appropriate in the American political environment. For others it meant putting aside Old World customs and language. For still others it meant the enthusiastic assumption of practically all the values and culture of American society. In later years it would come to mean great optimism about the possibility of massive conversions to the Catholic Church. For most it involved a support, theoretical or practical, of the separation of Church and state in the United States. A good number would interpret it to mean an openness and willingness to experiment with new methods and structures. By the end of the nineteenth century, the more enthusiastic of the Americanists saw great possibilities for cooperation with non-Catholic churches and schools. Unfortunately a number of those who claimed to be Americanizers acted as though it was essential for the good American Catholic to become an Irish-American Catholic.

In the course of this volume, we will attempt to specify which manifestation of the Americanizing tradition is under discussion. It ought to be remembered, however, that a common theme runs through most of the diverse elements in the tradition—an enthusiasm for the United States and the possibilities for Catholicism in the United States.

II

THE CARROLLS
First Bishop and "First Citizen"

If there is a special providence presiding over the destiny of American Catholicism, then that providence must have been keeping a close eye on the little town of Saint-Omer in France in the year 1748. For to that town had come two teen-aged boys, friends and distant cousins, who would together shape the beginnings of the Catholic Church in the as yet unborn American nation. One of them, Charles, became the richest man in the United States, a signer of the Declaration of Independence, a distinguished ally of George Washington through the Revolutionary War, a member of the United States Congress, and almost President of the United States. He would earn the title "First Citizen" from a political-religious controversy in which he used the name in an argument with another citizen who was called "second citizen," but later the title would come to indicate the position of dignity and respectability he had in the new republic toward whose foundation and development he had contributed so much of his time and energy. Through the long years of the nineteenth century when American Catholicism was largely the church of the poor and the working-class immigrant, Charles Carroll of Carrollton could be pointed to with pride as proof that the Catholic laity could be patriots and distinguished public servants.

The other cousin, "Jacky," was, if it be possible, an even

more distinguished figure than Charles. He would go on from
the College of Saint-Omer to the Jesuit seminary in Belgium
to be ordained, and serve for many years as a teacher in the
schools which the remnants of the English Jesuits maintained
on the Continent to educate the well-to-do sons of the English
and American Catholic families. When the Society of Jesus
was suppressed in 1773, he would return to the United States
after an absence of twenty-seven years at the age of forty with
his life's work in shambles. With the Society of Jesus suppressed and its educational vocation in Europe eliminated, it
would have appeared to John Carroll that there was nothing
left to do but to settle at his mother's home in Rock Creek,
Maryland, and play the role of parish priest for the Catholics
in the surrounding countryside. But in 1773, Carroll's life was
only half spent. In the remaining half he would shape American Catholicism and set it on its way down a path from which
it would rarely wander. If the Jesuits had not been suppressed
and John Carroll had not returned to Maryland, the story of
American Catholicism might have been quite different from
what it is.

The most important fact to be remembered about the
Carroll clan was that they were members of the aristocratic
colonial establishment. They may not have been quite full-
fledged members because their religion was to some extent
held against them. But the grandparents and the parents, and
the cousins and the uncles and the aunts of the Carrolls were
not prevented by their religion from becoming extremely
wealthy and active participants in the social and economic if
not the political life of the Maryland colony. One has the impression that their peers in the Maryland establishment were
quite willing to accept the Carrolls despite their religion and
then gradually be persuaded to give the Roman Catholic
Americans a chance at equal citizenship because no one in his
right mind could have questioned the patriotism of the Carrolls and their Catholic colleagues in Maryland.

Charles Carroll's first public involvement in politics began
as a spirited defense of the colonial cause against the royal
governor. It ended by a strange twist which he must have
rather enjoyed, with partial vindication of his religious beliefs.

Carroll, along with many of his friends and business associates, had been violently opposed to the Stamp Act and the Townshend Act and quite dissatisfied with Governor Robert Eaton, whom Lord Baltimore, the proprietor of Maryland, had sent to represent himself and the Crown in the colony. The Maryland Council passed a law substantially reducing the fees that government officials (and clergymen) could charge, but the governor dissolved the legislature and re-established the fees at the original price. The Marylanders, not liking taxes any more than any of the other colonists, began to engage in rebellious talk and express themselves in indignant publications though they were not yet ready to go as far as physical violence.

In January, 1773, the Maryland *Gazette* carried an unsigned dialogue between "First Citizen" and "Second Citizen." Second Citizen, defending the governor's position on the fees, ably presented the Royalist line, but First Citizen, who was a proponent of the patriot side, was permitted to be little bit more than a straw man. It was an open secret in Baltimore that the author of the article was one Daniel Dulany, an extremely talented lawyer and public official. Many colonists would have been willing to reply to him save for the fact that Dulany was such a master at rhetoric. However, a month later there appeared a second dialogue in which First Citizen was given more than an opportunity to defend himself. In fact, First Citizen remarked, "The sentiments of the first citizen are so visibly mangled and disfigured that he scarce can trace the smallest likeness between those which really fell from him in the course of the conversation and what has been put in his mouth. Since much depends on the manner of relating facts, the first citizen thinks he ought to be permitted to relate them in his own way." First Citizen then proceeded to devastate Second Citizen's argumentation. Dulany was quite upset by the audacity of his opponent and began to write a series of letters to the *Gazette* under the new pen name of Antilon. To these letters there came equally frequent replies from First Citizen. Under these assumed names, the Carroll-Dulany feud (which apparently had gone back several generations) raged for some months with Carroll slowly emerging as the more skilled contestant. Finally, Dulany made the mistake of letting his invective carry away his temper and turned from the arguments about the disputed taxation to a personal attack on Carroll and on his religion. He wrote: "After all who is this man that calls himself a citizen . . . who is he . . . he is disabled from giving a vote in the choice of representatives *on account of his principles* which are *distrusted* by those laws. He is disabled by an express resolve in interfering in the election of members [of the legislature] *on the same account.* He is not a Protestant."

Carroll of course was delighted and immediately wrote of his outrage and shock that Antilon would be so desperate in the argument that he would presume to attack a man for his religious beliefs. Apparently the outrage was widespread especially among those whose political opinions First Citizen was expressing, because Antilon gave up the controversy after one more letter and Carroll's party won an overwhelming victory in the council election. After having won the election, the anti-governor party filled the Maryland *Gazette* with letters of public tribute to First Citizen for defending their cause. By 1774, when the time had come for Maryland to set up Committees of Correspondence, one of the five committee members selected from Annapolis was Charles Carroll of Carrollton. Shortly thereafter, he was asked to serve as a delegate to the First Continental Congress. But Charles Carroll of Carrollton displayed the shrewdness which was to mark the rest of his career as well as that of his ecclesiastical cousin. He declined the appointment, arguing that his religion might serve as an impediment to his representing Maryland and chose rather to attend the meeting at Philadelphia as an unofficial representative. He hurried back from the Continental Congress to participate in Maryland's version of the Boston Tea Party —the burning of the ship *Peggy Stewart.*

By this time, Carroll's acceptance into the political as well as the social establishment was almost complete. He was elected and re-elected to the various colonial patriotic committees—the Committee of Observation, the Committee of Safety, the Committee of Correspondence—and finally to the Second Continental Congress, where he would become one

of the signers of the Declaration of Independence. But before
he would affix his name to that historic document, he and his
cousin Jacky, now a middle-aged ex-Jesuit returned from
Europe, would embark on one of the strangest missions of the
whole revolutionary conflict.

That Charles Carroll of Carrollton would be on the patriots'
side was not at all difficult to understand. He was a member
precisely of that merchant and landowning class which was
suffering the most from the British taxation and would be the
most likely to benefit from political and economic independence. But his cousin's position was something else again. John
Carroll had been away from America for all of his adult life
and had been in touch with American political developments
only through intermittent mail whose arrival was both de-
layed and problematic. (There were times when a whole year
would go by without any letters from his family getting
through to him.) His years in the Jesuits and traveling through
the European Catholic countries might have been presumed
to dispose him toward assuming if not a conservative at least
a Royalist position. But apparently it did not take him long
after he returned to Maryland to size up the politics of the
conflict between England and the colonies, and to make up his
mind on which side he belonged. In fact, one of the reasons
for his settling at his mother's home in Rock Creek rather
than at an established parish was that Carroll was extremely
reluctant to accept the authority of Father John Lewis, superior of the Maryland mission, and the Vicar-General of the
Bishop of London, who had ultimate authority over Catholicism in the colonies. Carroll was of no mind to associate
himself publicly with ecclesiastical authority that resided in
England. Thus when the peculiar request came for the Continental Congress for him to go on the ill-conceived mission to
Quebec, there was no doubt in anyone's mind that Carroll was
a man that could be trusted.

Why the Continental Congress thought it could win the
Catholics of Canada to the colonists' side is difficult for us to
understand in retrospect. The reaction of the colonies to the
Quebec Act giving religious freedom to Canadian Catholics
ought to have left no doubt in the mind of Bishop Briand and

his faithful about what the colonies thought of Roman Catholicism. Nonetheless, the Congress decided that such a flip-flop
was at least worth a try and the committee was put together
in early 1776 to visit Quebec and attempt to persuade the
Canadians that the Protestants to the south had undergone a
conversion. Benjamin Franklin was the obvious choice since
his diplomatic skills at making black look gray were well
known to all; and Samuel Chase of Maryland, since he had a
number of Catholic friends, seemed also to be a sound choice.
In the finest tradition of a "balanced ticket," which would
mark later American politics, a Catholic was added—the respected and trustworthy Charles Carroll of Carrollton. Then
someone, apparently Charles Lee, got a really bright idea. In
a letter to Hancock, Lee observed: "I should think that if
some Jesuit or religious of any other order (but he must be a
man of liberal sentiments, in large mind and a manifest friend
of civil liberty) could be found out and sent to Canada he
would be worth battalions to us. This thought struck me some
time ago and I am pleased to find from the conversation with
Mr. Price and his fellow travelers that the thought was far
from a wild one. Mr. Carroll has a relative who exactly
follows the description."

One wonders whether the good Protestants of the Continental Congress felt a bit squeamish at swallowing this notion;
but in any case, the Congress resolved on February 15, 1776,
"that Mr. Carroll be requested to prevail on Mr. John Carroll
to accompany the committee to Canada." John Carroll was
not terribly enthused about the appointment since he was not
at all convinced that the Canadians could be budged from
their position. Also, he was reluctant as a priest to become
involved in such overtly political activity. As he noted in his
reply to the Congress, "I have observed that when the
ministers of religion leave the duties of their profession to take
a busy part in political matters they generally fall into contempt and sometimes even bring discredit to the cause in
whose service they are engaged." Exactly where Carroll did
observe this, he doesn't say, but it would be most interesting to
know what experiences he had in Europe that led him to this
rather wise conclusion. Nonetheless he accepted the mission

and he and his cousin along with Chase and Franklin set out
for Canada. There their reception was not exactly overwhelming and Bishop Briand's reaction to the Maryland priest was,
if anything, more frigid than the Canadian winter. Abandon-
ing their unsuccessful mission, the commissioners returned to
the United States with John Carroll traveling with the sick
and discouraged Franklin and supervising that aged gentleman's deteriorating health. Franklin was considerably impressed with the patient and resourceful Catholic priest and
did not hesitate to tell his friends that if it had not been for
Mr. Carroll's ministrations he doubted if he would have survived the ordeal. Some ten years later, Franklin would repay
the favor (in a manner of speaking) by enthusiastically promoting the name of his friend John Carroll to be the first
Catholic bishop in the United States.

After the Canadian fiasco, John Carroll returned to Rock
Creek to continue his parochial ministrations. Charles Carroll
stayed in Baltimore, where he would serve both in the Maryland legislature and the national Congress through the rest of
the war.

Charles Carroll was elected officially to the Continental
Congress only after the Declaration of Independence had
been voted on on July 4. Nonetheless he arrived in time for
the formal signing of the document on the second day of
August. There was no one among the signers who risked more
in the way of financial loss since even at this time Charles
Carroll was one of the richest men in the United States if not
the very richest. Carroll managed to shuttle back and forth
between Philadelphia and Baltimore, serving both in the
Maryland State Senate and as a member of the Board of War
of the Continental Congress. He didn't have much of an opinion in Congress and much preferred service to his own state.
Nonetheless his presence on the war board enabled Carroll
to defend his good friend and business associate George
Washington from the plots of the so-called Conway Cabal to
replace Washington as the commander of the Continental
Army with either Horatio Gates or Charles Lee. Washington's
opponents managed to take control of the Board of War in
November, 1777, with Gates as president and Conway as

inspector general. Carroll served on the committee that Congress sent to investigate the situation of Washington's army at Valley Forge, helped turn the tide of the conspiracy in Washington's favor, and obtained support for him in the difficult winter. The picture of Charles Carroll visiting Washington in winter at Valley Forge and supporting the general against his disreputable opponents is not likely to be blotted out of the American Catholic conscience for a long time to come.

Carroll's services to the Congress were so impressive that in 1778 he was offered the presidency of the Continental Congress, which in some fashion nearly would have made him the chief executive of the revolutionary cause. But Carroll was not a particularly ambitious man, didn't think much of the Continental Congress, and hence he declined the offer and resigned from the Congress to return to serve in the Maryland legislature.

In the years afterward, Carroll became a stanch Federalist and bemoaned the weakness of the central government under the Articles of Confederation. He was elected to the Constitutional Convention but again declined to serve since he felt his presence in Maryland was more important. However, the Carroll clan was by no means unrepresented at the Constitutional Convention. Daniel Carroll, the younger brother of John Carroll, saw that the family name was affixed not merely to the Declaration of Independence but also to the Constitution of the new republic. The Maryland legislature would not permit Charles Carroll to stay out of national politics, and he was elected the first United States senator from Maryland and was on the committee that received George Washington (with whom he had been engaged in several business ventures since the end of the war) when the first President arrived in New York for his inauguration. Among his other services in New York (the national capital at the time), Carroll served on the committee on titles, where he managed to sidetrack the quaint notion that the President of the United States ought to be known as "His Highness" or "His High Mightiness." Carroll wanted him to be called simply the President but was willing to compromise on "His Excellency." Presumably in whatever section of the hereafter Carroll now resides, he is pleased by the fact that history permitted his suggestion to win. But even in this life, it must have given him a great deal of pleasure to vote on the First Amendment to the Constitution, which bestowed religious freedom finally and definitively on his coreligionists in the United States.

Carroll later resigned from the U. S. Senate to return to take up his seat in the Maryland Senate, which he always considered to be more important. It was from this position in 1792 that in a little-known interlude in American political history Carroll was almost summoned back to the national capital to become the second President of the United States.[1] Washington had not been an unqualified success as President and didn't particularly like the job. The Federalists were not eager to engage in an election campaign against Thomas Jefferson and were quite certain that if Washington did not run such a campaign would occur. Hence the suggestion was made to Alexander Hamilton that Charles Carroll might be the kind of candidate who could rally national support that was sufficient to guarantee victory over Jefferson. Hamilton wrote that if Washington should choose not to run, then he would have given his unqualified support to Carroll. Carroll's biographers suggest that if Washington had not run and if Hamilton had supported Carroll, he would have certainly received the Federalist nomination, in which case he probably would have been able to defeat Jefferson, who was defeated four years later by the much less popular John Adams. However, there was every reason to expect that Charles Carroll would have refused this nomination too. Carroll was through with national politics and had returned to Maryland to live to an advanced old age, dying in 1832 at the age of ninety-five. He was revered in the last years of his life not only as "First Citizen" but also as "the last of the signers." Charles Carroll was not at least by contemporary standards a devout Catholic; all of his children married non-Catholics; and apparently very few of his grandchildren, if any, were reared Catholics. But

[1] The details of this incident are reported in Allen Hart Smith's *Charles Carroll of Carrollton* (Cambridge, Mass.: Harvard University Press, 1942), p. 245.

in an age such as our own when it is claimed that the layman is at last emerging, it is worth-while to note that Charles Carroll of Carrollton had emerged even before the founding of the republic. His influence on American Catholic history must be deemed great, if indirect. Perhaps Catholicism would have acquired respectability in the new nation in some other fashion had it not been for the life of Charles Carroll, but he in fact was the one who persuaded his fellow Americans that it was possible to be a sincere practicing Roman Catholic and at the same time an unquestioned patriot. The "First Citizen" was also the first Catholic.

It was an extraordinarily helpful thing for the Church that its first bishop in the United States was a member of the Carroll clan and hence part of the Maryland establishment. If Protestant Americans were somewhat reluctant to accept John Carroll as head of the Roman Catholic Church, they would at least accept him as a Carroll and eventually exercise some toleration toward the Church because John Carroll was its leader. Thus in 1790 when John Carroll made a journey to Boston, the Boston *Herald of Freedom* had these comments to make about him: "As a preacher, his talents were admired; as a companion, his society was sought; as a man, he was esteemed, revered, and honoured. The narrow prejudices entertained by the ignorant or the illiberal, vanished from the radiance of his candour, and shrunk from the test of his piety. Under his auspices, even the prejudiced view with more favorable eyes, a religion which he so truly adorned . . . Boston would congratulate the hour of this Gentleman's return, and will remember with gratitude and pleasure, his visit to the State."

Obviously there were other factors at work in obtaining religious toleration for Catholics in the United States besides the personality of the first bishop. But his personality and his family connections were undoubtedly of considerable importance. If it was not the only cause of the spirit of toleration, Carroll's behavior must have accelerated the pace of acceptance of Roman Catholics. The Canadians had been greatly skeptical when Carroll had predicted to them at the time of his mission in 1776 that the emerging nation would grant religious freedom to all its citizens particularly if it was allied with a Catholic country during the war. The Canadians could see nothing in the behavior of either the Continental Congress or the American people which would justify such a prediction, but Carroll knew Americans extraordinarily well and three years after his Canadian mission he was able to write to his former Jesuit friend, Charles Plowden in Rome, "You inquire how congress intends to treat the Catholics in this country. To this I must answer you that congress has no authority or jurisdiction relative to the internal government or concerns of the particular states of the Union. These are all settled by the . . . states themselves. I am glad, however, to inform you that the fullest and largest system of toleration is adopted in almost all the American states; public protection and encouragement are extended alike to all denominations, and Roman Catholics are members of congress, assemblies, and hold civil and military posts as well as others." Having said these things to Plowden, Carroll couldn't resist making another point, and he added, "I'm heartily glad to see the same policy being adopted in England and Ireland and I cannot help thinking you are indebted to America for this piece of service." About all Plowden could have possibly replied was "Touché."

The change in the space of less than a decade from Catholics being under civil disability in all the colonies to the measure of toleration Carroll described to complete religious freedom in the new nation in another decade was a rapid and dramatic one. And the behavior of the Maryland Catholics, particularly the Carrolls, if it was not directly responsible for the legal change, at least enabled the small American Church (less than 1 per cent of the population of three million) to obtain social acceptance as rapidly as it had obtained legal acceptance. Thus when John Carroll wrote to George Washington congratulating him on becoming the first President of the new republic, Washington did not have to puzzle over who this obscure man was, who, representing such a small proportion of the population, dared to write such an elaborate letter. Washington knew full well who he was. Mr. Carroll was Charles Carroll's cousin and a gentleman and more than a gentleman—he was also a patriot and along with his friends and relatives in Maryland had served the patriot cause well. Washington's reply was every bit as gracious as Carroll's congratulations. When he replied, "I presume that your fellow citizens will not forget the patriotic part which you took in the accomplishment of the revolution and the establishment of our government of the important assistance they received from a nation in which the Roman Catholic faith is professed," he was not merely being courteous but simply speaking the truth.

The Carrolls were landowners and businessmen, men of sense and property and organizational skill. Charles Carroll helped organize the army during the Revolutionary War and John Carroll organized the property holdings of the ex-Jesuits and later the hierarchy of the American Church. They were calm, confident, competent men who took leadership positions for granted and whose self-assurance was so immense that no one dared question it. There seems to have been no criticism at all when John Carroll from his Rock Creek headquarters began the attempts to establish a Body of the Clergy to hold the corporate property of the suppressed American Jesuits. He was not the superior of the former Jesuits but neither the superior nor any of the others seemed to have minded Carroll's interventions. One imagines that Carroll himself would have been shocked beyond belief if anyone had objected. At no time in the life of either himself or his cousin does anyone seem to have seriously questioned the Carroll clan's right to command. Even the lay trustees who were to give John Carroll so much trouble in the years of his episcopacy seemed always to be just a little bit in awe of him.

Thus while the early American Church was small and suffered acute shortages of churches and clergy, it was thoroughly American and possessed an elite and aristocratic leadership which would compare favorably with any other of the churches in the colonies. As long as the Carrolls were around, American Catholics felt that they had nothing to be ashamed of and the question of acculturation of Catholicism to American life did not even arise. The Roman Catholic Church in the United States was American, as American as anything else, and Carroll's famous prayer for civil authorities could hardly have been written by a man who had the slightest sense of alienation in his personality. The Catholic Church of the Carrolls was a native American church presided over by leaders lay and clerical who yielded to no one in being respectable members of the American establishment.

A school of American historians has argued that the basic political tradition of the United States has been liberal; that is to say, the United States was a country that was "born free" and its basic political experience has been to conserve the liberalism with which it was founded. It can be argued analogously that in the United States Catholicism was born American and in its history has been essentially an effort to remain American while assimilating massive waves of immigrants. Catholics may well have had to be acculturated to American life but their church was American from the beginning. John Carroll had seen to that.

His basic principle in establishing the Church in this country was that it should be organized in the fashion most appropriate for the American environment. He was appointed vicar apostolic in 1794, and only five years later after much political maneuvering was Rome ready to establish a formal hierarchy in this country and appoint a bishop. Carroll, as a highly successful prefect apostolic, was absolutely certain to be selected. But he insisted to Rome that, given American beliefs and culture, it was appropriate that the American clergy elect their own first bishop and have this election confirmed by Rome. Carroll, of course, was too intelligent a man to think that there was any doubt that his colleagues would elect him but nonetheless insisted on an election. The first American bishop was elected by his fellow clergy with only two dissenting votes (presumably one was his own). Rome also permitted an election for Carroll's two coadjutors—Graessl, who died before the papers confirming his selection returned from Rome; and Neale, whose papers took five years to arrive in the United States. Despite the requests of Carroll and his fellow priests that this privilege of electing bishops be continued, Rome did not agree. Apparently there was no desire to concede to the priests of the new country such privileges, which already existed in some fashion or other in many

European nations. Rome was not about to let the Americans get out of control. In retrospect, this position seems most unfortunate, as did many other Roman decisions of the day concerning the American Church. Carroll's instincts were correct. The selection of bishops by the clergy (and one presumes eventually by the laity) would have been most appropriate in the American environment, would surely have increased the acceptance of the Catholic Church by other Americans, and probably would have in the long run produced a more distinguished hierarchy.

Church property in the new republic was not owned directly by the Church as it is today but rather by boards of lay trustees elected by the people of the parish. Carroll had no choice but to accept such a procedure since church organizations could not legally own property in the new states. But he also felt that this manner of holding property was more fitting in the United States than other forms of ownership. He was to be plagued later by this arrangement as schisms broke out in New York, Philadelphia, Charleston, and Norfolk over the control of church property, with lay trustees assuming the right to appoint pastors, and unstable and renegade clergymen conspiring to challenge the authority of Carroll in the appointment of the clergymen. In later years John Hughes, bishop of New York, was to criticize Carroll—though somewhat gently—for the system of lay trusteeship. But the idea was a basically sound one and worked well in most of the parishes. Unfortunately a careful study of the lay trustee system in the United States has not been done and most American Catholics know only of the abuses of the trustee system. Even today when lay participation in parish administration is discussed, it is frequently apt to be dismissed as a return to trusteeism—as though the very use of the word were enough to settle the controversy. Lay trustees are permitted by canon law, and the French-Canadian Church seems to prosper very well under such a system. It was a great historical misfortune that the few schisms which did occur in the United States prevented more experimentation with lay participation in church property administration in this country. Trustees were eventually abolished as bishops became fearful of the possibilities of even greater trouble. John England alone seemed to have devised a plan which would preserve the good aspects of the trustee system and eliminate the problems. But as we shall see in the next chapter, most of the American hierarchy were anything but willing to listen to John England.

Carroll's dealings with the government were also thoroughly American. He would congratulate public officials when they were elected, he would offer prayers for them, and he was friendly with them on a personal basis, but he would respect their pleas of having no competence in religious matters and would insist on this in his communications with Rome, where such a notion of the relationship between Church and state was almost inconceivable. He was a patriot and would support the War of 1812 even though his Federalist background certainly must have made him less than sympathetic with it. Support for the government was one thing, asking special favors was something else. Carroll must have known, of course, that he couldn't win any such favors since his church was so small, but he did not resent the fact that Catholicism could not become the established religion in the United States. One suspects that having experienced what established religion could do to the Church during his European travels Carroll's enthusiastic acceptance of the American situation was not only sincere but also expressed with something of a sigh of relief.

One of the more amazing aspects of his Americanism was his support for vernacular liturgy. In 1787 he observed:

I consider these two points as the greatest obstacles to Christians of other denominations to a thorough union with us, or at least to a much more general diffusion of our religion, particularly in N. America. . . . With respect to the latter point, I cannot help thinking that the alteration of the Church discipline ought not only to be solicited, but insisted upon as essential to the service of God and benefit of mankind. Can there be anything more preposterous than an unknown tongue; and in this country either for want of books or inability to read, the great part of our congregations must be utterly ignorant of the meaning and sense of the publick office of the Church. It may have been prudent, for aught

I know, to impose a compliance in this matter with the insulting and reproachful demands of the first reformers; but to continue the practice of the Latin liturgy in the present state of things must be owing either to chimerical fears of innovation or to indolence and inattention in the first pastors of the national Churches in not joining to solicit or indeed ordain this necessary alteration.

Such words are clearly very strong ones and it is interesting that it took Carroll's successors in the American hierarchy almost two hundred years to agree. But he would use even stronger words to describe the effects of the Latin liturgy in his country: "For I do indeed concede that one of the most popular prejudices against us is that our public prayers are unintelligible to our hearers. Many of the poor people and Negroes generally not being able to read have no technical help to confine their attention." It was not the time, however, for drastic liturgical reform. But Carroll would do what he could in the Agreement of 1810 signed by Carroll as archbishop and the suffragan bishops of the newly constituted dioceses. It was agreed that the sacraments would be administered in the vernacular with the exceptions of the essential "forms." Thus the first liturgical regulations in the United States conceded to American clergy the same privileges which were to be won again only with great difficulty in the *collectio rituum* of the 1950s and then to be taken away again until after the Vatican Council. One wonders what Carroll would have thought of the disgraceful episode of the *collectio rituum*.

Carroll was a firm believer in meetings of the clergy to establish some sort of uniform regulation for his sprawling church as well as to engage in joint deliberations about the problems the Church faced. He was instrumental in establishing the chapter meetings for the Select Body of the Clergy which replaced the Jesuits. He summoned the national synod in 1791 and had plans for a national council in 1812 (two years after his archbishopric came into existence), although his plans were frustrated by the War of 1812. Part of the desire to govern by consensus came from Carroll's own personality, part of it from the political and social culture of the country, and part of it from the sheer practical realization that in a missionary country like the United States, there wasn't any other way to govern.

Carroll left no doubt even as early as 1785 what he thought ought to be the policy in the American Church: "We desire that the faith in its integrity, due obedience towards the Apostolic See and perfect union should flourish; and at the same time that whatever can with safety to religion be granted, shall be conceded to American Catholics in ecclesiastical affairs. In this way, we hope that distrust of Protestants now full of suspicion will be diminished and that our affairs can be solidly established."

Carroll's thirty years as prefect apostolic and bishop were very difficult times for him, for it seems reasonably certain that he did not enjoy the job and all the discouragements it involved. But he had set out to establish Catholicism in the new nation and never relaxed his efforts. Schools were founded, religious orders were brought in, priests were recruited, dioceses were created, schisms were fought, laws were passed, and the size of the Catholic population grew at a fantastic rate. John Carroll, who had to go to Europe to receive his higher education, was determined that this should no longer be necessary in the United States, and the first love of his life was Georgetown College—later Georgetown University, in Washington, D.C.—which was founded in 1789 and which was always the object of his special attention. During Carroll's administration, a characteristic which was to mark Catholic higher education for its whole history began to appear: colleges were founded with great rapidity and went out of existence with almost as great rapidity. During Carroll's administration several were founded—St. Mary's of Baltimore, Mount St. Mary's of Emmitsburg, St. Thomas of Kentucky, and New York's Literary Institution. Only the two first mentioned of the five schools survived. In addition, Carroll founded a seminary, several academies for girls, and a number of parochial schools. His interest in education was so respected by the non-Catholics of Baltimore that he was selected to serve on the board of directors of Baltimore College and later was offered (but declined because of age) the office of provost of the University of Maryland. (Similarly, Father Gabriel Richard, a priest in Detroit, was the first vice-president of the University of Michigan.)

Carroll had proposed the founding of Georgetown in his original plan of organization in 1782 and never flagged in his devotion to the school, in spite of the opposition of many of his fellow ex-Jesuits, who feared that the construction of the college would in some fashion or other impede the eventual restoration of the Society, and although the lack of finances to keep the school running efficiently made it a considerable burden for Carroll for most of his episcopacy. Nor was he always happy with his presidents, at least two of whom (Neale and Molyneaux) were not nearly energetic enough for Carroll's taste. He was also troubled by Neale's approach to religious education. In a letter to Plowden in 1802, Carroll said, "Its president, my coadjutor, and his brother Francis . . . both of them as worthy men as live, deter parents from sending their sons thither by some rigorous regulations not calculated for the meridian of America. Their principles are too monastic and with a laudable view of excluding immorality, they deny that liberty which all here will lay claim to." Nor was Carroll particularly enthused about the notion of trying to isolate young men from the world in which they would live. He continued in his letter to Plowden, "Theory and experience are constantly at variance in this case; for tho the principles of religion and morality command or seem to command the Instructors of youth to restrain their pupils from almost every communication with the men and things of the world, yet that very restraint operates against the effects intended by it, and it is too often found, that on being delivered from it, young men, as when the pin that confined a spring is loosened, burst out of confinement into licentiousness, and give way to errors and vices, which with more acquaintance with the manners and language of the world, they would have avoided."

There are times when John Carroll's careful restraint and dignified eighteenth-century prose seems to be dealing with remarkably modern situations. The two paragraphs just quoted from his letters to Plowden could be applied without changing a single comma to a good deal of contemporary Catholic college education, to say nothing of seminary training.

Carroll was, in short, an American, about as thoroughly American as anybody could be. His philosophy about the Church in the United States was expressed to a Roman friend when he wrote that "toleration is a blessing and advantage which it is our duty to preserve and improve with the utmost prudence, by demeaning ourselves on all occasions as subjects zealously attached to our government and avoiding to give any jealousies on account of any dependence on foreign jurisdiction more than that which is essential to our religion, an acknowledgment of the Pope's spiritual supremacy over the whole Christian world."

But while Rome attempted to be sympathetic and helpful, it was often hard put to understand the American situation and puzzled by the behavior of the forthright and outspoken Americans. Peter Guilday, Carroll's biographer, in the midst of the description of the machinations that preceded Carroll's appointment as vicar apostolic, finally loses his temper and makes the following comment: "The interest in these early years was mainly political and financial, and from this date down to the first Provincial Council of Baltimore in 1829, no impartial reader will be able to accuse the Roman authorities of accurate knowledge of American Catholic affairs in general or of American conditions geographical and otherwise, in particular. The American clergy will be at the mercy of meddlers and at the mercy of badly informed chiefs in the Congregation to which they are obliged to look as to their superiors, until an Archbishop of Baltimore breaks the restraint the American clergy must have felt, and appeals directly to the Pope in a letter which lacks nothing in its indignation at the sad situation in which Roman curial ignorance had placed them."[2]

Unfortunately, the impartial reader of the history of American Catholicism is likely to make the same judgment on many other occasions.

---

[2] The archbishop here referred to is Archbishop Leonard Neale, Carroll's successor.

The situation that occasioned Guilday's outburst was a series of negotiations being carried on in Paris between the papal nuncio at Paris and Benjamin Franklin as to the leadership of the Catholic Church in a new country. While Franklin informed the nuncio in the name of Congress that the new country could take no official interest in the appointment of a bishop for the Catholic Church, he was able to also assure the nuncio unofficially that there would no longer be serious opposition to the appointment of a Catholic bishop (since an Anglican bishop had finally become acceptable) so long as any appearance of foreign domination was avoided. But it was a jerry-built ecclesiastical structure that Franklin and the nuncio had conceived. A French priest would be appointed vicar apostolic or bishop and would be in his turn subordinate to the papal nuncio to Paris. A French seminary would be set up to train priests for the United States. It is curious to speculate on how Benjamin Franklin could be so confused as to say that the United States was not officially interested in the leadership of the American Church but that unofficially Americans would welcome a leader who did not represent foreign domination, and at the same time engage in lengthy negotiations (which surely to some extent were official) on a plan that would establish foreign domination.

The whole story of this French intrigue is a complicated one and recent historians are inclined to exonerate the French hierarchy from undue interference in American affairs. It is more difficult to exonerate Franklin or the papal nuncio. However, Carroll's friends in Rome and England, particularly Charles Plowden, were highly incensed and wrote to Franklin protesting and wondering why it had not occurred to him to recommend his good friend John Carroll as the head of the American Church. As soon as the name of John Carroll was raised, Franklin became enthusiastic about his good friend and companion on the Canadian mission and the matter was very quickly settled with Carroll being appointed prefect apostolic in June of 1784. One wonders what went on in Franklin's mind. It is quite conceivable that this crafty old man had planned on Carroll all along but had been afraid to suggest him for fear that his suggestion of a native American by a representative of the American government would not be received favorably by papal officials. Hence, he bided his time, waited until someone else mentioned Carroll, and then jumped enthusiastically on the bandwagon. Of course, this is sheer speculation, but it is difficult to conceive that Benjamin Franklin could have acted as ineptly as the history books would have us believe he did in the matter of the appointment of the first American bishop.

Carroll was something less than wildly enthusiastic about the appointment when he received it. He did not like the severe limitations placed on the authority of a prefect apostolic by the document and was also quite dubious about the manner of the appointment, feeling strongly that the United States required a bishop and a bishop elected by the clergy of the country. It later turned out that the so-called "cramping clause," the clause that restricted Carroll's power as prefect apostolic, was not the intention of Rome but a mistake of a notary in the Curia who had used the wrong form letter to send Carroll his powers. This mistake must have caused Carroll some ironic laughter. But, as he wrote to Cardinal Antonelli in accepting the prefecture, there were other problems which troubled him. He did not think that either a prefect or a vicar apostolic was appropriate for the United States but that the new nation ought to have a bishop of its own "which will conduce more to the progress of Catholicity, which will contribute most to remove Protestant jealousy of foreign jurisdiction. I know with certainty that this fear will increase if they know that an ecclesiastic is so appointed as to be removable from office at the pleasure of the Sacred Congregation of Propaganda Fide or any other tribunal out of the country or that he has no power to admit any priest to exercise a sacred function unless that congregation has approved and sent him to us."

Nor was he satisfied with this quite blunt statement to the Holy See. He added, "As to the method of nominating a bishop, I will say no more for the present than this—that we are employing God in his wisdom and mercy to guide the judgment of the Holy See, that if He does not deem proper to allow the priests who have labored for so many years in this vineyard of the Lord to propose to the Holy See the one whom they deem the most fit, that some method will be adopted by which a bad feeling may not be excited among the people of this country, Catholics and Protestant."

It was a gentle and clever way of putting it but there was no doubt what Carroll meant. The United States needed a full-fledged bishop and a bishop selected by democratic process if American Catholicism was not going to make its beginning under very unfavorable circumstances. It took five years for Rome to agree but finally Carroll won completely.

However, this was not the end of his troubles with the Holy See. Scarcely two years after the formal establishment of the diocese of Baltimore, Carroll and his ecclesiastical colleagues became concerned about the condition of the diocese. It was still too big to be administered by one man, and Rome was petitioned to consider the matter of the division of the diocese or the appointment of a coadjutor. Obviously a division would make much more sense, but Rome, having established one diocese in the United States, was not terribly eager to immediately set up another one and advised Carroll rather to seek a coadjutor. It took eight years before complications of elections and communication permitted the installation of Leonard Neale as Carroll's coadjutor. In the interim, Lawrence Graessl was elected and confirmed by Rome but died before the papers of confirmation came. However, the letter confirming Graessl's appointment surely rates a high place in the list of masterpieces of confusion in the relationship between the Church in America and Rome. It was first of all addressed to Reverend Charles Carroll (if the lord of Carrollton ever heard of this, he must have howled with laughter). But there was worse to come. The letter said, "The Supreme Pontiff reserves full liberty to himself for the welfare of souls anytime it is demanded of dividing your very extended diocese into other episcopal dioceses even during your own lifetime and even should you be unreasonably opposed to such a step." Carroll was then adjured "never to put himself in opposition to the erection of new sees." These words must have seemed quite ironic to John Carroll who several years before had already suggested the division of the diocese.

It was not until 1808 that Baltimore was finally made an archdiocese and suffragan bishops were appointed—John Cheverus for Boston, Michael Egan for Philadelphia, Benedict Joseph Flaget for Bardstown, and Luke Concannen for New York. The first three were priests working in the United States while Concannen was an Irish Dominican of advanced years in Rome who was appointed without Carroll's knowledge or consent and who unfortunately did not live to come to the New World to assume his diocese. Concannen's successor was another Irish Dominican, John Connolly, who was also appointed without consultation with Carroll and indeed was made bishop of New York at a time when the United States was at war with England even though he, Connolly, was a British citizen. Prudently he did not come to the United States until after the war was over. Early Catholic historians were inclined to blame the Irish hierarchy and particularly Archbishop John Thomas Troy, the Dominican archbishop of Dublin, for interfering in American affairs in the appointments of Concannen and Connolly.

However, more recent research exonerates the Irish on this charge but does not exonerate them on the charge of attempting to promote the troublemaking Irish Dominican William Vincent Harold of Philadelphia to succeed Bishop Michael Egan of Philadelphia. Carroll had more than enough of Harold and his uncle James Harold, a secular priest. Both gentlemen had brilliant but erratic talents, and to turn a diocese over to one of them after the trouble they had created in the United States would have been disastrous. The Americans were highly incensed. Bishop Cheverus of Boston commented, "It is certainly astonishing that prelates and friends in Ireland should recommend subjects for the mission here and be listened to rather than you and those you are pleased to consult." Carroll wrote to his friend Plowden, "How any of these prelates could determine themselves to interfere in affairs so foreign to their concern and to which they are so incompetent is a matter of surprise. Intrigue must have been very active." And he wrote to the Archbishop of Dublin, "Would it not be resented as a very proper interference if the bishops of the United States should presume to suggest to the Holy See persons to be appointed to fill the vacant sees of Ireland?" And he added in a letter to Bishop Flaget, "It seems that several Irish bishops have interfered with a matter which concerns them not but I still hope that some copy of my dispatches to Rome have been at length received. It is still uncertain what will be the effect comparatively with that of the Irish prelates." The Harold appointment was prevented and for five more years after Carroll's death Philadelphia remained vacant until Bishop Henry Conwell arrived in December of 1820. Conwell quickly proved to be one of the most incompetent bishops America has ever been afflicted with.

Thus John Carroll's attempts to establish a loyal but independent American Church were not always crowned with complete success. He had to contend with inept American diplomats (Franklin), scheming Irish prelates, uninformed and ill-advised Roman curial officials, and perhaps conniving French clerics as well. It was by no means an easy war he had chosen to wage.

And the internal problems were immense. There were fewer than thirty priests—and many of them were quite advanced in years—when Carroll became superior of the American mission. There was little or no choice but to accept almost any European cleric who arrived on the scene with some kind of credentials. Some of these were dedicated missionaries but others were malcontents, misfits, alcoholics, and psychotics. When these kinds of clergy were combined with the communication problem, the vast territory of the Baltimore diocese, the uninformed laity, and the restless trustees, it becomes marvelous to observe that Carroll was in fact able to hold the American Church together through its first three decades. While this is not the place to detail all of Carroll's troubles, at least one more exotic character must be described—a Father de la Poterie, who arrived in Boston in 1789 and issued a pastoral letter which was described as "given in Boston, North America under our hand and seal of our arms, the twenty-second of February, signed La Poterie, Vice Prefect and Apostolic Missionary, Curate of the Holy Cross at Boston." He also announced that he was a doctor of divinity, prothonotary of the Holy Church, and apostolic vice prefect of Boston, none of which, incidentally, he was. Carroll's letters to Plowden on this situation give a good indication of the terribly awkward position he found himself in frequently with itinerant clerics:

Some time ago I was much pleased with the letters (which were written in the language of an apostle) of a French priest, who had wandered to Boston. I received several letters of strong recommendation, testimonials, &c., all which joined to his own sentiments of submission, induced me to grant him faculties for a short term. He proceeded with great rapidity to open divine service, introduced music, celebrated all the ceremonies of a cathedral, &c., and he proceeded to make some publications which soon convinced me of his imprudence. He soon after discovered himself to be an infamous character, his faculties are revoked, and he now proceeds to every abuse against me, as a Jesuit, aiming at nothing in my manoeuvrings, but to re-establish the order here, under the title of American clergy. It is singular enough that some of our own friends are blaming me for being too irresolute or indifferent, for not adopting their most intemperate counsels with respect to restoring the Society, whilst on the other hand Smyth, the Abbe, and others, are accusing me of sacrificing to this intention the good of religion. The Abbe has been at Rome, and pretends an acquaintance with Cardinal York, and other consequential characters there; he is exceeding insinuating, and as great a hypocrite in his letters as I ever knew. If he be only slightly known, he may impose, but I am sure that he has resided no where long, without betraying his infamy. I think he has lately discovered such knavery, that I should not wonder at his using the most iniquitous means of pursuing his resentment. Before his faculties were recalled, I directed him not to use, as he had done, public prayers for the king of France in the Sunday service, as is done for our own ruling powers, because a government jealous of its independence might construe it into an undue attachment of American Roman Catholics for a foreign prince. He at first acquiesced in the propriety of my direction, but he now says I forbade prayers for the king of France because the French expelled the Jesuits; and I think him capable of writing such falsehood to Europe, even to his ministry. His name is La Poterie.

Luckily the French corps diplomatique here are well acquainted with his character. Mr. Thayer will have much to do to repair the scandals committed by this man.

This letter to Plowden shows another one of Carroll's constant problems. As an ex-Jesuit, he was always suspected by the enemies of the order of being interested in restoring Jesuit power while his own former Jesuit confreres on the other hand felt that he was not nearly interested enough in working for the restoration of the Society.

It was a stormy, rocky thirty years during which Carroll directed the American Church and there were more problems and difficulties than there were successes. Guilday goes so far as to say that when Carroll died he felt he was a failure because his attempts to preserve the independence of the American Church had been frustrated by the intervention of the Irish hierarchy in the appointment of American bishops. However, Carroll was anything but a failure. John Gilmary Shea, the first historian of the American Church, summarizes Carroll's accomplishments in a rather flamboyant passage that is often quoted but deserves to be quoted once more:

When Archbishop Carroll resigned to the hands of his Maker his life and the office he had held for a quarter of a century, the Church, fifty years before so utterly unworthy of consideration to mere human eyes, had become a fully organized body instinct with life and hope throbbing with all the freedom of a new country. An archbishopric and four suffragan sees, another diocese beyond the Mississippi, with no endowments from princes or nobles, were steadily advancing: churches, institutions of learning and charity, all arising by the spontaneous offerings of those who in most cases were manfully struggling to secure a livelihood in modest competence. The diocese of Baltimore had theological seminaries, a novitiate and scholasticate, colleges, convents, academies, schools, a community devoted to education and works of mercy; the press was open to diffuse Catholic truth and refute false and perverted representations. In Pennsylvania there were priests and churches through the mountain districts to Pittsburgh; and all was ripe for needed institutions. In New York, Catholics were increasing west of Albany, and it had been shown that a college and an academy for girls would find ready support at the episcopal city, where a Cathedral had been commenced before the arrival of the long-expected Bishop. In New England the faith was steadily gaining under the wise rule of the pious and charitable Bishop Cheverus. In the West, the work of Badin and Nerinckx, seconded and extended by Bishop Flaget, was bearing its fruit. There was a seminary for priests, communities of Sisters were forming, and north of the Ohio the faith had been revived in the old French settlements, and Catholic immigrants from Europe were visited and encouraged. Louisiana had been confided to the zealous and active Bishop Du Bourg, destined to effect so much for the Church in this country. Catholicity had her churches and priests in all the large cities from Boston to Augusta and westward to St. Louis and New Orleans, with many in smaller towns, there being at least a hundred churches and as many priests exercising the ministry. Catholics were free; the days of penal laws had departed; professions were open to them, and in most States the avenue to all public offices.

The native American Church which John Carroll had founded, organized, and shaped for three decades had been, despite all the obstacles, shaped pretty much in his image and likeness. It was loyal to Rome but fiercely and independently American and its institutions were as American as Carroll could possibly make them. His position in the Maryland establishment enabled him to gain acceptance for Catholicism among influential public figures, and his unquestioned ability and zeal made it possible for him to obtain at least some kind of acceptance for *American* Catholicism in Rome. It was no mean feat. What sort of man was it who could accomplish this? A young man who knew him describes him:

I was too young when he came to reside here in 1786 to know much about him. It was somewhere between '95 and 1800 that I became intimate with him, from the kindness which he always showed to young people which won their affections. He was so mild and amiable and always cheerful, that we all took delight in his society. My father esteemed him highly, and I have often met him at his table, as well as those of most of the gentlemen in town. He had great conversational powers, derived from his extensive reading and his long stay abroad in England and on the continent. There were few subjects he was not master of. He enjoyed the pleasures of the table in moderation, and cheerful as he was, he never lost his dignity, but always commanded respect and attention without the slightest appearance of claiming either. It was impossible to treat him with disrespect or even levity, for he had spirit enough to resent any improper liberties taken with him and awed by his manner any approach to impertinence. . . . The Archbishop in fact was a thoroughbred, and a polished gentleman who put everybody at their ease in his company while delighting them with his conversation.[3]

Even after 150 years John Carroll still looks impressive. In many ways he still must be rated as the greatest of the American bishops. He did not have John England's brilliance and flair but he was able to gain acceptance for his ideas, which England rarely was. He did not have nearly so complex a church (or complex American society, for that matter) to cope with as did James Gibbons. But when the chips were down, Carroll demonstrated far more courage than Gibbons did. After the death of Charles Carroll of Carrollton, American Catholicism did not see his like again until the Kennedy clan arrived on the scene. But of Charles Carroll's cousin John, it seems safe to say that the American Church has yet to see his like.

[3] Peter Guilday, *Life and Times of John Carroll.*

III

JOHN ENGLAND
Super-American from County Cork

On the morning of December 28, 1820, the ship *Thomas Gelston* anchored in the port of Charleston, South Carolina. Standing on the deck as the ship worked its way up the channel were two young priests and a girl. One of the priests would be dead within the year and yellow fever would prevent the girl from seeing her twenty-eighth birthday, though in the seven years that remained to her, she would become the managing editor of the first Catholic newspaper in the United States. The other priest had twenty-two years of life ahead of him—twenty-two years in which he would shake the American Church as it had never been shaken before and has not been shaken since. John England, age thirty-four, the closest thing to an ecclesiastical genius that American Catholicism has ever seen, had arrived to take possession of his diocese. A few days later the Jesuit Father Fenwick, who had presided over Charleston awaiting the arrival of the new bishop, wrote to an anxious Archbishop Maréchal in Baltimore of the new bishop: "He will, I think, answer the place." These words may well go down as the biggest understatement in the Catholic history of the nineteenth century.

John England was an incredible man. To say that he was born ahead of his time would be to put the matter mildly indeed. He was probably even born ahead of our own time and one has the strong impression that England would be little more welcome in the American hierarchy of today than he was in 1820. He represented an option for American Catholicism, an option that was rejected. But even if the Catholicism of the first half of the nineteenth century would not listen to John England, he still stands as one of the mighty giants of the American Church; and the message he preached, this super-American from County Cork, rings out as loudly and clearly today as it did in Charleston in the 1820s.

The native American Church of John Carroll was in the process of being swamped by waves of immigrants, most of them Irish like John England. There was no question but that the American Church would become and remain for almost another 150 years, predominantly an immigrant church, indeed predominantly an Irish church. But there was question as to which aspect of the Irish personality would dominate this new immigrant church, whether the freedom-loving, open-minded, generous elements of the Celtic tradition would become characteristic or rather the narrow, defensive, militant, and angry aspects of the Irish soul would characterize the Church in the New World. It is to be feared that at least until the time of the Americanists toward the end of the century, Irish liberalism was not successful. However, John England stands as solid evidence that there was another option than the narrow defensiveness which characterized much of Catholicism from 1820 to 1880, that it was possible and would be possible once again to effect a marriage between the best traditions of the native American Church founded by John Carroll and the best traditions of the swarms of Irish immigrants. Even today, when many of the faults of American Catholicism are blamed on the militancy and the narrowness of the Irish, the voice of John England can still ring out and insist that there remains an alternative.

American Catholic Church history, as we have noted before, is not a well-developed, scholarly discipline, and it is difficult to find much in the way of conflicting theories as one goes through the literature. But there does at least exist a conflict over the years of the Church after the demise of John Carroll and before the Civil War. The so-called "Catholic University" school of historians presided over by Peter

Guilday and John Tracy Ellis seems to be inclined to the view that the successors of Carroll were not adequate to the tradition he began, and that the baton laid down by John Carroll was not picked up until John England arrived in Charleston. The "Notre Dame" school, led by the Reverend Thomas McAvoy, on the contrary, viewed Carroll's successors—Neale, Maréchal, Whitfield, and Eccleston—as not only the legal but also the existential successors to Carroll. McAvoy contends that the Guilday school ignores the existence of a cultivated, sophisticated Anglo-American Catholic minority and insists that the French bishops (mostly Sulpicians) who had come to the United States in the wake of the French Revolution were actually the defenders of the Anglo-American minority against an Irish invasion. He notes that the French Catholic clergymen were readily received by Anglo-American Catholics and even by non-Catholics because of their learning and culture. The sympathy of the French clergy was with the native Americans, with whom they generally associated and with whom they shared relatively the same social class, whereas the Irish, on the contrary, were generally antagonistic toward the English and had lost most of the traditions of Irish culture and lacked all social position. According to McAvoy, Maréchal and the other French looked upon the Irish as foreigners and a threat to the freedom and the dignity of the native American Church. Thus when Maréchal proposed Benedict Fenwick as bishop of Charleston, he was acting to protect the native American Catholicism from an Irish invasion.

The appointment of Irish bishops and the increasing number of Irish priests constituted in Maréchal's eyes the first threat of a foreign domination of the American Church. England, for all his talent and all his enthusiasm for the United States, was not as much a part of American Catholicism as the French-speaking Maréchal and the French Sulpicians of St. Mary's Seminary. They simply were not the social equals of the older English immigrants of the country. In this perspective, Maréchal's refusal to call a provincial council was a last desperate attempt to prevent the Irish led by John England from taking over the American Church and inundating it with

Irish Catholic immigrants whose cultural level was not as high as that of the Anglo-American group.

McAvoy goes on to rejoice that England's influence was checked at the various provincial councils of Baltimore and that the native American establishment continued to dominate the archdiocese of Baltimore and the Church for several more decades until finally, with the appointment of Francis Patrick Kenrick as Archbishop of Baltimore in 1851, the Irish ascendancy began. As McAvoy observes, there were

> some definite advantages and disadvantages in the composite American Catholic culture that was created before 1860. If the Anglo-American group led by Maréchal, Whitfield, and Eccleston, and later by Spalding, had retained the dominance over the Catholic minority, perhaps Catholic colleges and American Catholic literature English might have flourished more readily. Instead the energies of this smaller American group that might have developed into higher cultural reforms were absorbed in educating and absorbing a larger group which was without means and in great numbers had been deprived of education for generations. Likewise Catholics in politics might have even advanced more quickly in public office if they could have escaped the stigma of foreign culture which [in] confusion of religion and politics of this nativistic period was ascribed to all Catholics.

It is difficult to argue with this comment of McAvoy's but still one wonders how relevant it is. If there had not been waves of immigrants indeed the native American Church would have developed differently, but in point of fact there were waves of immigrants and the failure of the Maryland establishment to deal with these waves of immigrants made their downfall inevitable. The question was not in the final analysis between the Sulpician-dominated tradition of Baltimore and the wild, aggressive Americanism of John England. The sophisticated, cultivated, aristocratic Maryland Church was doomed in any event. The question was whether Irish-American Catholicism would follow the trail blazed by the liberal, imaginative, open-minded John England or would rather go down another path of narrowness, aggressiveness, and insecurity. It is hard, for the present writer, to escape the judgment that if the Anglo-French Church of Baltimore had spent more time worrying about the problems of the Irish immigrants and less time trying to fight John England, the latter option would not have been chosen.

American Catholicism had more than its share of problems in the years between the death of John Carroll and the beginning of the second half of the nineteenth century. At the root of the problem was the sheer overwhelming fact of physical growth. It is estimated that the Catholic population in 1790 was 35,000. By Carroll's death in 1815, it had increased to 90,000. By 1820 it was up to 160,000. Ten years later the Catholic population was estimated at well in excess of 600,000; and by 1840 the size had doubled once again with 1,300,000 Catholics within the borders of the United States. At Carroll's death, the Church structure consisted of the archdiocese of Baltimore and the dioceses of Bardstown, Boston, New York, and Philadelphia. Fifteen years later there were thirteen dioceses, and by 1838 there were fifteen dioceses, over four hundred clergymen, eleven seminaries, and fifteen colleges for young men. By the time of John England's death in 1842, there were 512 parishes, 545 priests, 24 colleges, 31 academies for girls, 72 charitable institutions, and a Catholic population moving rapidly toward the two million mark.

The doubling of a population every decade had been an immense problem in itself. But in addition the immigrants were not warmly welcomed in the American society. Many American Protestants who were quite capable of accepting, albeit on occasion reluctantly, the infinitesimal native American Church of John Carroll, were not at all sure they could tolerate such a fantastic growth in the Catholic population, and religious bigotry began to reach floodtide proportions. According to Ray Allen Billington, the objective and unbiased historian of nativism and Know-Nothingism, the Protestant crusade against Catholics began in 1820. The magazine *The Protestant,* published by George Bourne, began its attack on the papal menace in 1830, and in 1834 the first convent was burned by Protestant mobs. Punitive measures, legal and illegal, against Catholicism, were to rage until the Civil War temporarily brought them to a close; but in the meantime, churches and convents were burned, nuns were driven out of town, Catholics were killed, and books purporting to reveal the hidden secrets of convent life were best sellers. Anti-Catholicism was becoming a way of life for many Protestant churchmen and a not altogether unprofitable way of life either.

To make matters worse, internal problems of the Church grew more serious, with schism or near-schisms happening in New York, Philadelphia, Norfolk, and Charleston—schisms which were made more serious because in most instances they were on ethnic lines with French bishops and French priests at odds with Irish lay trustees and Irish clerics. Some of these latter were incredible troublemakers, with Fathers William Hogan in Philadelphia and Simon Felix Gallagher in Charleston being the worst of the lot. There wasn't much doubt that the very worst of the Irish clergy were being shipped off to the United States, where it was felt they wouldn't do much harm. The Irish malcontents were excellent symbols for the dissident laity to rally around with the claim (based on a misunderstanding of the ancient *jus patronatus*) that they who paid the pastor had the right to select him. They also furnished Archbishop Maréchal with the ideal explanation of all his problems. The good archbishop repeated several times that if he was not beset by so many drunken Irish clergy, most of his problems would have been solved. Finally, Rome could be counted on to do inept and unperceptive things, of which the most notorious was to order Archbishop Neale to reinstate the incredible Father Simon Felix Gallagher as pastor in Charleston despite his persistent refusal of obedience to the archbishop. Neale, who was an old man and would only survive his predecessor John Carroll by eighteen months, worked up enough strength to write the following words in reply:

Most Holy Father, is it thus the faith is propagated? Is this the way to treat archbishops who in penury, amid countless difficulties and miseries, labor for the faith and salvation of souls even to decrepit age, and who sink under the bitter burthen? I can scarcely believe that such an order emanated from the Holy See, or surely if it did emanate, it must have been obtained surreptitiously: for by this course, the door is opened to every rebellion in this distant country, and means are given, as I think, for the destruction of religion, for the children of this world are more prudent than the children of light. Before truth can reach Rome deceit and falsehood have already occupied the ground, and because they are supported by the testimony of faithless men, they find credit and advocates, my declarations being neglected because they are not upheld by the number and zeal of men without faith, or because my poverty does not permit me to have a procurator or a defender at Rome, for I and my brethren, bishops of this country, are much poorer than the rest of the clergy. Would that your Holiness had leisure to examine my letters and documents forwarded to the Sacred Congregation; I might hope for a prompt remedy for our evils.

These were extremely strong words and one presumes that Neale felt that he had a right to be angry. However, it is worth noting that he had not bothered to send to Rome the papers on the Gallagher case and that until he wrote the preceding irate letter, Rome had only heard one side of the story. Apparently it never occurred to Neale that Gallagher was capable of appealing over his head to Rome.

This brings us to what may be the most critical element in the problems of American Catholicism in the early half of the nineteenth century. Most of those who write on the subject point to the standard reasons—waves of immigrants, the prejudice of Protestants, the rebelliousness of the lay trustees, the erratic and unpredictable clergy, ethnic differences, and misunderstandings in Rome. But there is one other point that must be made. In all charity, most of the American bishops who came after John Carroll were anything but competent men. Indeed, at one time after Carroll's death and before the arrival of John England, all but one of the bishops in the United States were French refugees. These were intelligent, well-educated, pious men, but for the most part incapable of dealing either with their Irish subjects or with the fantastically complicated problems of their rapidly growing church.

Maréchal's consistent refusal to summon a national council (which often caused John England to wonder how such a pious Sulpician could ignore the requirements of the Council of Trent) to organize a national hierarchy that might cope with the new problems strikes the modern reader as little short of criminal negligence. John Dubois in New York was at a loss as to how to cope with the problems of that rapidly growing city. Flaget and David, whatever their unquestioned personal merits and ability to suffer incredible hardship, displayed little or no understanding of the possibilities of frontier Catholicism, and the sending of the aged Bruté to be the first bishop of Vincennes was quite incredible. Two of the other bishops, Connolly of New York and Conwell of Philadelphia, were if anything even more incompetent, although their appointments cannot be blamed on the French. Conwell, who was suspended from his office by Rome and then broke Roman orders to return to the diocese, where he plagued his successor and the other American bishops for many more years, surely was one of the most disgraceful bishops the United States has ever known. At a time of extremely difficult transition, the American hierarchy was presided over in large measure by ecclesiastics who at best were pious Frenchmen who did not understand their people or their problems and who at worst were disgracefully and ludicrously incompetent.

Maréchal's railing against *sacerdotes Hiberni intemperantiae aut ambitioni dediti* [Irish priests given to intemperance or ambition] might have provided him with all the explanation he needed for his problems but it surely didn't offer any solutions to the problems. Apparently it never occurred to the good archbishop that he could with relatively little effort recruit Irish clergy who were neither ambitious nor drunkards and who could serve their confreres with dignity and diligence. The truth of the matter is that Maréchal and some of his colleagues were snobs who did not take seriously the possibility that the Irish were capable of producing mature and intelligent ecclesiastical leaders.

Father Harold, who it must be confessed would hardly have a charitable view of the French clergy, describes the problems as follows:

I know some of the French Bishops in America, and I can say with pleasure and with truth, that their Zeal, their piety and learning are such as would have qualified them to govern with honour and advantage any church in their native country, but I can assure your Eme. with equal truth, that I could address a congregation of polished Italians in their own language, with as much effect as these worthy Prelates can produce on a congregation of enlightened Americans, and they are enlightened much more generally than any nation I have yet visited. The learned in Europe are far advanced above the learned in America, but knowledge is far more universally diffused among the people in the United States than thro' any nation in Europe. Any one with moderate talents and application may acquire such a knowledge of our language as may enable him to understand what is written in English, he may even converse so as to make himself well understood, particularly if he begin the study at an early age, but our pronunciation is so difficult, and the meaning of our words depends so much on the manner in which they are pronounced, that I have never heard a foreigner attempt to speak in publick in the English language who did not commit such blunders as it was impossible not to laugh at. Words of double meaning are in every language proportioned to the simplicity or corruption of a people—Your Eme. may well believe that in the language of England, such words cannot be few. These are never known at least by a foreign priest; and I have heard from the pulpit such words uttered as nothing but the ignorance to which I allude could have excused—To speak our language is most difficult to all foreigners, but to a native of France the difficulty is almost insuperable. The very serious inconvenience of preaching on controverted points of doctrine, in such a way even tho' none but Catholicks were present, must be evident to your Eme. The Catholicks do not, indeed they cannot disguise their feelings on such occasions. This produces a coolness between the flock and the Pastor which often ends in fatal and scandalous hostility. The foreign Pastor attributes the discontent of his flock to national prejudice, when in reality it is excited by the blunders which he unconsciously commits, and which expose himself, his people and their Religion to the sneers and contempt of the heretick.

The Sulpicians and their Sulpician-trained successors such as James Whitfield and Samuel Eccleston, archbishops of Baltimore, were able to keep control of the American Church long after its size had far exceeded their competence, and in the name and tradition of John Carroll seriously threatened the vitality of the work which he had begun. John England, who also was no friend of the French, prepared a statement for the Holy See in 1834 summarizing his view of the problems the American Church faced. Cardinal Weld of the Curia summarized the points that England made:

1. The lack of a sufficient clergy.

2. The evil conduct of some priests who had come from Europe not so much out of zeal as by necessity, and were accepted by our prelates because of the need of missionaries.

3. The ignorance of so many priests in America of the language, customs and laws of the United States; so much so that the people believe our Church is more a foreign institution in the land than a part of the American Republic.

4. The lack of theological training in many other priests.

5. The unfortunate efforts made by others of the clergy to accentuate in the Catholic Church here an affinity to certain foreign ecclesiastical institutions. The Americans are not suspicious of our spiritual dependence upon the Holy See; that they understand, knowing it to be essential to the organization of our Church; but their suspicions and jealousy are easily aroused, if that dependence seems to be given to other foreign centers. Such dependence involves direction and overseership from foreigners.

6. The absolute lack of any co-operation or understanding between the American bishops. Dr. England had grave reason to believe that the Philadelphia schism

would still be in full swing, had it not been checked by the Council of 1829.

7. Although the successors of John Carroll in the archiepiscopal See of Baltimore have been excellent men, nevertheless the opinion is quite general that the Holy See had not selected prelates of a very high order for that important post. Moreover, one grave evil is the perdurance of private nominations to American Sees.

8. The nomination to American Sees is a much more important affair than in any other part of the Church. Owing to the extraordinary powers and authority of the bishops here, great care must be taken in their selection.

9. The American people are intelligent; well educated, and keen observers, and personal qualifications for any office rank high in their estimation of that office itself. To send among them prelates whose personal deficiencies are noticeable to all, will only ruin respect for the episcopal office itself.

10. The Americans are extremely patriotic; and are not inclined to be hospitable to foreigners who may be placed over them. Some of the priests in the United States not only do not become citizens but also declare their preference for foreign institutional methods. Nothing convinces the American people more quickly of the alleged incompatibility of Catholicism with the American Republic.

11. Another grave cause of disorder is the absence of any legislation in the American Church for the protection of the priests. Having only delegated jurisdiction in their parishes *ad nutum episcopi,* they are at the mercy of a bishop's whims and fancies, and have no means of appeal from unjust censures or penal inflictions.

12. The American people are a law-abiding people, and the laws are respected so long as the voice of the people is had in its making. They will not obey whimsical legislation and to a certain extent, in the absence of Provincial Councils, ecclesiastical legislation is of that kind.

13.   The lack of any clear and defined status in the management of church property.

While Weld was a Roman official and performing a bureaucratic task in summarizing England's report, it is worth noting that as a young man he was an altar boy at John Carroll's consecration and his family and the Carrolls were close friends. One wonders if he would have so sympathetically summarized John England's position if he thought that England was attacking the legitimate successors of Carroll's tradition.

The critical question, then, it would seem to us, of early nineteenth-century Catholicism was not whether the Maryland establishment would be swamped by immigrants but rather whether that establishment could graciously yield power to the most enlightened and farsighted of the new wave of Irish bishops who might be able to continue in the best spirit of John Carroll's Americanism. When John England, Dennis Corkery, and Johanna Monica England arrived in Charleston in 1820, the Anglo-French establishment in Baltimore had its chance. They blew it.

John England was a man bigger than life; indeed, there were occasions when he seemed twice as big as life. Born in County Cork and ordained at the age of twenty-two, he served in that diocese for ten years, during which time he was chaplain of the city prisons, chaplain of the convent of nuns, chaplain of the Magdalene Asylum, a Sunday lecturer (preacher) of the diocesan cathedral, rector of the diocesan seminary (and professor of philosophy and theology there), inspector of the poor schools of the city, secretary to the Fever Hospital, secretary to the board of examiners of candidates for holy orders, diocesan superintendent of schools, and editor of a newspaper. It should be pointed out that England didn't hold these jobs successively but rather all at once. In addition, he managed to be a fiery Irish patriot, a friend of Daniel O'Connell, a promoter of Irish nationalism in a controversy over whether the British Crown was to have veto power in the appointment of Irish bishops, and a shrewd political leader of the Irish peasantry. But after eight years

of such frantic activity, he was appointed pastor of a parish
in Brandon some distance from Cork, probably because even
though his bishop was on John England's side politically, the
young priest had simply become too fiery a patriot to be
trusted in the city of Cork itself. There also seems to be
some reason to think that he was appointed a bishop in the
United States at least in part to get him out of Ireland because
there was considerable fear that his great talents would lead
to his rapid promotion in the Irish hierarchy where he would
make even more difficulty for the more conservative and less
patriotic of his fellows. His appointment to Charleston came as
a complete shock to him and apparently not a pleasant shock.
But John England was not a man to hesitate for long when
faced with a new challenge.

And Charleston would certainly be a challenge. For almost
two decades, Simon Felix Gallagher had made trouble in this
city, and by the time of the establishment of the diocese
Gallagher's followers in Charleston were in open schism and
were talking seriously about having a bishop consecrated by
the Jansenist Church in Utrecht, Holland, and setting up an
"independent Catholic Church." This may have been mere
bluff to persuade Rome to set up a separate diocese for
Charleston free from the French domination in Baltimore. In
any case both the schismatics in Charleston and Maréchal
wanted a separate diocese for Charleston (though Maréchal
was not prepared to have a bishop appointed to Norfolk,
where another group of schismatics were demanding their
own bishop too). The Charleston schismatics were hoping that
the new bishop would be a Dominican named Carbry or
their own clerical leader Gallagher or Robert Browne.
Maréchal, on the other hand, was deeply afraid of an Irish
bishop and was pushing a native American candidate, Father
Fenwick. Both sides were happy that a separate diocese was
established but neither was particularly satisfied with the
bishop that was assigned to the diocese. Maréchal was skeptical of him because he was Irish and the schismatics were
skeptical of him because they did not know where he would
stand on their demands for control of ecclesiastical appointments. To say the least, both sides got far more than they

bargained for. Indeed one is permitted to suspect that if Maréchal and the schismatics of Charleston had any inkling of what John England would turn out to be they would have settled their difficulties long before his arrival.

His performance in the first year in Charleston was sufficient indication of what was to come. Two weeks after his arrival, having issued a lengthy and eloquent pastoral on the nature of the bishop's office, England set out on a visitation of his huge diocese. During the winter and spring as he traveled at breakneck speed around the southland, he also found time to make plans for the construction of a cathedral, to found a Catholic book society, write a lenten pastoral, publish an English catechism, put the skids permanently under the rebellious trustees in Charleston, preach in Episcopalian and Presbyterian churches, write a letter to Maréchal suggesting a national council, prepare for publication and translation of a missal with an introduction and explanation of 120 pages that he himself had penned, make plans for a new translation of the Bible into English, and begin to lay the groundwork for a weekly Catholic newspaper and for a constitutional convention in his diocese.

England was discouraged periodically through his frustrating years as bishop of Charleston, but never for long, and the fantastic activity of the first year would continue virtually unchecked until his death. As can well be imagined, the very conservative and proper Sulpician hierarchy was anything but pleased with England's activity, especially since he had bothered to check none of his plans with them. An attempt was made unsuccessfully to ban his publication of the missal in English. The rigid and haughty Bishop John Baptist David (a close friend of Bishop Flaget, whom he succeeded as bishop of Bardstown, and who previously had tried to take control of Elizabeth Seton's religious community away from its founder) was eager to point out that some of the expressions that England used in his introduction to the missal might contain doctrinal error. Maréchal succeeded in persuading Archbishop Curtis of Ireland to write a letter to Rome blocking England's idea for a translation of the New Testament:

I have often heard [Curtis writes], that Dr. England is a man of the keenest intellect and piety and a man of great zeal, but that he lacks sacerdotal meekness, and prudence, and that in political matters he does not act with equanimity and sufficient caution. He should at least consult his metropolitan and his fellow bishops before he begins anything new, or he should propose his plans to the Holy See, lest he upset the Church, which must needs be administered with peace, harmony, and prudence. I do not know how he acts towards these prelates, but I have before me his letters recently printed in which he criticizes us Irish Bishops (without even a shadow of reason), and submits us to the ridicule of our people. It is your Eminence's duty to restrain these and similar acts of his impetuous temper, and to teach him at the same time not to be more wise than it behooveth to be wise, but to be wise unto sobriety.

One senses from the good Archbishop's letter not only why England was to be a constant thorn in the side of the American hierarchy but why he was far too hot to handle in Ireland.

But if England's activities in the southland were to cause consternation among his fellow bishops, his journey to the north would be viewed by them as almost disastrous. Since he had within the space of a very short time eliminated the problem of two decades' standing over the Charleston schism, England not unnaturally thought he might be able to lend a hand to the bishops in the north with their own particular schisms and became involved in seeking solutions to the problems of both Philadelphia and New York. His help was not exactly welcomed. And after discovering, much to his surprise, that his charming reasonableness and his ready solutions to old problems only angered the northern bishops, he discreetly withdrew from trying to arrange peace. But perhaps "discreetly" is not the right word, since even though he affirmed frequently that he had not the slightest intention of interfering ever again in the Hogan schism in Philadelphia, he could not restrain himself from commenting on it quite frequently in the pages of his newspaper. Later in his life, England was to claim, and perhaps with considerable reason, that if he had been given a chance he could have settled the

New York and Philadelphia problems in short order. The ultimate measure of the incompetency of the French-dominated hierarchy at this time in the United States was that a newcomer like England could resolve so very quickly the extremely troublesome Charleston schism. If he could do it in six months, there was no reason save their own ineptitude which prevented them from doing it long before.

There can be no doubt that the fiery, energetic, imaginative John England, for all the great charm which made him so popular with non-Catholics (he was preaching in the South Carolina House of Representatives but a year after his arrival), was quite incapable of adopting the discretion that would be required to win the cooperation of his stodgy and fussy colleagues in the national hierarchy. England never understood them and they never understood him. He was too much for them and they were too small for him. One must concede that if England had matched his other talents with prudence and tact, he would have accomplished far more. But it is also by no means obvious that all the prudence and tact in the world would have won over his brother bishops.

For John England committed the unpardonable crime—he was right. Almost every time he opened his mouth about the United States and the American Church he spoke truth, and such accuracy was intolerable in a man who had barely arrived on the shores of the new republic. One has the impression in reading of England's life that when he got off that boat in Charleston, he took one look around, sized up the United States, determined what had to be done, and then proceeded for the rest of his life to do it without ever a doubt that his analysis was right. As it turned out, there was no reason for him to doubt. Like everything else in his personality, England's respect for the United States was passionate. In a letter written to the Lyons Missionary Society in 1836, he summarized his feelings about the United States and Europe:

> The mind of Europe has been led to undervalue the nature of the American institutions, and to look upon the society of the United States as considerably under the standard of that in Europe. So far as religion, and especially the

ministry, is concerned, this mistake has not seldom led to very pernicious results. Frequently in companies, where upon most other topics I could receive great accessions to my little stock of knowledge, I have been led to doubt whether I heard correctly the very strange questions that were addressed to me respecting our laws, our manners, our society, our institutions, and our habits; I was frequently obliged to avoid enlarging upon the topics, and more than once to evade the questions, upon the very painful conviction that it would be worse than useless to give information to those who were determined not to believe. They could very readily admit all that I chose to say about Indians, huts, lakes, wild beasts, serpents, assaults, murders, and escapes, but it was out of the question that my assertions would be equally well received if I insinuated that anything in legislation, manufactures, literature, or the polish of society was comparable to even what was ordinary at this side of the Atlantic. In fact it would seem as if a century had rolled away, and left America and Europe in precisely the same relative positions as to improvement, as they were when the first European adventurers undertook to stem the torrent of the Mississippi, making a tedious and exhausting effort to overcome, in six months, the obstacles of a few days in a steamboat. *The result of this notion was that anything was good enough for America; and the Catholic Church has frequently felt the effects of this mistake.* It has more than once happened that men with acquirements and manners scarcely fit for Indians, have been deemed fit for any part of this region of Indians, and were thus inconsiderately sent into the midst of a community at least equally intelligent, and penetrating, and inquiring as any in the world.

But he formed his attitudes long before. His first year in the United States was not finished before he wrote to Archbishop Troy of Dublin asking for support in his new mission in the United States:

I have met some of the best Catholics in America, who see and deplore a thousand things like this; men who would sacrifice money most liberally where it would promote the good of religion, and who now would give nothing, for they are in despair of ever seeing religion flourish. What would your Grace think of a Prelate who has written to me in answer to my entreaty that he would leave me a priest to look after Charleston for a few months, whilst I visited a part of my Diocess to get a few Churches built and to give some instructions—"I cannot leave him, and you have here no business to think of building new churches or looking for Converts, you have more than enough to do in keeping up your duties." Yet I have been able, thank God, to make eleven new Congregations in my Diocess and have already had more than forty converts, some of them respectable and talented.

For God's sake and the sake of Religion, beg of Rome, for you know how, I wish I did also,—not to ruin this country by pouring in upon it a deluge of ignorance and folly which will not be received. There is here more information than in Ireland, more means than in Ireland, more fanaticism than in Ireland, more freedom than in Ireland, and more true search after religious truth than in Ireland. Nothing but knowledge and virtue will here command respect in religion, and yet one would think that the very off-scouring of the earth has been selected to plant Catholicity here. I may write with vain feelings, but your Grace must make some allowance; you would not be patient if you saw what I do, and if the Propaganda knew what I do, they love Religion too well to continue to act as they have acted hitherto. If your Grace be the means of their treating America in a more judicious way you will have great merit before God, and do an act which will be highly beneficial to millions. I may now safely say that my Diocess and another are the only two where there is peace. Priests and people in mine only wish to know what I desire and it is done, yet I have not found it necessary to say one harsh word, and mine has been the most turbulent in the Union. I am not known at Rome. I have nothing to communicate about Charleston but what is pleasant. You are known, you have weight and for God's sake obtain for America something like discipline and order, and you will deserve the blessings of millions, and you will have the lasting gratitude of

Your much obliged,
John, Bishop of Charleston.

He could not tolerate the haphazard selection of bishops for the critical roles in the American Church and in 1825 he inserted the following notice in the *United States Catholic Miscellany:*

> The Editor of the *Catholic Miscellany* will please to insert the following, and should he demand payment for three insertions, it will be sent to him by his stating the amount.

> NOTICE

> To the Roman Catholic Clergy and Laity of the United States.

> The Sees of Boston and New York are now vacant, or if Prelates have been appointed for them, I am not aware of who they are. They will both be filled before I shall probably address you upon the necessity of having some permanent and known mode of having our Sees filled, not by faction, intrigue or accident—but in a manner more likely to be useful and satisfactory than that which is now in operation.

> I give the present notice, in order that if I should see it necessary, or useful, to address you, after these Sees shall have been filled, it might be clearly known that my object will be independent of any personal consideration. AMERICANUS.

> We make no charge—Editor.

There wasn't much doubt among any of the readers of the newspaper who Americanus was or to whom he was speaking. The Anglo-French hierarchy might have been in the country long before John England but he had not the slightest touch of doubt in his mind that he was the real American and that they were not. It is terribly hard to prove that he was wrong; and when we turn to what was perhaps his most dramatic innovation in church government, the establishment of a constitution for his diocese, it becomes evident how fully American he really was.

The England personality and orientation being what it was, there is every reason to think that he would have come up

with some sort of democratic form for the diocese in any
case, but the occasion for his evolving his plan was an attempt
to find a way to resolve the awkward problem of lay trusteeship. England was not about to leave the control of various
churches in the hands of lay vestrymen who could with im-
punity defy the pastor and the bishop. But unlike many other
American prelates in his time and of succeeding generations,
he was not inclined to exclude laity from the governance of
the Church. On the contrary, what England had in mind was
a scheme which would not only eliminate the evils of trusteeship but actually give the laity more power in the policy-
making of the diocese than they had ever enjoyed in the past.
Only a brave man would try to accomplish such an apparent
contradiction and only a genius would have succeeded. But
England did it and indeed almost effortlessly.

The basic American inspiration of the constitution was clear
in England's mind scarcely two years after he arrived, when
he wrote to Cardinal Fontana in Rome:

> Having paid great attention to the state of several
> Churches in America, and studied as deeply as I could the
> character of the government and the people, and the cir-
> cumstances of my own flock, as well as the Canons and
> usages of the Holy Roman Catholic Church, and having
> advised with religious men and Clergymen, and lawyers, I
> this day, after consultation and prayer in the Church of
> St. Finnbar, published the Constitution by which the Roman
> Catholic Church under my charge is to be regulated, and
> I trust with the blessing of Heaven much disputation and
> Infidelity restrained. It was subscribed by the Clergy and by
> many well-disposed Laymen.

Nor did he have any doubt that the Constitution would be
popular both with Catholics and with those whom he came
close to describing with the modern term of "separated
brothers."

> Since your last meeting, our Constitution has been
> printed; and it is hoped that the members, being thus in pos-
> session of the details, they will be more than ever attached
> to those great principles of unity by which our strength is

consolidated, our efforts are made useful, our harmony is established, our body made respectable, and our charitable affections for each other enlarged and confirmed. The Catholic who peruses it will discover the ample, certain, easy, and efficacious mode in which provision has been made for the prevention of evils, or the remedy of such as may arise, as well as for the combination of our several efforts to produce whatever benefit we may desire. Our brethren of other denominations who may peruse it, will probably find that they have too often attributed to us tenets and principles which are not ours; and looked upon us as inimical to what we loved, and hostile to them upon account of principles which are common to us both, and to maintain which our ancestors and theirs stood in firm union, before that unfortunate separation by which we have been estranged from each other.

There were three critical elements in the Constitution. First of all, the bishop was assured of the ultimate control over church property. Thus schismatics would never again be able to deny to a priest legitimately appointed by a bishop control of the church to which he had been appointed. But secondly, a general "fund" was set up for the diocese, and the purposes of this general fund were quite inclusive:

1. The erection or improvement of the Cathedral, as being the great Church of the whole Diocess.

2. The aid of students in theology, especially by the erection and support of a Seminary, as being absolutely necessary to insure the Diocess a supply and succession of good clergymen.

3. Giving aid to missionaries to preach the Gospel and to administer the sacraments in remote, poor, and neglected parts of the Diocess.

4. Giving aid to small or poor Congregations or Parishes, in the erection of Churches, or other works of religion; but this should rather be by loan than by donation.

5. Giving aid to such religious communities, associations or establishments as are calculated to promote the interests of religion by public edification and instruction.

6. Giving aid to such schools as should be established, not merely to teach human sciences but also the knowledge of the true faith, and the way to eternal life.

7. The solace and aid of well-conducted destitute widows, or aged and infirm members of the Church.

8. The protection, education, and aid of orphans or destitute children of the Church.

9. Any other purpose that the principles exhibited in the above enumeration may justly embrace.

The trustees of the general fund were made up of a board of directors, composed of the bishop, the vicar general, five elected clergymen, and twelve elected laymen, and this board of trustees was in its turn explicitly informed that it had no power to spend money from the fund except "in conforming to an order or act of the general convention of the Church." Finally, it was required that each year there be a convention of the church of the diocese of Charleston, a convention made up of the bishop, the house of clergy, and the house of lay delegates. All of the clergymen in the diocese belonged to the house of clergy, and proportionally elected laymen from the various parishes and districts composed the house of lay delegates. The responsibilities of the annual convention were as follows:

1. To dispose of the general fund of the Church in the way that it may deem most advantageous.

2. To examine into and to control the expenditures made by its own order or by that of a former Convention.

3. To examine into, regulate and control, with the exception of their spiritual concerns, all establishments of its own creation; or which being otherwise created may be regularly subjected to its control.

4. To appoint the lay officers and servants of such establishments.

5. The House of the Clergy has power to examine into the ecclesiastical concerns of such establishments and to

make its private report thereon to the Bishop or Vicar, together with its opinion and advice, but such report or advice shall not be published in any other way, without the consent of the Bishop or Vicar first be had and obtained in writing under his hand and seal.

So the laity did not have direct control of parish property but they had something more important than that; they had a share in the board of trustees that supervised the expenditure of the general funds of the diocese. Even in the modern post-Vatican Church where diocesan senates of the laity and clergy are becoming frequent, American Catholicism still has a long way to go before it can catch up with the brilliant and ingenious scheme of Bishop John England.

The scheme worked marvelously well and through his whole administration England was bothered not in the least by trusteeship problems. But as can well be imagined, his fellow bishops wanted no part of the scheme. Bishop Conwell, who was in the process of making a complete fool of himself in the handling of the Hogan schism in Philadelphia, nevertheless had time to warn the Holy See that "if this constitution or *democratic* method of ruling the Church be approved by the Holy See, it might become necessary to extend it to all the dioceses here [;] it would mean the quick collapse of the American Church." It never occurred to Conwell that such a democratic method might have saved his diocese from utter chaos. Later he wrote to Rome warning them once again that England was violating the most sacred of ecclesiastical traditions and was threatening the American Church with ruin. Rome became somewhat curious but was for some reason not quite eager to ask England for a copy of his constitution and so rather asked Maréchal to send secretly a copy to Rome. Maréchal urged the Holy See not to approve the document because even though he had not seen it, he suspected that such a "democratic constitution" would do great harm to the prosperity of the Church.

Bishop David from Bardstown came through with his inevitable corrections of some doctrinal formulations in the document, which he thought lacked sufficient clarity. The

First Provincial Council of Baltimore in 1828 would acknowl-
edge England's method of government as a legitimate exception to that which was approved for the other dioceses. But
at least one Roman agent of the hierarchy attempted to persuade the Curia not to approve the act of the First Provincial
Council lest such approval be taken to be an implicit approval
of England's constitutional form of government. Rome, which
at this point had an uncanny insight as to what was going on,
replied that the wonderful tranquility of the diocese of Charleston was the proof of the wisdom of its bishops. As time went
on, at least some of the American hierarchy was persuaded
that England's radical innovation was a good thing for
Charleston but not a good thing for their own diocese. And
even though it worked with remarkable smoothness, it died
with England's death since his successor was afraid to continue it for fear that it would somehow or other interfere with
the financial retrenchment which he took to be the major
responsibility of his administration.

It is tempting to speculate what shape American Catholicism
would have taken if other bishops had been brave enough
to imitate England's ingenuity. We would certainly have had
a more democratic Church and a more American Church and
probably a far more successful Church. But such speculations
are idle. The constitution of the diocese of Charleston was
ahead of its time, and, just like its bishop, ahead of our time
too.

So too was his newspaper the *United States Catholic Miscellany*. England had a view of the Church which has since
been reinforced by the Second Vatican Council. A bishop was
not responsible merely for his own diocese but was to have
concerns for the church universal. Thus if you are to publish
a newspaper, you do not limit it merely to your diocese but
you make it a national newspaper and you comment on
national problems and comment on events not only in
Charleston but any other part of the country. It would also of
course be a thoroughly American newspaper and carry on its
masthead the words "Congress shall make no law respecting
the established religion or prohibiting the free exercise
thereof." Like everything else he did, England was not in-

clined to follow small plans, and the goals of the newspaper were almost as global as the goals of his constitution for the diocese of Charleston:

The principle of this publication will be candour, moderation, fidelity, charity, and diligence. Not that its conductors presume to attain the perfection of all or any of those qualities; but they will constantly keep them in view.
The topics which it will embrace are:

I. The simple explanation and temperate maintenance of the doctrines of the Roman Catholic Church; in exhibiting which its conductors are led to hope that many sensible persons will be astonished at finding they have imputed to Catholics doctrines which the Catholic Church has formally condemned, and imagined they were contradicting Catholics, when they held Catholic doctrine themselves.

II. The examination of history for the purpose of investigating the truth of many assertions which have been, perhaps, too lightly hazarded, and which have obtained too ready and general credence, and which have excited unfounded prejudice in the minds of many well-disposed individuals.

III. The correct statement of occurrences regarding the Catholic religion; for the purpose of better discharging which duty, communications and periodical publications from Rome, Paris, London, Dublin, Canada, South America, the various parts of the United States, and other portions of the world will be obtained, and are solicited.

IV. Memoirs and anecdotes of the several eminent persons who have distinguished themselves in the Church, or against it, in ancient or modern times.

V. A summary of political events and domestic occurrences.

VI. Occasional reviews of religious publication.

As Peter Guilday notes, the newspaper met with a frigid reception on the part of the other bishops of the country, and England did not wait long before he began to comment on the national scene, providing a weekly account of the developments of the Hogan schism in Philadelphia, beginning with his sixth issue in 1822. The work of keeping the *Miscellany* operating was turned over in great part to England's youthful sister who apparently had as much literary force as her brother and a great deal more patience and restraint. After her death in 1827, the paper lost much of its charm and some of its drive, and according to his friends, England's life lost much of its joy. But with interruptions due to shortages of finance, the paper continued for twenty years, commenting on the developing scene in the United States and in the American Church, arguing, pleading, cajoling, instructing, charming, and warning. If we are to judge by the quotations in the paper printed in England's biography, it was always ambitious and never dull, always vigorous and never hesitant. We can also suspect that the more conservative of the Catholics in the country viewed England, his sister, and their paper with the same lack of enthusiasm as the *National Catholic Reporter* receives today. But this was hardly likely to daunt England, because there were other plans that had to be pushed forward.

England did not, as one may have gathered at this point, like the Sulpician view of the world of the Church and he had no sympathy at all with the Sulpician seminary in Boston, which he thought had far too much influence in the American Church. So even though he had a diocese which in its beginning was composed of only six priests and would number but twenty at his death, he nonetheless determined to found a seminary that would be thoroughly American:

> I am daily more and more convinced [he wrote in 1835], that the genius of this nation and the administration of the French are not easily reconciled. Besides this, one of the strongest topics of prejudice against our Religion is that it is a foreign Religion, and it is not American, that it is the Religion of strangers, of aliens, etc. The Irish are easily amalgamated with the Americans. Their principles, their dispositions, their politics, their notions of government, their

language and their appearance become American very quickly, and they praise and prefer America to their oppressors at home. The French never can become American. Their language, manners, love of *la belle France,* their dress, air, carriage, notions, and mode of speaking of their religion, all, all are foreign. An American then says: "It might be very good, but 'tis foreign aristocracy." Trivial as this might seem, it has impeded the progress of our Religion here. And the French generally refer to France as the standard of perfection. The French clergy are generally good men and love Religion, but they make the Catholic Religion thus appear as exotic, and cannot understand why it should be made to appear assimilated to American principles. . . . You may use the contents of this letter as you please, as there is nothing in it I would not say in the presence of those of whom I write.

It goes without saying, of course, that the educational scheme for his seminary students was, at least by the standards of other contemporary seminaries, revolutionary. The seminary did not survive England's death but at least he had the satisfaction of knowing that he was the first American bishop to try to organize a clearly American seminary. It would take more than another century before it would be tried again.

The most serious battle England fought during his two decades in Charleston was for some form of collegial government for the American Church. He had been in the country less than a year when he wrote Archbishop Maréchal, pleading for a national synod which could draw up unified policy in dealing with the problems of the American Church. He kept on asking and Maréchal kept on refusing. In one letter he said, "I do not wish to be considered importunate though I am in earnest. May I request you will have the goodness to inform me whether you have any intention of immediately holding such a synod that will assemble before the fall. I shall await its issue before I proceed further and if it will not be held within the present year, I shall proceed to discharge what I conceive to be my duty to my diocese by making for it the best statutes that I can." The letter in the Baltimore archives has one word in Maréchal's handwriting on the back: *negative.* This word keeps recurring in Maréchal's comments on England's constant pleas for a council. Another point England observes:

> But viewing the whole state of the American church, I state that it has no discipline or semblance of discipline and that in my opinion most of the evils which affect it arise from this cause; that each Diocess is affected more or less by the disorder, or the other evils existing in any other; and that therefore the special evils in each are in some measure a common concern of the whole and that this has been acknowledged by the Church from the beginning, as an undoubted principle felt through all its Provinces. . . .
>
> That is my humble opinion. The deranged and unsettled state of the American Church can be reduced to order and peace and permanent system only by Provincial Synods of the American Hierarchy. That much as I would value even the temporary quiet and highly as I would esteem and reverence and faithfully as I would obey a Papal legate, I solemnly and earnestly deprecate and am averse to this extraordinary mode of doing what I think might be better done by the proper and ordinary mode of a Provincial Synod. Because the usual mode of a Synod has not been tried. Because the usual mode of a Synod is more congenial to the practice of the Church. Because the usual mode of a Synod is more congenial to the old canons of the Church. Because the usual mode of a Synod has been prescribed by the last general council. Because the usual mode of a Synod has been found most beneficial in those places in which it has been followed. Because the usual mode of a Synod has been preferred by most holy Prelates whose example is most precious and useful in the Church. Because the usual mode of a Synod is more in accordance with the spirit of our National institutions, and because it is the mode which will best please the flock and insure their support to its regulations. Whereas placing the power in the hands of an individual appears to me an encroachment upon the rights of Diocesan Bishops, and an attempt to reduce them to the level of Vicars-Apostolic. It destroys what Cardinal Bellarmine calls the republican part of Church government, and

properly states to be one of its characteristics, and is calculated in this country to create a great moral obstacle to the
continuance and progress of our Faith.

England's argument was clever. He pointed out to Maréchal,
who in some fashion or other was claiming to be the de-
fendant of the American tradition against the Irish invaders,
that the collegial governance of a national church was in accord not only with American institutions but also with the republican element of the church which even so respectable a
scholar as Robert Bellarmine had defended.

But England was wasting his breath. The "*negatives*" kept
appearing on the back of his letters to Maréchal and the
council was not called until Maréchal's death. His successor,
Archbishop James Whitfield (born in Liverpool), was no more
eager to face John England and a national council but finally
summoned one; there isn't much doubt from Whitfield's reluctance to summon another council that England completely
dominated the first one. Whitfield did his best to avoid the
requirements of the Council of Trent in convoking a Second
Provincial Council three years later, but by this time England
was in Rome on a visit and charmed the curial officials and
persuaded them to force Whitfield to call another council.
By this time (1833) the opposition was ready for John England, and England's friend and sometime ally, Bishop Francis
Patrick Kenrick of Philadelphia (later the first of the Irish to
assume the reins at Baltimore) wrote to Cardinal Cullen in
Rome his sad opinion of the whole proceedings:

Little was done in consequence of the suspicion with
which every measure emanating from Bishop England was
viewed. The prelates for the most part second the archbishop who felt mortified that he had been obliged by the
influence of Bishop England to call the council. Bishop Ro-
sati felt displeased at Bishop England's interfering at Rome
in regard to limits to his diocese though Bishop Rese and I
agreed perfectly with Bishop England on that point. . . .
The talents, learning, fame, eloquence of Bishop England
rendered him not an object of envy for I believe the good
prelates superior to this narrow passion but fear for they

dreaded lest his active mind and liberal views might lead
them into the adoption of measures which might weaken
their authority and disturb the repose of the Church. To me
they appeared to fear where there was not cause for fear.
Their votes could always outweigh his arguments. Had they
manifested a respect for his judgment, a disposition to hear
his reasons, and to adopt his suggestions if found correct,
had there been more personal courtesy, fraternal charity,
and less bias, less anti-Irish feelings, the results of the council would have been more consolatory. We would have not
seen the state of Virginia sacrificed by being made an ap-
pendage to the archdiocese when it might be a flourishing
diocese. A young man having no experience of the ministry
save that which he would have had within the college walls
[Eccleston] raised to the office of coadjutor to the archbishop and an old man [Bruté] with the most strange eccen-
tricities of mind sent in the decline of a life spent in col-
legiate exercises to be the apostle of a new diocese.

From a moderate, temperate man like Kenrick who would
have his own disagreements with Bishop England, such an
indictment of the American hierarchy is particularly damning.
The bishops led by Whitfield were more eager to block John
England than they were to govern the American Church, so
eager in fact that they selected a thirty-one-year-old coadjutor
for Whitfield, to lessen so far as they could the possibility that
Rome might be remotely tempted to make England the Archbishop of Baltimore. Kenrick was a far more generous man.
Later in his letter to Cullen, he remarked of England: "Besides, the Charleston Diocese is not a fit theater for a man of
his splendid talents. He would shine with great luster in some
of the eastern cities and I would at any moment resign my
miter to make place for him. This I authorize you to communicate to the Sacred Congregation." But both his enemies and
his friends were wasting their time in seeking promotion for
John England. Several times he refused to permit his name to
be considered for such promotions and even turned down the
opportunity to be considered as an archbishop in Ireland. He
was a man singularly without personal ambition, which is
quite astonishing in one so talented and dynamic. Even

though he knew the scheme to make Samuel Eccleston co-adjutor to Whitfield was directed principally at him, he rose up and promptly approved the scheme to make it clear to everybody that he was not motivated by any personal ambition. In a sense it is a tragedy that he was not, because ambition, while it would have made him somewhat more inclined to pull his punches, could also have made him more careful in the arts of ecclesiastical politics and would have eventually placed him in the See of Baltimore where his creative and visionary leadership would have been indispensable. But it was not to be.

However, his insistence on collegiality was at least successful. The provincial councils of Baltimore continued until the creation of other archdioceses made necessary the convening of the three plenary councils of Baltimore which are the landmarks of nineteenth-century Catholic history. And as the century wore on, the annual meeting of the archbishops and of all the hierarchy in the country become an integral part of the collegial life of the American Church long before the theologians of the Vatican Council had begun to use the word or think of the concept.

England had only limited success in his dealings with his fellow bishops. He was much more successful in his relationships with non-Catholics. He would preach wherever he was invited and sometimes would appear in three Protestant pulpits on a Sunday. Scarcely five years after his arrival in the United States, he was invited to address the federal Congress in Washington in 1826, becoming the first Catholic priest to speak as a priest to that body (Gabriel Richard had served as a member of Congress and presumably had spoken as a congressman). Interestingly enough, England delivered this oration but one month after receiving his citizenship papers. At least two passages from this thoroughly remarkable address deserve to be quoted in any publication dealing with the history of American Catholicism:

A political difficulty has been sometimes raised here. If this infallible tribunal, which you profess yourselves bound to obey, should command you to overturn our government, and to tell you that it is the will of God to have it modelled anew, will you be bound to obey it? And how then can we consider those men to be good citizens, who profess to owe obedience to a foreign authority, to an authority not recognized in our constitution, to an authority which has excommunicated and deposed sovereigns, and which has absolved subjects and citizens from their bond of allegiance?

Our answer to this is extremely simple and very plain; it is that we would not be bound to obey it, that we recognize no such authority. I would not allow to the Pope, or to any bishop of our church, outside this Union, the smallest interference with the humblest vote at our most insignificant balloting box. He has no right to such interference. You must, from the view which I have taken, see the plain distinction between spiritual authority and a right to interfere in the regulations of human government or civil concerns. You have in your constitution wisely kept them distinct and separate. It will be wisdom, and prudence, and safety to continue the separation. Your constitution says that Congress shall have no power to restrict the free exercise of religion. Suppose your dignified body tomorrow attempted to restrict me in the exercise of that right; though the law, as it would be called, should pass your two houses and obtain the signature of the president, I would not obey it, because it would be no law, it would be an usurpation; for you cannot make a law in violation of your constitution, you have no power in such a case. So, if that tribunal which is established by the Creator to testify to me what he has revealed, and to make the necessary regulations of discipline for the government of the church, shall presume to go beyond that boundary which circumscribes its power, its acts are invalid; my rights are not to be destroyed by its usurpation; and there is no principle of my creed which prevents my using my natural right of proper resistance to any tyrannical usurpation. You have no power to interfere with my religious rights; the tribunal of the church has no power to interfere with my civil rights. It is a duty which every good man ought to discharge for his own, and for the public benefit, to resist any encroachment upon either. We do not believe that God gave to the church any power to interfere with our civil rights, or our civil concerns. Christ our Lord refused to interfere in the division of the inheritance between two brothers, one of whom requested that interference. The civil tribunals of Judea were vested with sufficient authority for that purpose, and he did not transfer it to his Apostles. It must hence be apparent, that any idea of the Roman Catholics of these republics being in any way under the influence of any foreign ecclesiastical power, or indeed of any church authority in the exercise of their civil rights is a serious mistake. There is no class of our fellow-citizens more free to think and to act for themselves on the subject of our rights than we are; and I believe there is not any portion of the American family more jealous of foreign influence or more ready to resist it. We have brethren of our church in every part of the globe, under every form of government; this is a subject upon which each of us is free to act as he thinks proper. We know of no tribunal in our church which can interfere in our proceedings as citizens. Our ecclesiastical authority existed before our constitution, is not affected by it; there is not in the world a constitution which it does not precede, with which it could not coexist; it has seen nations perish, dynasties decay, empires prostrate; it has coexisted with all, it has survived them all, it is not dependent upon any one of them; they may still change, and it will still continue.

What was the religion of William Tell? He was a Roman Catholic. Look not only to the Swiss republics, but take San Marino,—this little state, during centuries, the most splendid specimen of the purest democracy, and this democracy protected by our Popes during these centuries. Men who make the assertions to which I have alluded cannot have read history! Amongst ourselves what is the religion of the venerable Charles Carroll of Carrollton? Men who make these assertions cannot have read our Declaration of Independence. What was the religion of the good, the estimable, the beloved Doctor Carroll, our first Archbishop of Baltimore, the founder of our hierarchy, the friend of Washington, the associate of Franklin? Have these men been degraded in our church because they aided in your struggle for the assertion of your rights, for the establishment of our glorious and our happy republics? No, they are the jewels which we prize, the ornaments of our church, the patriots of our country. They and others, whom we count as our members, and esteem for their virtues, have been the intimate and faithful associates of many of our best patriots who have passed from our transitory scene, and of some who yet

view in consolation our prosperity. What is the religion of
Simon Bolivar? What was the religion of the whole population of our republican sisters upon the southern continent?
We are always assailed by speculation. We always answer
by facts. Have we been found traitors in your councils,
unfaithful to your trust, cowards in your fields, or in correspondence with your enemies? Yet we have been con-
sulted for our prudence, confided in for our fidelity, en-
riched your soil with our blood, filled your decks with our
energy; and though some of us might have wept at leaving
the land of our ancestors because of the injustice of its rulers, we told our brothers who assailed you in the day of
battle that we knew them not, and we adhered to those who
gave us a place of refuge and impartial protection. Shall we
then be told that our religion is not the religion calculated
for republics, though it will be found that the vast majority
of republican states and of republican patriots have been,
and even now are Roman Catholics? It is true, ours is also
the religion of a large portion of empires, and of kingdoms,
and of principalities. The fact is so far an obvious reason,
because it is the religion of the great bulk of the civilized
world. Our tenets do not prescribe any form of government
which the people may properly and regularly establish. No
revelation upon which my eye has fallen, or which ever
reached my ear, has taught me that the Almighty God commanded us to be governed by kings, or by emperors, or by
princes, or to associate in republics. Upon this God has left
us free to make our own selection. The decision upon the
question of expediency as to the form of government for
temporal or civil concerns, is one to be settled by society,
and not by the church. We therefore bind no nation or
people to any special form, the form which they may adopt
lies not with us but with themselves. What suits the genius
and circumstances of one people might be totally unfit for
another; hence no special form of human government for
civil concerns has been generally established by divine authority; but the God of order who commands men to dwell
together in peace, has armed the government which has
been properly established by the principles of society, with
power for the execution of the functions which are given by
society to its administration; whilst it continues, within its
due bounds, to discharge properly its constitutional obliga-
tions, it is the duty of each good member of society to con-

cur in its support; and he who would resist its proper authority, would in this case resist the ordinance of the God of peace and of order, and as the Apostle says, would purchase damnation for himself. This principle applies alike to all forms of government properly established, and properly administered, to republics and to kingdoms alike. It is then a mistake to imagine that our church has more congeniality to one species of civil government than to another; it has been fitted by its Author who saw the fluctuating state of civil rule, to exist independently of any, and to be suited to either. Its own peculiar forms for its internal regulation may and do continue to be adhered to under every form of temporal rule.

The pages of the *Miscellany* are filled with England's controversial writings, because for all his charm and trust in Protestants and for all his ability to get along with them, he was a masterful controversialist and could, without losing his temper (as John Hughes did so frequently), produce utterly devastating prose. In one sermon to the Society of St. John the Baptist, England spoke the following powerful words:

> Within a period considerably later than my arrival here, I recollect one of our best scholars and well informed men, in an oration which he delivered in the city of Philadelphia, stated as an instance of the progress of our religion, that there were then about 100,000 Catholics in our Union, with as many as 100 clergymen and probably more than that number of churches. Our facilities and our resources are also comparatively more extensive. How many calumnies have we exposed? How many misstatements have been corrected? How have we, by plain exposition, by calm elucidation, by the very falsehoods of our opponents and the investigation of the candid enquirer gained upon the public mind? Our fellow-citizens have been misled in our regard. It requires patience, kindness, candour and the friendly communication of truth on our part to gain their affections. We have not exhibited those who have assailed us in false and odious colours. We have not gathered up the calumnies, of which the old world had grown ashamed, to cast against them in the new. We never imputed to them disaffection to

our State and National institutions and hostility to our civil liberties, that we may excite suspicion and hatred against their persons and their creed. We never sought under the pretext of patriotism to prevent the naturalization of their kindred, that we may deprive them of the just weight of their numbers, and keep them in helotage and degradation. We have not hired the polluted outcasts of society to libel the morals of their most exemplary members and to befoul their best establishments. We have not burned their religious edifices and turned their unprotected women and defenceless children to sicken under the dew of the night, in the fields, whilst we plundered their dwelling and scattered abroad the bones of their dead. It is not by such proceedings as these that we have made progress in these republics. Even though success should attend such misconduct, God forbid that we should be the perpetrators of crimes like these.

But for all his ability to charm those Protestants who were charmable, to persuade those who were persuadable, and to devastate those who merited devastation, England simply could not win over most of his fellow bishops and at times this was a great torment to him. In 1834, he told Cardinal Cullen in Rome what he thought of Archbishop Whitfield and his Sulpician friends:

I am under the impression and no doubt exists in my mind of its correctness, that the Archbishop, without being aware of it, is completely the tool of the Sulpicians, who have for a number of years created a government of faction and intrigue, instead of honest, open, strong administration, based upon the convictions, and sustained by the affections, of the Catholic body. The consequence is that the great body of the priests and the great body of the people are in secret opposition to the great body of the Hierarchy and their adherents; and on the other hand the power of administration being lodged in this few is regarded with jealousy and distrust by those who ought to support authority. Added to this, the prejudices of all our legal tribunals are arranged against our institutions, but the law sustains our rights. This faction, for in truth I can give it no better name, instead of sustaining itself by the force and by the provisions of the law, and thus standing upon firm ground, as they were repeatedly advised by the present Secretary of the Treasury, the late Attorney General, and several others of our best Catholic lawyers prefer a miserable course of evasion and chicane which fosters a spirit of intrigue, is more congenial to their habits and modes of thinking, and whenever we are forced into Court not only exposes us to defeat but to ridicule, and keeps up the impression that the Catholic religion is hostile to our political and legal institutions. These causes render a schism here very formidable; it might be created by the most chuckle-headed priest, and it would require more than I can easily find here to extinguish it. That in Philadelphia, which continued ten years, could by any other administration have been stifled at its birth; frequently I could alone have done it, but now I know and have the proofs abundant that at that very time *it was not desired to have it cease,* until by its means Irish influence should be destroyed. The history is melancholy; I hope I shall never be *forced* to give it to the printer.

By this time at least Rome was sympathetically disposed to John England, but it was not always so. In 1825 the Roman Congregation of the Propaganda had administered to him a stinging rebuke as a result of charges of interference leveled against him by the inept Bishop Conwell of Philadelphia. The Cardinal Prefect of the Propaganda had told England that the entire situation of the Church in America was well known in Rome and his advice was not needed. England was hardly to be daunted by such words and replied, *"Omnia Roma nota non esse ut ex litteris eminentiae vestrae patet"* (Rome doesn't know everything as your Eminence's letter makes evident). Five years later Rome was to retract the rebuke and send England on a diplomatic mission to Haiti which, while it was a tribute to his ability, consumed much of his time and sapped much of his energies with little practical purpose being served. However, his diplomacy was so skillful that it was rumored that the cardinalate would eventually be awarded him. If he had not died such an early death, worn out by his constant efforts, it is very likely that Rome would have overcome the opposition of his American enemies and England would have become an archbishop and probably the first American cardinal. However, he died in 1842 at the relatively young age of fifty-six, exhausted by his constant travel and his incessant labor. But characteristically he summoned his clergy around his bedside when it became clear that death was near and delivered a stirring oration, in which he pleaded among other things that they would keep alive the works they had begun in Charleston. Sad to say, it was a prayer that was not directly answered. England's enemies succeeded in blocking the appointment of the men he had suggested as his successors and instead sent Ignatius Reynolds as John England's successor "to clean up the mess" that England had made in Charleston. The Ursuline nuns were expelled from the diocese and the seminary was closed, the constitutional conventions were abandoned and even the *United States Catholic Miscellany,* which he had founded, ceased to mention his name. As Guilday says, "One by one during Bishop Reynolds' administration, his projects were abandoned and the unity of spirit he had given to the church in the three parishes constituting his diocese of Charleston began quickly to wane. Silence fell upon the long years of his episcopate, there were few to do him honor, none in fact to write the story of his life."

But Guilday's evaluation of John England undoes at least to some extent the injustice done to him immediately after death: "He was an American with the all mystical love for America which is visible in leaders in the earlier days of this nation's history. It is on account of his untrammeled Americanism, on account of his thorough grasp of American idealism, and above all because of the unique place he made for himself in American history by interpreting justly and accurately to his own epoch the harmony between Catholic principles and the constitutional bases of the American government . . . [that England will be long remembered]."

Guilday concludes his life of England by observing: "Had he been in one of the larger cities, or better still, had he succeeded Maréchal or Whitfield in the Metropolitan See of Baltimore, his splendidly equipped mind, his incisive, trenchant pen and his peerless ability as a public speaker might have

47011

prevented much of the animosity towards a Church of which he was then the honor and the pride."

American Catholicism had a splendid opportunity in John England and missed its chance. The opportunity would not return again for almost a half century.

IV

JOHN HUGHES
A "Fearsome" Man

The air was filled with tension at the Fordham College commencement in the year 1861. Orestes Brownson, the truculent convert philosopher, was to give the graduation address on the theme of American patriotism. Presiding over the commencement was Archbishop John Hughes, the equally truculent head of the New York archdiocese. The two had been together on the same platform in 1856. Brownson had spoken to the effect that "if the Catholic religion had been or could now be presented to the American people through mediums or under auspices more congenial with their national feeling and habits, the progress of the Church and the conversions of the Protestants would have been far greater." After Brownson had spoken, the Archbishop had privately whispered in his ear that what he said was pure speculation, that he, the Archbishop, did not agree but Brownson was perfectly free to hold the position. This did not prevent the Archbishop, who was often carried away by the powers of his rhetoric in times of anger, from rising up at the conclusion of the ceremonies and sarcastically denouncing Brownson, much to the amusement of the assembled students and faculty of Fordham. Everybody wondered whether the atmosphere of the Civil War and the need for national unity would prevent another such performance. A little thing like the Civil War would hardly cool John Hughes down. Once again, after

Brownson was finished, the Archbishop launched a violent diatribe, which, according to Brownson's biographer, caused "consternation on every side." Brownson this time arose and attempted to argue with Hughes, but Hughes ordered him to sit down, and continued his diatribe. After the ceremony was over, the Jesuit fathers took the Archbishop and the other dignitaries attending to a banquet that had been previously prepared. And Brownson was left sitting by himself in the auditorium until it was time for him to catch his train. John Hughes had struck again.

Hughes was to reign in New York from 1838 to 1864. During the last two decades of his administration he was to be easily the most powerful figure in the American hierarchy. By his own not too modest admission, he had influence far beyond the borders of the nation's largest city. At precisely the time when the crises of the immigration experience were most severe, Hughes's influence can only be considered a major disaster.

"Americanization" can and has meant many different things. For John Carroll it meant political independence from Rome, loyalty to the American republic, adjustment of the internal structure of the Church so far as possible to be at harmony with American society. John England was prepared to push several steps further. He argued for national collegial government of the Church as a manifestation of Catholicism's "Republican" principles, and introduced widespread democratic participation in the government of his diocese as being the way most suitable for Catholicism in the United States. In years to come other Americanizers would argue that the separation of Church and state and the religious freedom in the United States was a model to be looked at by the rest of the Catholic world. But Carroll was presiding over a native American Church, where foreign immigration presented no serious problem. And England's tiny diocese of Charleston was not terribly affected by mass immigration. The Americanists at the turn of the nineteenth century were representatives of a well-organized, highly successful, and reasonably unthreatened ecclesiastical institution. For John Hughes in New York two decades before the Civil War, the Amer-

icanization of the immigrant, at least as it was described by
the native Americans of New York City, seemed more frequently to mean that the immigrants must become Anglo-
Saxon Protestants or they would not be welcomed in this
country. John Hughes was not prepared to let this happen.

The native Americans were more than troubled by the massive immigrations from the old world. They frequently found
themselves terrified by it. The immigrants were uneducated
and frequently unruly. They were poor and worked for wages
lower than native workers. Their slums were dirty and un-
sightly. Their votes could easily be captured by a corrupt
political machine. They threatened the social structure, economic welfare, and the existing governmental system. They
were poor, intemperate, illiterate, frequently criminal. They
had street gangs, and in the coal fields of Pennsylvania, they
organized an underground army called the Ancient Order of
Hibernians or more popularly the Molly Maguires, which
for twenty years spread terrorism and death in the coal fields.
It was not safe to walk through their neighborhoods at night.
They were "a noisy, drinking, brawling rabble." Their illegit-
imacy rate was high and they were a tremendous drain on the
little social welfare services that were available in the years
before the Civil War. They did not respond to the instructions
of the native Americans that they should pull themselves up
and improve their lot as their predecessors had. They were
surly and uncooperative; their political and religious leaders
were frequently demagogues. They were also supposedly of
racially inferior stock and professed a highly superstitious religion. It was very doubtful in the minds of most native Americans whether it would ever be possible for the Irish (and
German) immigrants of this period to be assimilated into
American society.[1]

It has never really been clear how Anglo-Saxon immigrants have to become in order to be Americanized. The
melting-pot model, held implicitly in the nineteenth century

[1] Curiously enough, much of the same rhetoric would be used by
the descendants of these same immigrants against Negro Americans
one hundred years later.

and explicitly in the early twentieth century, has not been very useful, and the notion that it is possible to maintain much of one's own ethnic background and still be thoroughly American has considerably more popular acceptance now than it had at the beginning of the present century. For Hughes and his Irish flock in New York, there was not much question: they were going to be thoroughly American and still remain Irish. It turned out that they could get away with it, the native Americans in the country notwithstanding.[2]

One of the prices that had to be paid for success in the battle against the nativists was the adoption of an authoritarian and paternalistic style of ecclesiastical government quite at variance with the ideals of either Carroll or England, and quite foreign to American society. Another price was the aggravation of the strife and tension between the immigrants and the native Americans. Under any set of circumstances the transitions from the native American Catholicism to a largely immigrant Catholicism would have been a rough and rocky one. It is difficult to escape the conclusion that John Hughes may have made it much worse. Some of the negative effects of his leadership can still be felt a century later.

We are fortunate in having a clear statement of Hughes's own philosophy on his role as a bishop. In 1857 he was criticized by a Catholic writing to the *New York Times* on the grounds that he was guilty of "maladministration, nepotism, indolence, arrogance, and a meddling and petty spirit," and also of indifference to the Virgin Mary, "since he didn't celebrate with due solemnity the definition of dogma of the Immaculate Conception." Hughes was hardly one to ignore any opportunity for the fight, and apparently felt it necessary to deliver a long (eighty pages) document to Rome defending his administration.[3]

[2] No less than a half century later the Irish-Americans were not inclined to allow the German-Americans the same freedom.

[3] Along with the eighty pages of manuscript he sent a check for three hundred dollars to arrange for its translation into Italian. In this document he states with great clarity and vigor the authoritarian and paternalistic philosophy that was to mark his administration.

Now *my* lot was cast in the great metropolis of the whole country. My people were composed of representatives from almost all nations. They came under episcopal government in a new country, and in circumstances such as they had not been accustomed to in their own. It was necessary that they should be brought to coalesce as one Catholic flock. They were surrounded by many inducements to diverge from the unity of the Church, both in profession and in practice. Many snares were laid for them; and, under these circumstances, I found it expedient to adopt a mode of government resulting almost by necessity from the peculiarity of my position. I had to stand up among them as their bishop and chief; to warn them against the dangers that surrounded them; to contend for their rights as a religious community; to repel the spirit of faction among them; to convince their judgment by frequent explanations in regard to public and mixed questions; to encourage the timid, and sometimes to restrain the impetuous; in short, to knead them up into one dough, to be leavened by the spirit of Catholic faith and of Catholic union. Hardly anything of this kind was either expedient or necessary in any other episcopal see within the United States.

He looked on himself as the leader and champion of his people, the only one capable of defending them against the attacks of their enemies, a great and noble monarch leading and guiding these people in time of stress and difficulty without stopping to consult the people, much less to ponder the possibility of a negotiated peace with their enemies. And Hughes knew full well this style of leadership was imitated elsewhere. He went on to say:

As time went on, however, and the solution of different disputed questions here became public, and as it was always found in favor of the position I had taken, New York acquired a certain kind of general predominancy in the minds of the Catholics. What was done at New York, or said by me, was taken to be the true course for every place else as well as this. And thus, through the medium of the newspapers, rather than from any direct instruction or guidance on the part of the local ecclesiastical authority, a certain tone of action and feeling became prevalent among the

Catholics. . . . Even this it was not in my power either to
prevent or avoid. I wished to do my duty toward my own
diocese; and beyond that I desired neither praise, nor
censure, nor responsibility.

This self-image of the bishop as the father and protector,
of a flock not able to take care of itself and surrounded by
hostile enemies, was to persist in the Church for at least a
century after Hughes's death. It would lead to such absurd
situations as one cardinal in the American Church seeing, in
an amendment to the Constitution forbidding child labor, a
Communist plot from which he had to bend every effort to
protect his people. There would, of course, be many bishops
who were not paternalistic. And there would only be a very
few who would be such violent controversialists as John
Hughes was. But he nevertheless shaped a pattern of behavior
which many ecclesiastical leaders would find very easy to
imitate in the years to come. If John England thought that
American society was basically open and friendly, Hughes
viewed it as closed and hostile. If England thought within
American culture the Catholic Church could grow rapidly and
healthily, Hughes viewed the culture outside the Church as
dangerous to its very existence. There was only one way to
handle American society, and that was ultimately to convert
it. And to convert it not on its own terms, but on his. He was
fond of quoting a remark of Metternich's that "the Catholics
and the Protestants in your country are like the iron pot and
the earthen pot floating down the stream together: when they
clash, the earthen pot must be broken."

Nor was Hughes inclined to hide his plans from the American Protestant population. In 1850 he had informed the congregation at St. Patrick's Cathedral that Protestant nations
were crumbling before the forces of Rome and would continue to do so until all the world was under the spiritual rule
of the Holy Mother Church. He went on to add:

There is no secret about this. The object we hope to accomplish in kindness is to convert all pagan nations and
all Protestant nations, even England with her proud parliament and her imperial sovereign. There is no secrecy in all

this. It is the commission of God to his Church and not a human project. Protestantism pretends to have discovered a great secret. Protestantism startles our Eastern borders occasionally on the intention of the Pope with regard to the Valley of the Mississippi, and dreams he has made a wonderful discovery. Not at all. Everyone should know it. Everybody should know that we have for our mission to convert the world, including the inhabitants of the United States, the people of the cities, the people of the country, the officers of the Navy and the Marines, commanders of the Army, the legislatures, the Senate, the Cabinet, the President, and all.

One can imagine what comments like this did to nativists already fearful of Roman plots.

Hughes had no sympathy with people like Brownson, who found the American environment favorably disposed toward Catholicism. He could see nothing but hostility and persecution:

> Convents have been burned down, and no compensation offered to their scattered inmates; Catholic churches have been burned down, while whole neighborhoods have been, under the eye of public officers, reduced to ashes. People have been burned to death in their own dwellings; or if they attempted to escape, have been shot down by the deadly messenger of the unerring rifle. Crosses have been pulled down from the summit of God's sanctuary. Priests have been tarred and feathered. Ladies have been insulted for no crime except that of having devoted themselves to the service of their divine Master in a religious state, in the hope of conferring aid or consolation on their fellow-beings. . . . These things were the work of what is called mobs; but we confess our disappointment at not having witnessed a prompt and healthy, true American sentiment in the heart of the community at large in rebuke of such proceedings, and so far as reparation was possible, in making it to the injured parties whom they had failed to protect.

While John Carroll felt quite at home in the United States, and John England saw vast possibilities for growth and development in the new society, Hughes saw only enemies and persecutors from whom he would have to defend his people. Unquestionably there were far more enemies than either Carroll or England had to face. Prejudice and bigotry were violent, irrational, malicious, and incredibly ignorant. In some fashion or other, the Church had to resist them. The crucial question is not whether John Hughes was wrong in seeing enemies about him; it is rather whether Hughes's style in dealing with the enemies may not have, in the final analysis, played right into the enemies' hands.

He had the background and personality intended for a leader of warriors rather than a compromiser. He was almost killed by armed Orangemen during one of the periodic armed conflicts between Protestants and Catholics of Ireland. As he would tell it later, only when one of the men, one of five holding bayonets, had a chance to recognize him was he permitted to go free. He came to the United States during his teens in great poverty, and his education was erratic and incomplete. He had to work about St. Mary's Seminary as a gardener in order to finance his seminary training. His hostility toward Anglo-Saxons, English and American, for the suffering they had inflicted on himself and on his family, never was hidden very far beneath the surface of his personality. He was a fierce and angry man, who lost his temper readily and was not inclined easily to forgive, though sometimes after the heat of battle he would regret angry words. His biographer tells the story of the student in the seminary who was charged with a small infraction in discipline. Trying to explain to the bishop the unfortunate young man told what Hughes thought was a lie and Hughes in the presence of "some thirty other persons administered a verbal castigation which no one who heard it will ever forget. It was short, but in bitter sarcasm and crushing invective. . . . He drove the unfortunate offender from the house and would never consent to see him again." It is not exactly easy to reconcile such behavior with Christianity, but some of the other of Hughes's activities were equally difficult to interpret as befitting a Christian bishop.

On another occasion a clergyman who was promoting a Catholic colonization society hoping to establish an Irish village in Nebraska, made the mistake of attempting to give a lecture in New York. Hughes heard about the scheme, and agreeing with his auxiliary bishop Bayley, he determined to write a letter to Bayley condemning the project. But, thinking it over for a while, the archbishop decided that merely a public letter would not be enough. He attended the meeting, rose at the end of the talk, bitterly denounced the speaker, and then denounced even more bitterly the speaker's attempt to apologize. The bishop's biographer tells us that the audience, as if awestruck, withdrew in profound silence.

There weren't very many Catholics who were willing to risk John Hughes's wrath. As a priest in the Philadelphia diocese, he had been temporarily recommended by Bishop Francis Kenrick to become the first bishop of Pittsburgh, and then Kenrick under the influence of John England changed his mind about the formation of the Pittsburgh see. Hughes demanded, and in no uncertain terms, an explanation from both Kenrick and England, which these two gentlemen seemed eager to provide, as they wanted no part of Hughes's anger. And later, as auxiliary to Bishop Dubois, of New York, he was not above writing a letter to Rome in which he insisted that he was not trying to have Dubois's diocese taken away and conferred upon himself, but which in fact was designed to accomplish just that. It was time for Dubois to be retired (indeed he probably never should have been appointed), but Hughes's eagerness to replace the old man, although perhaps characteristic, was hardly admirable. He was a fierce and terrible man. One surely would not want to have him as an enemy, and it's not altogether clear that one would have wanted to have him as a friend either.

Hughes's great love was controversy. In his later years, almost all of his time was devoted to it. He sat up late at night every night writing or dictating controversial material. He read few books and magazines but read all the newspapers he could get his hands on and let no attacks on the Church or on John Hughes go unanswered. He was a brilliant controversialist, even more fierce in the written word than in the spoken. His powers of logic and ridicule were overwhelming. But his effectiveness as a controversialist was seriously impaired by his temper. He could easily win an argument but rarely a friend. Hughes's controversial style was not directed at convincing those he was arguing with, but rather at defending the Church and protecting those Catholics for whom he thought such defense was necessary.

An example of his style at its fiercest was a comment he made about a state legislator named Brooks. "Mr. Brooks is unworthy of notice. I take him consequently with covered hands to the nearest open sash of window with the single mental observation: go hence wretched and vile insect; the world has space for you as well as for me." In his early years he had written anonymous letters to a violently anti-Catholic journal called *The Protestant* under an assumed name so that when he revealed the trick he could ridicule its faults. When asked how he justified his behavior, he replied, "I was satisfied that no enlightened man would believe a line published in *The Protestant,* and that no modest woman who had read it once by accident would ever read it again by design. I wanted to ascertain whether or not conscience had anything to do with the columns of *The Protestant.* I found it did not. I found that from the moment I spoke against Catholics and adopted the signature of a coward, I might write anything, however false, nay the falser the better, and it was published under the sanction of your names. I could not find a line deep enough to fathom the editorial depravity of *The Protestant.*"

And of a Catholic priest who made the mistake of tangling with Hughes as a young man, he observed, "Experiences proved to my satisfaction the dread of scandal which usually restrains good men from defending themselves. There is in this operation the kind of encouragement, that progressive spirit which triumphs by its recklessness. If the birch had been applied to McAlpin's back ten years ago it would not be necessary for me as it now is to apply it. I have certainly been severe. However the present affair may terminate, still I am confident that McAlpin will take care how he meddles with what does not immediately concern him hereafter." John Hughes did not expect the meek ever to inherit the earth.

Again, he referred to his opponents as "voracious mongrels of heresy under the plea of propagating religion [who] are absolutely attempting to devour everything." He engaged in a long and violent series of written and then oral controversies with a Protestant minister named John Breckenridge, despite the fact that his bishop at that time, Francis Kenrick, was not enthused about the controversy. It all started out courteously enough. But like most things in which Hughes became involved, the courtesy did not last very long. At one point he said, "There are some men in whom vulgarity and pride are inseparably put into alternately betraying each other. Lest the gentleman should mistake my motive for abstaining, I wish him to know that as to family origin, good breeding, education, private history, public character, I have reason to shrink to a comparison with him."

Even though Hughes had initially supported the rising of '48, when it failed he turned against its supporters who blamed the failure on the clergy. He commented ironically, "Let us get priests and religious out of the way, as they make cowards of men. Let priests be removed. Let Popes be removed. Let everything that tends to create a conscience be abolished forever. . . . These are the political confectioners who threw up the poison of their infidelity and sugar plums of flattery to popular prejudice that they may throw them to the children of folly. They call themselves Catholics too, even as Voltaire said he was a Catholic. They say that they are Irishmen, and they may be Irishmen, but not Irishmen of a legitimate stamp. They are not of those Irishmen who have preserved the nationality and honor of their country by preserving their faith in the midst of every persecution."

There were few controversies which Hughes lost in the sense of the other man having the last word. An exception to this was Orestes Brownson. Brownson had opposed slavery in the Civil War years both as immoral (and urged the emancipation of the slaves as an act of morality) and also as a help to victory for the Union. Hughes in attacking Brownson allowed himself to be put in the position where he seemed not only to be defending slavery but could even be interpreted as defending the slave trade. Brownson promptly retaliated with a quotation from a papal document denouncing the slave trade and suggested that Hughes, pillar of orthodoxy that he pretended to be, was actually deviating from papal teaching. Hughes rather lamely explained that he didn't mean quite what it seemed that he meant, and later remarked to Brownson with some kind of graciousness that he was never going to get into a controversy with him again. This was as close to an admission of defeat as John Hughes would ever make.

Hughes was not a terribly effective administrator and was a very poor financial planner. He built a church in Philadelphia to replace one that rebellious trustees had commandeered. It was a magnificent church; but when he left, it was burdened with a forty-thousand-dollar debt which was to plague the parish for decades to come. In a very curious letter Bishop Kenrick wrote to Bishop Dubois, lamenting the fact that the loss of John Hughes was likely to make this parish quite bankrupt, but adding that he felt certain that Hughes's efficient administration would be a help to Dubois. Kenrick was too kind and charitable a man to be consciously ironic. But the thought of someone who had amassed such a huge debt, which the parish was not going to be able to pay, in his absence becoming an efficient administrator is at least curious. Hughes was a man given to mighty projects, such as the foundation of St. John's College at Rose Manor near Fordham Heights (the present Fordham University), but he was a disorganized and erratic man. His biographer, John R. G. Hassard, says:

He had no fixed time for any thing. He lacked all idea of order or system. He never followed a regular plan of action, and never laid out his work in advance. All his great achievements, such as the overthrow of the trustee system and the destruction of the Public School Society, originated by accident. He was not persevering; but he threw himself into difficult enterprises with a resolution which generally insured success. If matters went according to his wish, his application soon flagged; if he met with opposition, his energy was aroused, and he never rested until he had accomplished his purpose; but when the victory was gained he very often neglected to pursue it to its legitimate conse-

quences. He had a far-reaching, comprehensive mind, but
no head for details. Had there only been some practical,
hard working, clear-headed man whom he could have called
to his assistance, he would have accomplished much
more than he actually did; but his clergy were all busy
with their own duties, and as for laymen he never would
let them interfere in church matters if he could help it.

John Hughes, therefore, was essentially a warrior, a fierce-
tongued battler, with little financial or administrative acumen.
He had no talent for diplomacy or compromise with those
whom he considered enemies (though he could be very diplomatic on other occasions, as his mission to Paris would
demonstrate). It is very dubious whether Hughes was what
New York and the American Church needed in the antebellum
days but it's what they got.

It is customary in American Catholic history to see Hughes
as a fierce battler for the rights of his people. His handling
of the controversy with the Public School Society as well as
the nativist riots in New York in 1844 are cited as examples
of this vigorous and courageous leadership. But there is a
new school of thought among the younger Catholic historians
(such as these may be), who take a somewhat different view
of the matter. Hughes certainly put the Public School Society
of New York out of business. He forced the state to replace
this essentially private organization with a state-controlled
educational commission. David O'Brien, a historian at Loyola
College in Montreal, in an article in *Cross Currents* (Summer issue, 1966), argues that Hughes's action in the Public
School Society controversy did a great deal of harm to the
American Church. In 1840 the city of New York was exempt
from the common-school laws that governed the rest of the
state. Instead of money going directly to a public school
system governed by popularly elected trustees and presided
over by a superintendent of public schools, New York funds
for public education went to a private organization, the
Public School Society. This private, or at least only semipublic,
organization professed to impart a secular education and to
teach the general principles of religion, morality, which all

Christian denominations hold in common. The members of the Society were from various religious groups, and at least some of them were Catholic. Hughes was very suspicious of it because he was convinced that nondenominational Christianity was essentially Protestant Christianity and that "the books used in the public schools abounded in false and contemptuous passages concerning the Catholic faith."

When Hughes was in Europe in 1840, the laymen of the diocese began agitation that the Common Council divert some of the state educational funds to the support of Catholic schools. When Hughes returned to New York, he brushed aside the involved laymen and took command of the matter himself. As he explained, "There were not a few able gentlemen willing to enter the lists. But there is none who has studied the question so deeply as myself. And as I wish to make the argument consistent, I deemed it expedient to monopolize all the speaking." Monopolize he did, with several three-hour orations before the Common Council, as well as a number of fiercely demagogic orations at meetings of Catholics. When the Common Council rejected with one dissenting vote Hughes's petition, he formed a Catholic political party to run candidates for the state legislature. It was a *pro forma* candidacy since Hughes knew it was much too late to win the election. But at least it established his command of enough votes to be able to seriously influence the New York election and persuaded the state government to pass an act extending to the city of New York the provisions of the general act on the common schools which, in effect, would abrogate the Public School Society and turn the administration of the New York public schools over to the state administration. The Public School Society had prevented Hughes from getting money for Catholic schools and he had struck back by destroying the Public School Society. He himself admitted that he was "far from believing any form of common school education from which positive religious teaching was excluded could be a good one." But he also felt that almost any change from the system of the Public School Society would be for the better.

Hughes's rhetoric in the controversy was well calculated to stir up Catholic feeling:

Is this state of things, fellow-citizens, and especially Americans, is this state of things worthy of *you*, worthy of our country, worthy of our just and glorious constitution? Put yourself in the poor man's place, and say whether you would not despise him if he did not labor by every lawful means to emancipate himself from this bondage. He has to pay double taxation for the education of his child, one to the misinterpreted law of the land, and another to his conscience. He sees his child going to school with perhaps only the fragment of a worn-out book, thinly clad, and its bare feet on the frozen pavement; whereas, if he had his rights he could improve the clothing, he could get better books, and have his child better taught than it is possible in actual circumstances.

Nor did he seem to find it at all inappropriate that he should attend the meetings of the Common Council.

It has been suggested to me by a gentleman very deeply interested in the success of the question that it might not be expedient for me to appear in such a place on such an occasion. While it is possbile that some language might be used toward me which, though I might bear it with patience, might be painful for others. I replied that I was willing to give up my own opinion but at the same time I stated that I had no apprehensions of the subject either on questions of propriety or any other. I have, however, considered whether I should not there be out of place [or] whether even [at] meetings like the present I am not. But so vital and important do I consider this question that I conceive I cannot be anywhere more in keeping with my character as a bishop than when I stand before you pleading the cause of the poor and the oppressed. And so near is the question to my heart that I can burn myself from morning till night. For such a question I may venture to the furthest limits to which propriety will allow a Bishop to go.

It's worth noting in passing that only three hundred children of the New York Catholica were attending the schools administered by the Public School Society.

In the course of the controversy, the public school people attempted to make peace with Hughes by offering to submit their schoolbooks to the bishop and allow him to expurgate them. But Hughes was not about to concede their good faith. He observed, "As if we have nothing to do but to mark out a passage and it will disappear. Are we to take odium of erasing passages which you hold to be true? Have you any right to make such an offer? If we spend the necessary time in reviewing the books to discover offensive passages, you give us no pledge that you will even then remove the objectionable matter. After all that trouble you may remove them or not as you see fit. And even if you should remove it, another board of officers may succeed it tomorrow, and restore everything that you have marked out."

No good was to be expected from the Public School Society. "It was deemed expedient that the children from the earliest years should be brought up in blissful companionship without allowing any one religion to find place among them in public schools as an apple of discord. Such was the theory of what was called the Public School Society in the city, and Catholic parents to a great extent have fallen into the trap thus cunningly laid for them" (even though there were 5,000 children in Catholic schools, and only three hundred Catholic children in public school).

David O'Brien's comments on the whole controversy are devastating.

It was Hughes who forced the extension of non-denominational education to the city and then fought to remove even general religious teaching. Protestant groups who had long been at odds with the Society because of its non-sectarian policies rallied to its support, because they saw that Hughes's attack must eventuate with the removal of religious influence in public education. Not until it became clear that no such concessions would appease Hughes and his followers did the trustees give free reign to the nativists for whom the controversy was made to order. Their charges appeared to be verified by Catholic statements and middle class support now came to their movement which had been faltering for the latter half of the previous decade.

O'Brien continues:

The Bishop's actions and words indicate that he was skeptical of the possibility of receiving aid. He wished to destroy the Public School Society and replace it with a less objectionable school system and in the process, to build up Catholic support for parochial schools by emphasizing the dangers of non-sectarian education. In addition there is evidence to indicate that the Bishop hoped to break Irish-Catholic allegiance to the Democratic party in order to mobilize the Catholic population and its leadership as an independent political force capable of standing firm for their demands and commanding the respect and consideration of party leaders.

O'Brien concludes his account of the controversy by noting,

Of those involved in the 1840–42 controversy, Hughes's record is perhaps least attractive. . . . He is convicted of using the issue to unite the Catholic population under his leadership, to destroy the lay trustees within the Church and the Public School Society without. He helped force the non-sectarian education he decried onto his Protestant fellow citizens and then strove to remove even generalized religious instruction from the schools. The Catholic school system now seemed more necessary than ever to protect the immigrants against the hostility which Hughes and others helped to intensify. He added fuel to the fire of nativism by engaging in politics and denouncing both Protestant and public education. Remaining loyal to his primary responsibility, the spiritual welfare of his flock as he saw it, he did little to assist his immigrant followers to understand their surroundings and to live in peace with their neighbors. He taught them that a strong, militant and politically united Catholic bloc could defend its interests, but he neglected to instruct them in the requirements of the common good. . . . Hughes convinced Seward in 1840 that they shared a common devotion to tolerance and the ideal of universal education, but the bishop, unlike the governor, placed the interests of his particular group above the demands of the public welfare.

These are harsh words to be uttered against a man who has frequently been hailed as one of the heroes in the American Church. Hughes lived in troubled times. The Irish of New York did need dynamic and militant leadership if they were to survive the onslaughts of nativist bigotry, as we shall note in subsequent paragraphs. Hughes and his vigorous leadership probably protected New York from disastrous riots and murders similar to those that occurred in Philadelphia in 1844. It is unlikely that Hughes could have commanded the loyalty and power that he did in 1844 if he had not survived a long history of militant conflict with the native Americans. His former superior, Bishop Francis Kenrick in Philadelphia, was too meek and mild-mannered and scholarly a man to defend a Roman Catholic diocese from the nativists. But Hughes was far too militant. His controversial temperament simply did not know when to stop fighting and to begin negotiating with his enemies. There must have been some sort of middle way between Hughes and Kenrick. But by 1842 the man who best exemplified that middle way was buried next to his sister Joanna in the Catholic cathedral in Charleston, South Carolina. Curiously enough, that man was responsible for John Hughes going to New York.[4]

Ray Allen Billington argues that the mistakes of the American Church principally made by John Hughes in the late 1840s and early 1850s, led to a resurgence of nativism in the form of the Order of the Star Spangled Banner, or as it has become known in American history, the Know-Nothing party. The decade after the first controversy was

[4] When England had been in Rome in the late 1820s, he was asked whether John Hughes or John B. Purcell would be most appropriate to be the first bishop of Cincinnati. He recommended Hughes because he felt that Hughes's physical strength was stronger for the frontier than was that of Purcell. However, the Roman official misunderstood him and the next day informed England of the documents sending Hughes to New York. England thought the whole thing must be providential and refused to clarify the misunderstanding. If Hughes had gone to Cincinnati and the liberal (and pro-Negro) Purcell had gone to New York, or if England himself had gone there, the history of the American Church might have been very different.

over, Hughes once again through the *Freemen's Journal* began to argue that Catholics everywhere should unite in demanding public money for the support of their schools, or if this could not be obtained, the passage of laws forbidding the reading of Protestant Bibles in state-operated educational institutions. A number of campaigns were begun around the country for such aid, but they all proved to be disastrous. State legislatures found themselves first swamped with Catholic petitions and then Protestant petitions demanding that Rome's intolerable pretensions be rejected. The Catholic campaign was a dismal failure, and the nativist bigots could readily insist that it was one more part of a Catholic attempt to take the Bible out of the public schools.[5] The fires were fanned even higher when an ill-advised Catholic priest in upstate New York gathered several copies of the Protestant Bibles which had been distributed to his children in public schools and publicly burned them. Hughes's comment was scarcely helpful. "To burn or otherwise destroy a spurious or corrupt copy of the bible whose circulation tended to simulate erroneous principles of faith or morals, we hold to be an act not only justifiable but praiseworthy."

Billington argues that Hughes's attempt in 1852 to secure the introduction of a measure (the so-called Taber bill) by the New York legislature to enable the ecclesiastical authorities to hold title to church property, further played into the hands of the Know-Nothings. The Taber bill was harmless but it could easily be denounced by Protestants as selling out to the Pope and was badly beaten by the New York assembly. Protestants struck back by the introduction of the Putnam bill, passage of which was designed to force lay ownership of all church property, and to make clerical ownership definitely illegal. Previous legislation was obscure on the matter; the Taber bill would have clarified the right of the bishop to hold property and the Putnam bill would have made it very

[5] Curiously enough, a century later many Catholics, including some Catholic publications, would be horrified when the Supreme Court finally outlawed Bible reading in public schools. History not only makes strange bedfellows, it makes strange reversals of opinion.

clear that he had no such rights. The Putnam bill passed, but became a dead letter when New York authorities chose not to enforce it. However, Hughes's attempt to beat the few rebellious lay trustees still in existence in his diocese through legislative action almost disastrously backfired, and strengthened the hands of the Know-Nothings.

In 1853, at the height of the tension, Hughes issued a statement which he thought would ease tensions, but it was worded in such a way as simply to make them worse. "If there be, as it has been insinuated, a conspiracy against the civil and religious rights which are secured to you by our constitutional laws, defeat the purpose of that conspiracy by a peaceful and entirely equal deportment in all relations of life. But on the other hand, if such a conspiracy should arise unrebuked by the public authorities, to point really menacingly with destruction any portion of your property whether your private dwellings, your churches, your hospitals, orphan asylums, or other Catholic institutions, then in case of an attack, let every man be prepared in God's name to defend the laws of the country and the authorities of the city to stand by the laws of the country and the authorities of the city in the defence of such rights and property." But at this point the harm had been done and Hughes's statements couldn't make it much worse. Churches were burned and convents were stormed in New Orleans, Galveston, and Charleston; nuns were insulted in most of the cities of the country, more than a dozen churches were burned, crosses were stolen, altars were violated, windows smashed. Billington may be wrong when he implies that without the Catholic blunders largely to be laid at Hughes's doorsteps, the Know-Nothing passions would not have been inflamed. Nativist bigotry needed little pretext. The flames were there and would have been there no matter what Hughes or any other ecclesiastical leader did. But Billington is probably right when he argues that Hughes's attitude on the school questions and on trusteeship had the same effect as pouring gasoline on flames could be expected to have.

And yet when the flames finally did burst forth, Hughes surely knew how to behave.

In Philadelphia in 1844, when the nativists burned Catholic churches and destroyed several score Irish homes, Kenrick thought that the best move was to urge his people to peace and to leave the city. Hughes's reaction was considerably different. When the nativists from Philadelphia came to New York, Hughes was ready. He blamed the Catholics of Philadelphia and said, "They should have defended their churches since the authorities could not or would not do it for them."

Each church in New York was to be occupied in case of trouble by an armed force of one or two thousand men "resolved after taking as many lives as they could in defense of their property, to give up if necessary their own lives for the same cause." He informed the government of New York that "if a single Catholic Church were burned in New York, the city would become a Moscow." As the situation grew critical he descended upon the mayor of New York with the following conversation or with Hughes's interpretation of it:

"Are you afraid," asked the mayor, "that some of your churches will be burned?"

"No, sir; but I am afraid that some of *yours* will be burned. We can protect our own. I come to warn you for your own good."

"Do you think, Bishop, that your people would attack the procession?"

"I do not; but the Native Americans want to provoke a Catholic riot and if they can do it in no other way, I believe they would not scruple to attack the procession themselves, for the sake of making it appear that the Catholics had assailed them."

"What, then, would you have me do?"

"I did not come to tell you what to do. I am a churchman, not the mayor of New York; but if I were the mayor, I would examine the laws of the State, and see if there were not attached to the police force a battery of artillery, and a company or so of infantry, and a squadron of horse; and I think I should find that there were; and if so, I should call them out. Moreover, I should send [word] to Mr. Harper, the mayor-elect, who has been chosen by the votes of this party.

"I should remind him that these men are his supporters; I should warn him that if they carry out their design, there will be a riot; and I should urge him to use his influence in preventing this public reception of the delegates."

It is hard to say, at this distance, to what extent Hughes's fierceness prevented rioting in New York. It could well be that police and the government of New York were much better organized than those of Philadelphia. And the different reactions of the different archbishops may have been only minor factors in determining the outcome of the conflicts. There is surely something impressive about Hughes telling the mayor of New York that he was more worried about the Protestant churches than he was about the Catholic churches. And in the situation even the most open-minded Americanizer might have wished he could have behaved the same way. Certainly there was plenty of provocation for Hughes to surround his churches with armed men, nor did it seem very likely that a completely different style to Hughes's whole administration would have substantially lessened the danger of violence in New York (and here we part company from David O'Brien's analysis). But the point is that Hughes's general behavior simply reinforced the prejudices of the nativists, and made even the more respectable and intelligent Protestants wonder whether any rapprochement between Catholicism and American society was possible.

One would suspect that even the most "ecumenical" of Protestant Church leaders, if the word had been in use in that day, would have found Hughes a very difficult man to deal with. But John Hughes was a product of his time. The tragedy for the American Church is not so much that he was a product of his time but that on only very rare occasions was he able to rise above his own times.

If John Hughes was a fiery crusader for the rights of his own people, it must be confessed that he and indeed virtually the entire American Church were much less concerned about the rights of others. Almost to a man, the Catholic hierarchy failed to give any sort of leadership on the slavery program. The Catholics, of course, lost no love on the abolitionists, who seemed to be exactly the same people as the nativists. Their concern about the sufferings of the black man was not matched by any concern at all about the sufferings of the Irish immigrants.

The bishops did not particularly like slavery (John England said that it was a great evil to introduce into a country) but neither were they willing to suggest that it was a grievous injustice and a terrible crime in American society. The Catholics of the antebellum era were concerned about their own rights but cared little about the rights of Negroes.

After an extended visit in the South, Hughes declared that the slaves were well treated, and argued with fantastic illogic for a man so proud of his logic that the slavery system, even though it was an evil, was nevertheless to be preferred to the condition under which the Negroes would have lived if they had not been brought from Africa. In the *Metropolitan Record,* official paper of the archdiocese, in 1862, we read, "A recumbent posture under a tropical sun is his conception of paradise. And to force upon such a people a freedom they neither desire nor can appreciate, hundreds of thousands of white men are to lose their lives upon the fields of battle. And is the Abolitionist clamoring about liberty to the black man? Who proposed to despoil men of their own race and color of their liberty and property? It is these men who prayed about universal brotherhood and preached confiscation and vent all their venom upon men guilty of skin that's colored like their own. They would have the Negroes escape the primal curse."

It goes without saying that Hughes had some reluctance about the Civil War. He wrote the Secretary of War, pointing out quite clearly that Catholics were willing to fight for the support of the Constitution, the government, and the laws of the country, but that if they were required to fight for the abolition of slavery they "will turn away in disgust and disparage what would otherwise be a patriotic duty." In spite of this reluctance to approve the emancipation of the slaves, Hughes was willing to send frequent letters to Secretary of State Seward advising him how to run the war and occasionally insisting that this advice be passed on to President

Lincoln. Lincoln and Seward must have respected some of the advice, because they sent Hughes on a mission to Paris to try to counteract the Confederate mission to Louis Napoleon. Hughes, even though now in his middle sixties, eagerly and cheerfully accepted the mission, and if he did not convince the French emperor, at least charmed Napoleon and the Empress Eugénie. It was the last of Hughes's trips to Europe, and he returned in poor health scarcely able to go to Philadelphia to report to Archbishop Kenrick. He returned to New York just as the conscription riots broke out and did his best to quell the mob with a speech from the balcony of his house. But those who came to listen to him were not the rioters. And Hughes was too tired and too old to be able to talk intelligently even to those who did. Nonetheless, he did note in a somewhat pathetic manner to the rector of the North American College in Rome that after his talk the violence in the city ceased. He still must have felt that the old magic remained. But six months later he was dead.

As we have noted, Hughes was not without personal charm and had many friends among highly placed public officials, particularly Governor Seward, Thurlow Weed, and Horace Greeley. He rose to the leadership in the American Church at the time he did largely because his controversial abilities and his refusal to be cowed by recalcitrant trustees or bigoted nativists marked him above the ineffectual and pious men who sat in many of the other American bishoprics in the 1830s and the 1840s. He certainly was a symbol around which the harassed immigrants could rally. And he could on occasion be perfectly splendid in his confidence and courage. But Hughes's influence on the American Church was for the most part negative. He was the forerunner of many other ecclesiastical leaders who for all their patriotic loyalty to the American republic were to assume only a posture of pugnacious militancy vis-à-vis non-Catholics in an American society and who could grasp no other relationship with their own people besides authoritarian paternalism. None could come anywhere near to Hughes in sheer vitriolic power but many others would imitate his obstinacy and his narrow parochial viewpoint. They were, of course, playing a role not dissimilar to that which

many of the clergy played in Ireland. Unfortunately they did
not realize that a different style would have been much more
appropriate in the United States and that at least some Irish
clerics were capable of fulfilling it. Even more unfortunately,
their stubborn and insecure narrowness often reinforced the
prejudice of the natives, be they the ignorant rabble or the
sophisticated liberal. John Hughes was not so terribly different from other Counter Reformation hierarchs to be found in
the Catholic world of the nineteenth century, save that his
own personality contributed a great deal more anger and
violence to the posture of the Church. It was unfortunate that
Hughes did not realize that other courses of action were
feasible in the American society, or that there was not an
archbishop in New York who could have understood as did
Carroll and England and the Americanists later on in the
nineteenth century, that even though America was presumably
a Protestant society, it was also a society where many of the
assumptions of the Counter Reformation were no longer valid.

It is not difficult to say which side John Hughes could be
placed on in the long struggle between the Americanizers and
the anti-Americanizers. Despite his patriotism, he did not like
American society, and took it as his mission to protect his
flock from being corrupted and injured by that society. Whenever he deemed it necessary, he struck out violently against
those whom he considered to be the enemies of the Church.
John Hughes by himself could not create the defensive
"ghetto" mentality of American Catholicism but he symbolized it, reinforced it, and worst of all, failed to provide a
working alternative in precisely the time and the place where
such an alternative could have been of critical importance.

V

CONVERTS FROM BROOK FARM
Brownson and Hecker

In the late summer of 1857, an American priest sat in the anteroom of the council chamber of the Redemptorist Order in Rome. After a wait of several hours, he was admitted to face the stern and somber group. He was asked a few brief questions, but little attention was paid to his answers. Four days previously he had come as a representative of a group of five American Redemptorists, all of them converts, to plead with the superior general of the Redemptorist Order for the establishment of a Redemptorist house in Newark which would be American in its orientation. But in three interviews the general refused to discuss that issue, and insisted that Isaac Thomas Hecker had been gravely disobedient in coming to Rome to present his plea. Neither were the members of the council at all interested in the issue of whether the Redemptorist activities in the United States had to continue with strong German flavor. The only issue was whether Hecker was disobedient, and even that had been decided before he was admitted to the council chamber. He had begun to present his defense when the general of the Order preemptorily cut him short and asked the secretary to read a document. As Hecker listened in stunned disbelief, he realized that he was being expelled from this community, even though he was exercising a right to appeal to Rome that had been guaranteed by the Redemptorist constitution. He fell on his knees, then fled to a chapel for fifteen minutes of prayer. Returning once again to the council chamber, he asked for another hearing but his request was denied. In astonishment, Hecker asked, "Are you condemning me without a hearing?" They nodded in silent assent. The case was finished. The highest authority of the Redemptorist Order had, in what can only be considered in retrospect an act of blind and arrogant stupidity, expelled one of the great American converts of the nineteenth century. So much the worse for them; Isaac Thomas Hecker would go on to found his own community, which would do a much better job of capturing the spirit of American Catholicism than the nineteenth-century Redemptorists were even remotely capable of.

Hecker and his fellow convert from Brook Farm, Orestes Brownson, were unquestionably two of the outstanding Catholics of nineteenth-century America. But their careers, in addition to being of considerable interest in themselves, are of special interest to the concerns of this volume, because they emphasize some of the troubled problems and frustrations in the acculturation of the Catholic Church to the United States. In sociological theory, acculturation is a two-way process and involves not only the taking on of the traits of the host culture by the client culture but also the opposite process whereby the host culture is influenced to some extent by the client culture. There is little in the way of systematic research available on the extent to which American society has absorbed and integrated traits of the many non-Anglo-Saxon cultures which have invaded the shores of North America; but American society is not a purely Anglo-Saxon society in the sense that it was Anglo-Saxon at the time of the Revolutionary War. The immigrant ethnic groups have been permitted to live within a body politic and a body social in the United States; but more than this, some of their cultural traits have been absorbed by the larger society. Italian and German food, Polish dances, Irish songs, northern European Christmas customs, and Irish political style are obviously now the property of the whole American society. But there is little in the way of systematic knowledge available to us on either the phenomenon of reverse acculturation or the process. However, one could safely judge that in the give and take of acculturation, certain individuals would play critical roles as bridge builders.

Some members of the client culture are accepted by the host culture and are able to act as channels of communication between the two. Such was the role of John Carroll and the whole Carroll clan. On the other hand, some members of the host culture may choose to ally themselves with the client culture and to bring to it some of the values and orientations of the older culture, while at the same time dedicating their lives to persuading their former colleagues in the host culture that there need be no conflict between the two cultures. Nineteenth-century converts, particularly Brownson and his disciple Hecker, played the latter role. They were missionaries in two directions trying to persuade American society that the Roman Catholic Church responded to its higher aspirations and simultaneously trying to persuade the Church that American society, far from being hostile, represented great opportunity. The trials and tribulations of both of these converts from Brook Farm reveal much of the strengths and the weaknesses of the nineteenth-century Church.

Both were thoroughly American. Brownson, born in 1803 in Vermont, was as Yankee as the Green Mountains; and Hecker, born sixteen years later in New York City, was the son of a German immigrant who had prospered in the brass foundry business and then suffered economic setbacks which forced his three sons to become bakers. Both were involved in the radical political movement known as the Workingman's party. Both were associated with George Ripley's famous Brook Farm, a Utopian community in West Roxbury, Massachusetts—Brownson as a participant in its foundation and a frequent visitor (though never a member), and Hecker as a guest for almost a year. Both were deeply influenced by the transcendentalist movement, a religious and philosophical development which was an intrinsic part of the so-called "flowering of New England." Both went through arduous religious pilgrimages before entering the Church, though Brownson's was much longer and included several years of service as a Universalist and then a Unitarian minister. Both were close friends of many of the leading literary and philosophical lights of their day: Emerson, Amos Bronson Alcott, the Ripleys, Channing, and Thoreau. And some literary histories list Brownson as one of the transcendentalist writers, at least up to the time of his conversion.

Both were largely self-educated men, Hecker's schooling stopping at the age of twelve and Brownson's surviving only a few years into his teens. Both were vigorous original thinkers whose decisions to join the Church involved great personal sacrifice. Both were "diamonds in the rough": Brownson, a fiery, passionate, logic machine who could argue both sides of a question with equal conviction and even with some semblance of consistency; and Hecker, a poetic mystic who subsisted at one point on a diet of bread, nuts, and apples, and thought that he had learned through a vision in a dream that he was not to marry. To the rough-and-ready Irish ecclesiastics whom they encountered they must have been quite a trial. Neither of them seemed to have any doubts about the validity of Catholic claims, and both of them refused steadfastly to be disabused of the Protestant notions which they had never held. The American Church tried, often ineptly and on occasion brilliantly, to cope with these two strange visitors from another world. It was somewhat easier to deal with Hecker's gentle charm than Brownson's ferocious intellect, so there was more acceptance for Hecker in the American Church than there was for Brownson. Only after Hecker died would a cloud of suspicion and doubt descend upon his work. As for Brownson, he was temperamentally incapable of ever being out from under a cloud for very long. American Catholicism, while it learned something from these two transcendentalist converts, did not learn so very much and even today does not realize to what extent the lives and works of these two men prefigured many of the great reforms of the middle twentieth century.

While the backgrounds of the two men were similar, their basic approaches to the Church and indeed their essential contributions to the Catholicism of the nineteenth century were quite different. Hecker was a mystic who sought from a strong organized religion an external validation of the profound mystical experiences that stirred his soul. Brownson was a logician who had from reading and study arrived at a theory of "communion" which almost necessitated an organized church as the logical result of a thought process. Vincent Holden, one of Hecker's biographers, perceptively and neatly summarizes the difference: "Brownson's religion was of the head, logical and intellectual. Hecker's was of the heart, spontaneous and mystical. Brownson's religious advance was gradual, evolving slowly from one syllogism to another. Hecker's was sudden, awakened and quickened by the ever mysterious action of God. Brownson's religion was social, dealing in the interests of others. Hecker's was personal, dealing with his own soul."

Hecker said of Brownson, who led him to the Church, "He has the temperament of genius but more of a rhetorician and declaimer. He arrives at truth by a regular consecutive system of logic. His mind is of the historical rather than the poetic mold. . . . As a man, we have never known one so conscientious and self-sacrificing. . . . His love of right is supreme and his great horror, the thing he detests, is bad logic. . . . He is wholly wanting in genuine pathos. . . . His art is logic, but he never aims at art. . . . He is a man of the thirteenth or fourteenth century but not of the nineteenth. . . ."

Brownson said of Hecker, to whom he was to point the way to the Church, but whom he would follow into the Church, "Simple, uncomplicated, playful and docile child, warm and tender in his feelings, full of life, cheerfulness of manner, he infuses, as it were, his own sunshine into your heart. From his youth he has been remarkable for his singular purity of heart and gentleness of his soul and the earnestness of his spirit, his devotion to truth, and his longing after perfection."

For neither of these two men was transcendentalism anything more than a halfway house. Hecker, before he became a Catholic, when he was on friendly terms with Emerson, observed:

The Transcendentalist is one who has the keen sight but little warmth of heart. . . . He is in rapport with the spiritual world, unconscious of the celestial one. He is all nerve and no blood. Colorless. He talks of self-reliance but serves to trust himself to love. He never abandons himself to love but is always on the lookout for some new facts. His nerves are always tightly stretched like the strings of a bow, his life is all effort, and in a short period they lose their tone. Behold him sitting on a chair. He is not sitting but is braced upon his ankles as if his bones were of iron and his nerves of steel. Every nerve is drawn, his hands are clenched like a miser's. It is his lips and head that speak, not his tongue and heart. He prefers talking about love to possessing it and he prefers Socrates to Jesus. Nature is of the church and he is his own God. He is a deceptive critic, heartless, cold, and what would excite love and sympathy in others would but excite his curiosity and interest. He would have written a critical essay on the power of the soul at the foot of the cross.

For Brownson, on the other hand, the weakness of transcendentalism was that it regarded man as his own object. He held rather that "the Church must enlarge its ideal and purpose, not the progress of isolated individuals, but the progress of men in their union with humanity." And foreshadowing the doctrine of the mystical body by perhaps a hundred years, Brownson went on to say, "The profound truth of the solidarity of man in humanity and of humanity's from Jesus to God is only by a living community of the individual through humanity with Jesus and through Jesus with God that he can be redeemed and sanctified."

As a child, Brownson engaged in arguments with whomever he would encounter and indeed shortly after his conversion to the Church he would accost people on the ferryboat and attempt to argue religion with them, or create a scene in a restaurant that would not serve fish on Friday. Hecker, on the other hand, as a youth, would awaken at night with some thrilling mystical insight and dash out to look at the moonlight on the East River under the spell of some powerful and noble inspiration. For one, Brook Farm was too man-centered; and for the other, it was not rich enough in love. Almost despite themselves they saw in the Church of Rome an emphasis on the communion of the whole race with God and the profound validation for mystical love. But neither of them were exactly what the Irish clergy of New York and Boston were accustomed to dealing with. Thus Hecker could pour into his diary one night shortly before entering the Church:

> O Lord! my heart is choked from the utterance of its depth of thankfulness. O dear Christ! O sweet Christ! O living Christ! oh, more than brother, friend! oh, more than any other being can be! O Son of God! oh, Thou who showest forth the pure love of God! oh, Thou inexpressible Love! draw me nearer Thee, let me feel more of Thy purity, Thy love! Oh, baptize me with Thy Spirit and loosen my tongue that I may speak of Thy love to men! Oh, it cannot be spoken of, nor can our hearts feel its greatness. God! what is Thy mercy that Thou sufferest us to live? Our ingratitude is too great to be uttered. Lord, I am silent, for who can speak in Thy presence? O Father! O Love! O Loving-kindness! My heart could fly away!

And later on he would pen the following:

> Where shall we find God? Within.
> How shall we hear the voices of angels? Listen with the inward ear.
> When are we with God? When we are no more with ourselves.
> When do we hear the music of heaven? When we are entirely silent.
> What is the effect of sin? Confusion.
> Where does God dwell? In silence.
> Who loves God? He who knows nothing and loves nothing of himself.
> What is prayer? The breath of silence.
> What is love? The motion of the pure will.
> What is light? The shadow of love.
> What is force? The power of love.
> Where does God dwell? Where there is peace.
> Who is most like God? He who knows he is the least like Him.

What is the innermost of all? Stillness.
Who is the purest? He who is most beyond temptation.
What is the personality of man? The absolute negation
of God.
What is God? The absolute affirmation in man.
What is it to know? It is to be ignorant.
What should we desire? Not to desire.
What is the most positive answer? Silence.
What is the truest? That which cannot be proven.

One would hardly know what to do when somebody like that
came into the parish rectory.

But neither was Brownson easier to deal with in the rectory
culture since the twists and turns of his powerful mind were
terribly difficult to follow. Shortly after his conversion, he
would embarrass American Catholics by insisting with vehe-
mence that all those who were not Catholics were doomed to
perdition and would write of his sometime friend, Ralph
Waldo Emerson, as a man "who in his own character is a
striking proof of the falseness of his theory. In the very
tempest and whirlwind of his passion to the very excess of his
madness, uttering the incoherent ravings, the wildest extravagances, Mr. Emerson is eminently himself, perfectly cool and
self-possessed, and proceeds deliberately as a mathematician
to solving his problems or as a stonecutter in squaring his
blocks. . . . We seem to feel his intense personality, that he is
master of his thoughts, and that he knows what he says and
intends to say it. Here is a man to whom Almighty God has
given ability and genius of the first order and of whom we
will demand a large account."

One wonders if even John Hughes, who was generally spoil-
ing for a fight, did not wince slightly at such gratuitous treatment rendered to a popular American writer. But if Hughes
held his peace when Emerson was attacked, he did not remain
silent when Brownson several years later went even further
and began to extol the Pope's right to depose temple rulers,
a stand which was bound to stir up nativist antagonism. Even
for Hughes this was too much and he wrote Brownson telling
him that such statements were "inopportune," to which
Brownson replied that the very fact that assertion of a truth

aroused opposition was indication of its opportuneness; however, Francis Kenrick, by now Archbishop of Baltimore, was so upset that he suggested to Brownson that he "voluntarily" remove from the cover of his journal (Brownson's *Quarterly Review*) a letter of praise he had received from the American hierarchy. Brownson was clearly a difficult man. He antagonized the nativists by insisting on the temporal power of the Pope, and simultaneously he antagonized the Irish by describing them as a "miserable rabble, a noisy drinking and brawling rabble," and went on to say, "It must be conceded that the great body of foreigners naturalized is simply resident among us [and] are not republican in their spirit, their interior habits, and their interior life and discipline." He also referred to Irish writers as "bombastic orators and ignorant editors." It was truly difficult to deal with a man who could make enemies of virtually everybody in sight.

Even though both the two converts were firmly convinced of Catholicism almost before they had talked to any Catholics, it was not particularly easy for them to get into the Church. Hecker approached Hughes about the possibility of his becoming a Catholic and a priest, and was informed "their Church was one of discipline." Hecker noted that, "He seemed to think I had some loose notions of the Church . . . I am not prepared to enter the Roman Church at present. It's not natural with us since it does not meet our wants nor does it fully understand and sympathize with the experience and disposition of our people. It is principally made up of adopted and foreign individuals."

Hecker would later change his mind but Hughes was certainly no help. Walter Elliott, Hecker's first biographer, commented, "To us this is exceedingly instructive for it tells us how *not* to meet the earnest seeker after Catholic truth. Even a good-natured dog does not show his teeth when caressed. . . ."

Nor was Brownson's experience with Bishop John Fitzpatrick in Boston much better. The great New England philosopher was viewed by the auxiliary bishop of Boston as "proud and conceited." It was necessary that he be forced to bend in his own style and approach to Catholicism and accept the traditional approach. He was not the least bit interested in what had brought Brownson to the Church, but in simply making sure that Brownson had been completely purged of all his Protestant errors. Brownson so desperately wanted to be a Catholic (he was convinced his eternal salvation depended on it) that he docilely accepted a style of thought which was completely foreign to him. As Hecker observed of his friend's experience with Fitzpatrick, he was forced to "adopt a line of public controversy foreign to his genius and one which had not brought him into the Church and perhaps could not have done so." Brownson's own comments are more than a little pathetic. "I really thought that I had made some philosophic discoveries which would be of value even to Catholic theologians in convincing and converting unbelievers and I tried to have them accepted by the Catholic Bishop. But I perceived almost instantly that he either was ignorant of my doctrine of life or placed no confidence in it. . . . My trouble was great and the bishop could not relieve me so I dared not disclose to him its source."

Hecker, who himself found that most of his convert instructions with Bishop Fitzpatrick had involved an attempt to "purge him from communism," which Fitzpatrick assumed he had practiced at Brook Farm, commented on the sad effect on Brownson of being under Fitzpatrick's instruction and then censorship for a decade. "Dr. Brownson, by shifting his argument . . . lost never to regain the leadership Providence had designed for him. I always maintain that Dr. Brownson was wrong in thus yielding to the bishop's influence and he should have held on to the course Providence had started him in. Had he held on to the way inside of the Church which had interested him outside of the Church, he might perhaps have carried with him many non-Catholic minds of a leading character." At another time Hecker observed with perception and perhaps more anger than one would have expected of so gentle a soul, "Dr. Brownson . . . found that he could not solve the problem of even a destiny in harmony with reason without the aid of Catholic teaching and discipline. For this applied only after he had settled the philosophical question of objective reality in the facts of con-

sciousness. These branches of philosophical controversy were
the providential theses of his life. By means of them he could
have cleared away passion, prejudice, ignorance in the minds
of his fellow countrymen, especially in New England, and
brought them to a position in the multitudes correct and inevitable as his own. What Dr. Brownson was best able to do
he was not called upon to do enough of."

To put the matter more bluntly, Hecker was saying that the
treatment Brownson received in coming into the Church and
being forced to submit to intellectual discipline which wasn't
part of the essence of Catholicism alienated him from the
American environment, and produced an erratic and irascible
militancy. For a brief number of years during and after the
Civil War, Brownson suffered what he would later call "a
lapse into liberalism"; but these years marked a return to his
authentic genius and produced a tremendously important philosophical contribution to American Catholicism.

Brownson was of course a difficult man and one must be
careful of blaming Bishop Fitzpatrick for completely maiming
him. Hecker, on the other hand, was a gentle, sensitive soul,
who could have been easily hurt and for whom harsh treatment would have been particularly blameworthy. Harsh treatment he did receive, but beneath the gentle exterior it turned
out that there was a will of iron which could not be bent from
the great vision that Hecker had. His experience with the
Redemptorist spirit in the seminary in Belgium was peculiar
but on the whole pleasant. His superiors recognized him as a
man of extraordinary gifts of prayer who could withstand all
the tests of obedience which were taken to be part of the
development of the good religious. They were so impressed
with him, in fact, that they were willing to overlook his
pathetic inability to comprehend classroom work, an inability
in part attributed to his inadequate schooling in his earlier
years and in part to the fact that mysticism interfered with his
study.

The real problems came after his return to America when
he and a group of other Redemptorists who were also converts
began to preach missions in various cities of the United States.
Clarence Walworth, Augustine Hewbit, George Deshon, and

Francis Baker all shared Hecker's vision of the possibilities of immense conversions in the United States but they all agreed that the strong Germanic flavor of the American Redemptorists was a distinct disadvantage in working with those beyond the boundaries of German ethnic groups. They were particularly confident that there would be many more vocations to the Redemptorist Order if it were not virtually required of the young men to become Germans to be accepted into the community (German was the official language of Redemptorist houses in the United States). The provincial was a timid, insecure man who didn't quite know how to cope with these enthusiastic, unorthodox Americans, especially since the new general of the Redemptorists had insisted that only the most rigorous kind of discipline and most unquestioning obedience would be necessary to restore vitality to the order. Bishop James Bayley of Newark was eager to have an American Redemptorist house open in his diocese but the Redemptorist superiors did not approve the project and rather proposed to send the American missionaries to Quebec and to an island in the Caribbean. After considerable soul-searching the five converts delegated Hecker as the representative to Rome to plead the case for an American house and for better understanding of the nature of the American mission. They based Hecker's mission on the provision in the Redemptorist constitution which permitted an appeal to Rome. However, as described earlier, Hecker had scarcely arrived in the Eternal City when he discovered that the case had been decided and that not only were his petitions to be denied, but he was to be expelled from the Order for even daring to present them. There was a great deal of self-righteousness in the way the Redemptorist superior pronounced his death sentence on Hecker's dreams, and also a great deal of stupidity.

Fortunately there were others in Rome who could not stomach the harsh injustice worked on Hecker, and under the guidance of the sensitive and fair-minded Cardinal Barnabo, Hecker managed after six months of maneuvering to have himself and his colleagues released from the Redemptorist vows (hence implicitly his expulsion from the order was revoked) and authorized to establish a new missionary community to work in the United States. For all practical purposes, it can be said that the Paulists were not founded because they wanted to leave the Redemptorists, but because they were thrown out on their ears.

John Hughes's behavior in the case was characteristic. Hecker had visited him before going to Rome to inform him of the full nature of the problem and Hughes had approved not only the appeal for an American house but also the appeal for better understanding of the work of the American fathers. However, when he received a letter later from the Redemptorist general announcing Hecker's dismissal, he wrote to Rome that he was completely uninformed about the precise nature of Hecker's visit. But worse than that, several weeks after replying to the general's letter the Archbishop would tell Fathers Deshon and Baker that he had not replied to the letter from Rome. The two Paulists left the Archbishop's house quite disappointed. Deshon remarked, "If we succeed without him, he will be our friend. If we do not, he will be ready to lend a parting kick." Father Walworth characterized Hughes as "a heartless friend as well as an ungenerous foe." The absence of support from the Archbishop could have weighed heavily against Hecker's cause in Rome had not the other members of the American hierarchy come to his rescue. Archbishops Kenrick of Baltimore, Spalding of Louisville, Purcell of Cincinnati, and Bishop Lynch of Charleston all wrote extremely strong letters in support of the American missionary. Kenrick's letter was particularly surprising because he was heavily dependent on the Redemptorists for work among the German-speaking people in his archdiocese. The support of the archbishop of Baltimore and of the highly respected Spalding plus Cardinal Barnabo's shrewd advice assured Hecker of victory and the Congregation of St. Paul was born. In the midst of the battle, however, it became evident that the mystic was also an extraordinarily able politician and there wasn't much doubt about his being elected the first superior of the new congregation. He and his colleagues determined that New York was the place where they would be most effective, and despite their unpleasant experience with Archbishop Hughes, they

chose to begin their work of converting America on Fifty-
ninth Street in New York City.

As long as Hecker lived, the American bishops knew what
a prize they had, and he was recommended at least once for
promotion to the hierarchy and attended the Vatican Council
as a delegate for an American bishop who could not attend.
But while the hierarchy respected Brownson's talents they did
not understand his doctrine (especially since it seemed to be
changing so frequently) and could not cope with him as a
man. American Catholicism in the middle of the nineteenth
century had room for Isaac Thomas Hecker but it had no
room for Orestes Brownson. The latter's ideas would be almost completely lost while the former's would be listened to
(especially as expressed in his highly influential journal, *The
Catholic World*) and admired until a dark cloud fell on them
in the Americanism controversy at the end of the century. The
net result was virtually the same. American Catholicism
moved into the twentieth century having learned very little
from these two thoroughly American giants who had tried to
build bridges between Catholicism and America. Hecker left
after him a religious community which even though it has had
a number of identity problems has found most recently in the
ecumenical movement a work that is particularly in keeping
with Hecker's genius. Orestes Brownson, however, left behind
him only twenty volumes of collected works that practically
nobody reads any more.

Such a fate for these two nineteenth-century converts was
unfortunate. Both had much to say that was relevant to the
Church in their day and which even in our day seems still to
be quite pertinent.

Like the other Americanizers of the nineteenth century,
Brownson was a strong advocate of the relationship between
Church and state that existed in the United States. In the
American Republic, perhaps his greatest book, he observed
that

the Church being free and the state harmonizing with her,
Catholicism has in the freedom of both all the protection
it needs, all the security it can ask and all the support it

can in the nature of the case receive from external institutions. The religious mission of the United States is not to establish the Church by external law . . . but to maintain Catholic freedom, neither absorbing the state in the Church nor the Church in the state, but leaving . . . each to move freely according to its own nature. It is a sincere sign of the internal order of things. The effect of this mission on our country fully realized would be to harmonize Church and state, religion and politics, not by absorbing either in the other or by obliterating a natural distinction between them, but by conforming both to the real or divine order which is supreme and immutable.

Under such circumstances Brownson, like Hecker, had a very strong faith in the appeal of Catholicism to the American mind and the possibility of the eventual conversion of the country. He said, "Our own belief is that very few would reject our religion." He felt the real problem was caused by those within the Church who "believe or feel or imagine that the Church is a . . . spiritual despotism." Therefore he felt that it was his role to make it clear that "in her teaching, faith and reason are reconcilable from the start; authority and private judgment when rightly understood are harmonious. When they are not so, the fault is that of Catholics, not of Catholicity."

One of Brownson's biographers suggests that Brownson had John Hughes in mind when he wrote those words. But if he did, Brownson was being too optimistic when he thought that a mere reformation of the structure and attitudes of Catholic Church government and attitudes of Catholic leaders would win over American society. Nonetheless, he was in the process of adopting attitudes which a century later would appear again as cornerstones of the Catholic ecumenical movement. One of the statements could easily have been made by Pope John: "We must be allowed to make those modifications in the human elements of the beliefs and doctrines of Catholics which the present state of non-Catholic thought and intelligence render necessary." He further argued, "We do not refute false doctrines simply by putting out their falsehood; we must do it by distinguishing between the true and the false, and by showing that we accept the true and integrate it into a higher unity. In the early numbers of our review[1] we wrote not a few articles against Protestants and unbelievers in favor of Catholicity which were perfectly satisfactory and conclusive to our Catholic friends but which had little or no effect on those who held the errors we labored to refute except to puzzle and bewilder them. There was something not unjust in the reply. 'Your arguments are logical; they are well put; they silence; they do not convince.' "

He further insisted that Catholics could not ignore the progress of physical sciences. "We must beat the heterodox and unbelieving on their own ground, with their own weapons. We must be more scientific than they, and more perfect masters of science. . . . Of all the people in the world, we Catholics are the most blameworthy of the neglect of the sciences on which civilization more immediately depends. We have no excuse. The world can be saved only by the faith which we alone have in the unity and integrity in God and demand the strict reckoning of us for the use we make of it."

During the time of his freedom from Bishop Fitzpatrick's censorship, Brownson returned to his doctrine of communion. In his autobiography, *The Convert,* he describes the insights of the doctrine which had brought him into the Church but which he had abandoned under the belief that he could not be a sincere Catholic and follow this line of theologizing. One of the few American theological studies of Brownson (the Doctoral dissertation of Rev. George K. Malone, *The Apologetics of Orestes Brownson*) summarizes the apologetic of *The Convert* in eleven points:

1.   It is assumed that man can and must make progress.

2.   By its nature progress is in some way supernatural.

3.   The doctrine of life by communion, by showing that man can make progress through contact with a superior or supernatural object, shows that the supernatural elevation of man is possible.

[1] When Bishop Fitzpatrick was still peering over his shoulder.

4. The testimony of the human race asserting the elevation of certain Providential Men, of whom the epitome is Jesus Christ, shows that the supernatural is a fact.

5. Moreover, Jesus Christ is the *only* mediator between God and man.

6. Since man cannot commune directly with Jesus, he needs a mediator, who is provided through Apostolic succession.

7. Since the followers of Christ lead one life, they form an organism, to which it is necessary to belong.

8. Since this body lives Christ's life, it must have divinely commissioned authority.

9. Since the life is transmitted by communion, the Church must have been uninterruptedly operative from Christ's time to modern times.

10. Because of the difficulty created by schisms and the resulting separation from Rome of the dissident Orientals and the Protestants, this necessity of uninterrupted operation makes it clear that the current of Christian life has flowed and still flows only through the Roman Catholic Church.

11. Therefore the Roman Catholic Church is the true Church of Jesus Christ to which all must belong in order to live supernatural life.

It is reasonably easy to demonstrate, as Malone in fact does, that Brownson's apologetics of communion can have an unorthodox interpretation. Presumably if we were to take the words of many great theologians at exactly their face value, it can also prove that they do not measure up to the strict standards of orthodoxy, at least as found in the pre-Vatican theological manual. But one would think that the most useful approach to Brownson's apologetics is not to apply rigorous tests of precise orthodoxy to them, but rather to attempt to understand the point he was making. Three-quarters of a century before the doctrine of the Church as the body of

Christ was to become popular once again, Brownson had argued his way into the Church on the basis of the intuitive comprehension of the importance of that doctrine and was contending that the appeal of Church as body and Church as community would be the most effective way of presenting Catholicism to American non-Catholics. It was a magnificent insight and its magnificence was not diminished by the fact that Brownson was forced to suppress it for more than a decade and that few, if any, people who listened to him perceived the importance of what he was saying.

Hecker, too, was delighted with American governmental forms. "The form of government of the United States is preferable to Catholics than other forms. It is more favorable than others to the practices of those virtues which are necessary conditions of development of a religious life in man. This government leaves men a larger margin for liberty of action, and hence for cooperation with the guidance of the Holy Spirit, than any other government under the sun. With these popular institutions men enjoy greater liberty in working out their true destiny. The Catholic Church will therefore flourish all the more in this republican country in proportion as her representatives keep in their civil lives to the lines of the republicanism." Of the members of his own religious order he argued: "A Paulist is a Christian man who came to a Christian perfection consistent with his natural characteristics and the type of civilization of his country." Hecker would then have his followers develop the best that was within their own human personality in order to most adequately relate that which was best in the culture around them. He contended, "So far as it is compatible with faith and piety, I am for accepting the American civilization with its usages and customs. Leaving aside other reasons, it is the only way in which Catholicism can become the religion of our people. The character and spirit of our people and their institutions must find themselves at home in our Church in the way those of other nations have done. And it is on this basis alone that the Catholic religion can make progress in our country."

It is therefore necessary in the Paulist community that there be tremendous emphasis on initiative and responsibility. "A

Paulist is to emphasize individuality, that is to make individual liberty an essential element in every judgment that touches the life and welfare of the community and its members. Those who emphasize the community element are inclined to look upon this as a dangerous and impractical experiment. . . . Individuality is an integral and conspicuous element in the life of a Paulist; this must be felt. One of the natural signs of a true Paulist is that he would prefer excesses of liberty than the arbitrary actions of tyranny. . . . The individual man cannot be too strong or his liberty too great when he is guided by the spirit of God. When one is easily influenced from below rather than from above, it is evidence that the spirit of pride and of the flesh is not of the liberty and the glory of the children of God."

Hecker felt that this emphasis on individuality was distinctive to his own order. "Many other communities lay the main stress on community life as the chief element giving it control as far as it is consistent with the fundamental individual right. Paulists, on the contrary, give the element of individuality the first place and put it in control as far as is consistent with the common life." However, there was still a necessity for community discipline. "When it comes into conflict with the common right, the individual must yield to the community. The common life outranks the individual life in case of conflict, but the individual life should be regarded as sacred and never be effaced."

Hecker was convinced that the delicate balance that must be be kept in all communities between freedom and unity would not be difficult within the Paulists; the superior was indeed a "true Paulist." And subordinates were also "true Paulists, that is to say, keenly sensitive of personal rights, as well as appreciative of such that are common." He then raises a critical question that would certainly be asked anybody pushing such a revolutionary emphasis in the religious life. "How about persons of dull minds or of little spiritual ambition coming to the use of this freedom?" Hecker's answer was perfectly simple. "No such person should be allowed to enter the community." In other words, it would not be difficult to maintain the balance between individual freedom and community responsibility so long as those who were chosen to be admitted into the order were mature, dedicated individuals.

The superior's job was to facilitate the work of individuals within the community. "It is the duty of Paulist superiors to elicit spontaneous zeal of the fathers to further it with his authority. . . . But the center of the action is individual, is in the soul moved by the Holy Ghost; not in the superior of the community. . . . If he be moved by the Holy Spirit, he will be most obedient to his superior and will not only be submissive to the authority of the Church, but careful to follow out her spirit."

Hecker may have been unduly optimistic about how easy it would be to reconcile freedom and authority, but insisting on the need to respect the dignity and the uniqueness of individual members of the community was a Christian insight that had been overlooked through the Counter Reformation centuries. It was particularly important in the society of the United States in the nineteenth century. It would take another hundred years for the church universal to rediscover the wisdom of this insight.

Hecker also insisted that the spiritual director ought not to attempt to dominate or manipulate the soul under his guidance. "True spiritual direction consists of discovering the obstacles in the way of divine guidance in aiding and encouraging the penitent to remove them and in teaching how the interior movement to the Holy Spirit may be recognized as well as in stimulating the soul to fidelity and docility. The director is not to take the place of the Holy Ghost. . . ."

"The primary worker of the soul sanctification is the Holy Spirit acting interiorly. The work of the director is secondary and subordinate. To overlook this fundamental truth of the spiritual life is a great mistake, whether it be on the part of the director or the one under direction."

Obviously, Hecker's notions about the governance in the religious communities and the direction of the individual person put tremendous emphasis on the importance of the Holy Spirit working in the soul. So it would not be easy for individuals to deceive themselves into thinking they were being led by the Holy Spirit when in fact they were not. Hecker's response to this was an indication of his own path to the Church.

> The solution of the difficulty is as follows: The action of the Holy Spirit embodied visibly in the authority of the Church and the action of the Holy Spirit dwelling invisibly in the soul form one inseparable synthesis; and he who has not a clear conception of this two-fold action of the Holy Spirit is in danger of running into one or the other, and sometimes into both, of these extremes, either of which is destructive of the end of the Church. The Holy Spirit, in the external authority of the Church, acts as the infallible interpreter and criterion of divine revelation. The Holy Spirit in the soul acts as the divine Life-giver and Sanctifier. It is of the highest importance that these two distinct offices of the Holy Spirit should not be confounded.

Hecker emphasized very strongly the need for the "natural virtues" such as "honesty, temperance, truthfulness, kindliness, courage and manliness." He contended not only that these virtues were essential if one was to be effective in American society, but also that just as the exercise of reason is necessary to faith, so the integrity of natural virtues is the best preparation for the grace of God.

"Catholicity is that religion which links itself to all the faculties of mind and proofreads all the instincts of human nature, and by thus comparing with the work of the Creator, confirms its own divine origin."

The ultimate reason for Hecker's insistence on the importance of the natural virtues was another theological insight which was to become much more popular a century later; Hecker saw no conflict between the workings of the Creator and the Redeemer.

> And we further insist on the natural virtues because they tend to place man in true relations with himself and with nature, thus bringing him into more perfect relation or union with God than he was by means of the creative act—a

proper preliminary to his supernatural relation. Who will deny that there were men not a few among the heathen in whom Prudence, Justice, Fortitude, and Temperance were highly exemplified? They knew well enough what right reason demanded. Such men as Socrates, Plato, Epictetus, and Marcus Aurelius had by the natural light of reason a knowledge of what their nature required of them. They had faults, great ones if you please; at the same time they knew them to be faults, and they had the natural virtues in greater or less degrees. Thus the union between God and the soul, due to the creative act, though not sufficient, never was interrupted. The Creator and the Mediator are one.

Hecker's emphasis on freedom, the natural virtues, and the inspiration of the individual by the Holy Spirit was perfectly orthodox, though it was an emphasis which had not been made for several centuries. In the Americanism controversy after his death (occasioned by a French translation of Elliott's *Life of Hecker*), Pope Leo XIII would condemn in his encyclical letter *Testem benevolentiae* certain aberrations from sound doctrine which many enemies of the Americanists thought was a condemnation of Hecker, but the Holy See declined to place either the English or the French version of Elliott's book on the Index. Any fair and open-minded reading of Elliott's book and the encyclical letter would demonstrate that the condemned doctrines were not held by Hecker and do not appear in Elliott's biography. One could, by pulling some of Hecker's statements out of context, draw conclusions from them which might not be orthodox. But such manipulations can be performed on any work, including the New Testament.

While Hecker's orthodoxy may have been questioned by French monarchists, who used the American controversy as a means of punishing French republicans, and by the American opponents of Archbishop Ireland and Bishop Keane, Rome apparently had no doubt about the orthodoxy of what Hecker had written. In our own age, Hecker's words seem not only orthodox but prophetic. Unfortunately, the Americanism controversy permitted a cloud to descend upon Hecker's memory, a cloud not of suspicion but rather of uncertainty and doubt.

For a generation and even two generations, American Catholics and scholars would not be terribly concerned about developing and exploring his insights. In the long run, Hecker's work would suffer the same fate as Brownson's, except that Hecker would be spared the necessity of seeing his ideas ignored in his own lifetime.

Most of the books written about the American Church in the nineteenth century point with pride to these two great converts from Brook Farm and from transcendentalism. But what such accounts overlook is the fact that the major efforts of Hecker and Brownson were not successful. Their goal of converting America to Catholicism was in retrospect naïve; and their mission to modify the American Church so that it could have much wider appeal among non-Catholic Americans was conspicuously unsuccessful. Hecker and Brownson were trying to do no more than John Carroll had done, though having come in to the Church from the outside in adult life they had more fully developed ideas of what form Catholicism ought to take in American society. If they had been professional theologians, they might have been more precise in choosing the terms to describe a transformation which they desired. And if Brownson had been a less irascible man, his confusing ability to argue both sides of the question might not have so puzzled American ecclesiastics. But it seems rather certain that it would not have made much difference. Brownson and Hecker were not listened to not because they were imprecise, or occasionally self-contradictory, but because American Catholicism thought it had no time to listen. Even though they were both largely self-educated men, Brownson and Hecker were men of ideas, men who could step back from the hustle of everyday activities and think about ultimate goals. In the mushrooming Catholicism of the middle nineteenth century there was precious little room for such people. There were new dioceses to be formed, new churches to be built, new immigrants to be cared for, new locations to be sought, new schools to be opened. The church leaders of the middle nineteenth century were not on a priori grounds opposed to men with ideas, nor even suspicious of them. But they really didn't quite know what to do with such men, just as they really didn't know quite what to do with John England.

Hecker was valued and respected, one suspects, not so much because of his theories but because of the invaluable service that his new religious order provided. Paulists preached missions, gave retreats, and administered parishes, which was the sort of activity that ecclesiastical leaders of the middle nineteenth century could value. His ideas were harmless enough and could be reconciled with the propositions in theology manuals, so they caused no great concern. Indeed, many of the bishops must have thought that they were very fine ideas. They sounded so thoroughly and patriotically American.

Similarly Brownson at his patriotic best was a real asset to the American Church though one could not be sure how long he would be on the patriotism emphasis before he shifted to exactly the opposite. Of course both men were converts. "You can never really be certain what a convert would do"; but such distinguished converts were proof that Catholicism was making great progress. And so the clergy and hierarchy were reasonably content with the two strange men from Brook Farm, though frequently puzzled by them.

But that their ideas might open vast new horizons to the Church of the United States, which might require drastic internal reorganization and perhaps completely new methods of dealing with religion in the American environment—such thoughts simply did not occur to most American Catholics, clerical or lay, in the middle of the nineteenth century. Unfortunately, they would not occur until the middle of the twentieth century either, not until the Second Vatican Council began to emphasize some of the same things on which Brownson and Hecker had insisted. It is ironic that American Catholics are unaware of the importance of the two converts from Brook Farm and that very few realize how much of the Vatican renewal was anticipated in the thinking and the writing of Brownson and Hecker. They are still names in history books and not prophets. But these voices ought to ring out as loud and clear today as they did at a time when even Abraham Lincoln attended a lecture by Orestes Brownson.

VI

THE AMERICANISTS
Gibbons, Ireland, Keane, Spalding

In the decade that passed between the end of the Third Council of Baltimore and beginning of the twentieth century, American Catholicism went through a period of excitement and crisis. From 1880 to 1900, the Catholic population jumped from six million to twelve million as immigration reached close to its all-time high. New dioceses were founded almost every year and the expansion of the Church went ahead at a pace even more rapid than in previous decades. There was a different atmosphere about this late-century expansion: for by 1880 the American Church was serenely confident it could handle any conceivable expansion. Indeed one of the reasons for the German controversy was the suggestion by German welfare organizations that large numbers of immigrants had left the Church. By this time the American Church had little self-doubt about its ability to survive in the United States and had bright dreams about its prospects for fantastic success; the suggestion that it was failing the immigrants was unthinkable (and as it turned out, untrue).

A good deal of the new optimism that characterized Catholicism at the end of the nineteenth century was similar to the optimism of the whole country in the years at the close of the century. Some of this naïve faith in progress had rubbed off on the liberal segment of the Catholic hierarchy. The wounds of the Civil War had been healed (at the price of permanent segregation of the Negro). The frontier was about to be closed; America was becoming a great power, industry and commerce were expanding at a fantastic rate only slightly affected by the periodic depressions. It seemed to some Catholics that the manifest destiny of the United States suggested the manifest destiny of American Catholicism. It is not surprising then that during these years there rose up a group of ecclesiastical leaders who represented the Americanizing trend in Catholicism at its strongest and most brilliant. It is also to be expected that opposition to these confident and at times arrogant Americanists could be found among the more hesitant members of their own Church, to say nothing of ecclesiastical leaders in Europe. The four principal Americanists were James Gibbons, John Ireland, John Keane, and John Lancaster Spalding. Whether Spalding was an Americanist or not is hotly debated. He broke with John Ireland on the school issue; on the other hand, on the question of the apostolic delegation, Spalding was even more of an Americanist than Ireland. Perhaps it can be said about Spalding that he was a maverick Americanist.

They were gifted men with splendid oratorical skills, great capacity to stir up support, and sublime self-confidence. Two-thirds of a century later they still are held as among the greatest figures American Catholicism has ever known. They fought a series of running battles with their domestic and foreign opponents, winning many of the battles and definitely losing none of them. But it cannot be contended that the Americanists triumphed. Even without the condemnation of a heresy called "Americanism," the Americanists probably would have been beaten; but the condemnation of this "phantom heresy," even though none of the Americanists held it, for all practical purposes meant defeat for their cause. The condemnation had effectively put out most of the fires that the Americanists lighted. Their brilliant and imaginative campaign to finally Americanize the Catholic Church in the United States at best could be called openly a partial success, and leaders of their splendor have not again appeared on the ecclesiastical scene.

1. *John Ireland*

John Ireland was born in Kilkenny, Ireland, in 1838. In the midst of the potato famine a decade later, the Ireland family migrated to the United States, first to Chicago, and then in 1852 to Minnesota. He was in the city but a year when he decided to study for the priesthood and was sent by Bishop Cretin to a seminary in the diocese of Belley in France. While there, the future archbishop of St. Paul began a romance with the French nation and the French culture that was never to end. He returned in 1861 to be ordained in time to serve as a chaplain in the Civil War and to become something of a hero at the Battle of Corinth, where he helped to rally the Union troops after a surprise Confederate attack. He attended the Vatican Council as a representative of his bishop, Thomas Grace, who was seriously ill; was named auxiliary bishop in 1875; and after a decade of service in the St. Paul diocese, he became its bishop in 1884. In 1888, St. Paul became an archdiocese and John Ireland its first archbishop.

During his years as priest and a bishop, he was active in two social programs that had great popularity with progressive Catholics of the time: the colonization movement, which hoped to settle immigrants in rural communities made up entirely of members of their own faith; and the temperance movement, which intended to eliminate the sufferings created by the immigrants' passion for John Barleycorn. Neither movement proved to be conspicuously successful but Ireland's enthusiasm for them never waned.

Ireland was also tremendously interested in politics and was perhaps more involved in it than any other American bishop before or since. He was an intensely partisan Republican who took it as his mission in life to lead Catholics from the Democratic party to the Republican. He was not content merely with campaigning openly for Republican presidential candidates. He was also quite capable of interfering in New York politics. When a Catholic member of the State Board of Regents died, the New York Democrats chose Bishop Mc-

Quaid as their candidate to fill the vacancy. And the Republicans rather cleverly proposed as their candidate Father Sylvester Malone, who was a friend of Ireland. The Archbishop of St. Paul (McQuaid's bitter enemy), thereupon descended upon New York and campaigned for Malone, who was swept into office in 1894. McQuaid rose in his pulpit, denounced him for meddling in another bishop's territory, as an enemy of the parochial schools, and as one who supported the American Protective Association (A.P.A.). He was also charged with accepting bribes from Republicans, and his conduct was described as "undignified, disgraceful to his episcopal office, and a scandal in the eyes of all right-minded Catholics." Rome rebuked McQuaid this time and Ireland fancied himself a victor. He continued to bait McQuaid and the other bishops who refused to even vote in a national election for fear that this would encourage criticism of the Catholic Church by observing that any American who refused to vote deserved disenfranchisement or exile. This led a Chicago newspaper to respond that Ireland was "the one metropolitan of all whose intense devotion to American institutions has been constantly conspicuous."

John Ireland therefore was a flaming, outspoken progressive who never suffered a moment of self-doubt and had all the tact and diplomatic skill of an enraged bison. His flashing oratory and his great dramatic flair made him many friends but his cutting wit and his intolerance of disagreement made him many enemies. It is most unlikely that the controversies of the end of the nineteenth century would have been nearly as violent as they were if it had not been for the fierce temperament of the archbishop of St. Paul.

One of the things that John Ireland never doubted was his devotion to the American republic:

Republic of America, receive from me the tribute of my love and of my loyalty. With my whole soul I do thee homage. I pray from my heart that thy glory be never dimmed. *Esto perpetua.* Thou bearest in thy hands the hopes of the human race, thy mission from God is to show to nations that men are capable of highest civil and political liberty.

Be thou ever free and prosperous. Through thee may liberty triumph over the earth from the rising to the setting
sun. *Esto perpetua.* Believe me, no hearts love thee more
ardently than Catholic hearts, no tongues speak more honestly thy praises than Catholic tongues, and no hands will
be lifted up stronger and more willing to defend, in war
and in peace, thy laws and thy institutions than Catholic
hands. *Esto perpetua.*

He had great sympathy also for the spirit of the age and
urged the Church not to be afraid of it. He argued:

It was the religion of Christ first whispered into the ears
of the world the sacred words charity, brotherhood, liberty.
It was the religion of Christ that took to its bosom bleeding,
agonizing humanity, warmed it with divine love, healed its
sores, and breathed into it health and vigor. And only under
the blessed guidance of the religion of Christ can humanity
proceed on the road towards greater progress . . . whisper
in tender accents to liberty that religion cherishes it, go
down in sympathy to the suffering multitude, bring to them
charity and what is more rarely given justice. Let them
know what religion will ward off the oppression of capital
and will teach capital that its rights are dependent upon its
fulfillment of duties. . . . Laymen need not wait for priests
nor priests for bishops nor bishops for Pope. The timid
move in crowds, the brave in single file, the Church must
regain the sceptre of science which he wielded for ages.
To sing lovely anthems in cathedral stalls, wear coats of
embroidered gold . . . while the world outside is dying of
spiritual and moral starvation, that is not the religion we
need today.

In another, more sophisticated and cynical age, Ireland's
rhetoric may frequently seem to be a bit too much; but his
ideas, if they can be separated from the flamboyant mode of
expression, are not a bit old-fashioned. His pleas for social
and racial justice indeed seem quite modern: "Into the arena!
Priests and laymen, seek out social evils and lead in movements that tend to rectify them, speak of vested rights for that
is necessary but speak of vested rights and strive by word and

example, by enactment and enforcement of laws to correct them." He supported the Knights of Labor in their struggle to avoid a condemnation by the Holy See and was bitter in his denunciation of racial injustice. In 1890, he observed that prejudice against men because of their color made him ashamed as a man, a citizen, and a Christian, and added that every prejudice entertained, every breach of charity and justice against a man because of color, has stained for them the banner of our liberty that floats over us. "They who compel a man because of his color to betake himself to a corner marked for his race contradict the principle of justice and right established by the God of Mercy." His enemies, Archbishops Patrick J. Ryan of Philadelphia and Michael A. Corrigan of New York, were quite upset because they thought Ireland's enthusiasm had led him too far, that is to say, far enough to demand social equality for Negroes. Ireland was quite perceptive about the unpopularity of his stand and about its future timeliness: "Untimely today, my words will be timely tomorrow, my fault if there be a fault would be that I'm ahead of my day." Ahead of his day on many issues John Ireland was, but it did not make him any more acceptable to his enemies that he was serenely confident that history would justify his every word. More often than not however, he was right.

He could not abide those Catholics who were opposed to the spirit of the times and especially to the boundless optimism of the concluding decade of the nineteenth century:

What! The Church of the Living God, the Church of ten thousand victories over pagans and barbarians, over heresies and false philosophies, over defiant kings and unruly peoples—the great, freedom-loving, truth-giving civilizing Catholic Church—this Church of the nineteenth century afraid of any century, not seeing in the ambitions of the nineteenth century the fervent ebullitions of her own noble sentiments, and in its achievements for the elevation of mankind the germinations of her own Christlike plantings, this Church not eager for the fray, not precipitating herself with love irresistible upon this modern world to claim it, to bless it, to own it for Christ.

I preach the new, the most glorious crusade. Church and age! Unite them in the name of humanity, in the name of God.

And the best manifestation of the spirit of the nineteenth century was the United States of America. Between Catholicism and this republic there could be no contradiction:

> I can truly say that my Catholic heart and my American heart are one, and I am delighted to say that the free air of America has cheered the soul of Leo XIII, and that he has not been without guidance from our institutions. When the question is asked, "Do you put Church before country or country before Church?", I say that one is not to be put before the other. They are in different spheres altogether, and so far as principle goes, the Church tells me that service to the State and country is a solemn, sacred, religious duty. I do not think that anyone is fit to enter the kingdom of heaven who is not capable of taking care of, so far as the opportunity affords, this magnificent kingdom given to us here, the republic of America.
>
> Church and Country; soul and body; the one is necessary to the other, and there is no distinction between the love we owe to the one and that which the other demands. Church and Country; nature and grace; and grace demands as its soil a thorough and well prepared field, and a field made thorough and beautiful by nature is enhanced when the dews of supernal grace fall on it.

And he could not abide the accusation that Catholicism was a "foreign institution":

> Yes, if the Savior of the World is a foreigner, and the Bishop of Rome as His vicar is a foreigner. The Catholic Church is extra-American, supra-national, begotten for all nations—a foreigner on no spot of the earth's surface. Catholics demand no special power—merely equal rights for all. The rights of Catholics are the rights of the personal conscience of the Catholic citizen. It is not the Catholic Church in its official name that comes into issue—it is the American citizen, whose religious faith is the faith of the Catholic

Church. Not to know one's rights is lowmindedness; not to defend them is cowardice.

He was willing to do battle at the drop of a coin, and the Lucerne memorial of Peter Paul Cahensly (which will be discussed later), even though relatively harmless in its actual words, was enough to send John Ireland off into a paroxysm of rage (in a letter to Gibbons):

Is there no protest to be made by us as regards what has been so aptly called the "Lucerne conspiracy"? Is Mr. Cahensly, Herr Schlosser [sic], Premier Mercier etc., to go on telling Rome how the Church in America is to be ruled, with our silence and apparent approval? Are we, by saying nothing showing ourselves worthy of the trust which our people put in us? Will not Rome herself deem us worthless men, whom she need not consult on this or any other matter, in which we are concerned? I am reading the late book of "Drumont" in which you are quoted as the model bishop because of your courage to speak out in the case of the K[nights] of L[abor]—your action being in contrast with that of the Cardinal of Paris, who is by nature all submission, and who is, on consequence, utterly ignored by Rome. The American Church has been deeply insulted. We look to you as our leader to invite the Archbishops to meet with you and counsel with you. The time fixed for our November meeting is too distant. By that time the whole value will be lost to our protest.

I know your delicacy of sentiment, which might tempt you not to act, lest jealous minds complain. I honor this delicacy. Yet, it must at times yield before stern duty. Ask the Archbishops to meet you, if convenient to them, and, if not, to write to you. A certain number will come—sufficient to take action. You will say I am hasty and need to be repressed. Not so, this time I think. We are American bishops; an effort is made to dethrone us and to foreignize our country in the name of religion. The question will not be as to quarrels between us and Germans—or Canadians in America—that is a home question. But it will be as to men daring to rule us from Germany or Canada. Our non-Catholic fellow-citizens can well call us traitors if we are silent.

If German-American Catholics were upset by this kind of rhetoric, it is perhaps understandable. But John Ireland was so thoroughly American that he could not abide any influence which would isolate the Church from contact with all that was best in American society:

> We desire to win the age. Let us not, then, stand isolated from it. Our place is in the world as well as in the sanctuary; in the world, wherever we can prove our love for it or render it a service. We cannot influence men at long range; close contact is needed. Let us be with them in the things that are theirs—material interests, social welfare, civil weal —so that they may be with us in the things that are ours, the interests of religion. Let us be with them because their interests are ours, and ours are theirs, because nature and grace must not be separated.

His desire to defend the best in American society often angered his ecclesiastical opponents. Few pronouncements got him into more trouble than the speech he gave at the 1890 convention of the National Education Association, in which he defended the public school as the pride and glory of the country. The words which were constantly used against him in years to come were: "the free school in America, withered be the hand raised in sign of its destruction!"

Strangely enough, for one so American, John Ireland was not above yearning for papal honors, and was apparently quite brokenhearted that several attempts to obtain the red hat for him were unsuccessful, though apparently he was about to be made a cardinal by Pope Benedict XV at the time of Ireland's death in 1918, long years after the fires of the Americanism controversy had gone out.

Ireland was a magnificent man whose magnificent virtues and talents and also magnificent faults might have profited from humility, more self-questioning, and more tact in dealing with enemies. But even his enemies, such as Archbishop Sebastian Messmer of Milwaukee, could not hide their admiration for, as Messmer put it, "the much misunderstood and misrepresented prelate of St. Paul," and when one of the attempts to obtain the red hat for Ireland failed, Messmer conveyed regrets that are so sincere as to be unquestionable. "For many years German-American Catholics had not very much love for the Archbishop of St. Paul, I am only too happy to say that the sentiment has changed very much of late." But it was too late.

2. *John J. Keane*

John Keane was born in Ireland a year after his colleague of St. Paul and came to the New World three years earlier in the first phases of the potato famine. In 1848 his family moved from Canada to Baltimore, where Keane was ordained in 1866. Keane served in St. Patrick's Parish in Washington for twelve years until his appointment as bishop of Richmond in 1878. Keane was in many ways the most admirable of the Americanists. He was a much more gentle and tactful man than John Ireland and had more courage than did his great patron the cardinal archbishop of Baltimore, whom he would frequently urge to more decisive action. Keane's famous letter from Rome to Gibbons at the time of the Knights of Labor controversy reveals the personality of both the bishops very clearly:

> . . . As an American citizen, I rejoice at every advance towards the perfect realization of that truest and noblest ideal of social organization and government; and therefore do I rejoice to behold you and the vast body of working men at your backs banded together, not for violence or injustice, but for the calm, orderly, dignified assertion and vindication of your God-given rights. The Catholic Church is the old Church of "the gospel preached to the poor." As a Catholic Bishop I welcome whatever really improves the poor man's condition, whatever lifts poverty out of squalor and degradation, places it beyond the power of oppression, and makes it worthy of the Divine Carpenter of Nazareth, who chose poverty for His Bride and deified labor in His sacred person; therefore do I hail this organization of the intelligence, the energy, and the conscientiousness of the

sons of toil, which, if faithful to intelligence and conscience, cannot fail to win for them the respect as well as the justice that is their due. . . .

Like his fellow Americanists, he was particularly enthusiastic about American freedom: "The fathers of our country proclaimed to all the world that it is the land where humanity shall ever be free to pursue the end and enjoy the rights bestowed on man by his creator . . . and the world proclaims his first principle that man is dependent upon God alone, has all his rights from God, that fellow men must respect them and the law protect them, but the Creator whose bounty is alone their origin and his omnipotence they guarantee." He concluded therefore that it was "no wonder that the Church of God feels so entirely at home in such a country. She too has known what it is to be fettered and hindered and treated shamefully in the old world both by open enemies and by falsehearted self-seeking believers."

In one lecture he argued that Leo XIII's support of the rights of the workingmen was in effect an endorsement of American democracy:

> This is the era of democracy, the day of absolute government is over and never again will a nation's laws be made by one man, or set of men, other than the agents of the people, for whose welfare alone laws should be made. . . .
> . . . He [Leo XIII] has laid down the law, the only law that laborers should have a just recompense for their work and has warned them to keep themselves within the circle of the law. He has said that Governments must protect them in their rights. Some may imagine that he is drifting away from the landmarks of his predecessors—what a mistake! He has simply laid down the only laws of the Democracy of the age. His unbounded love for America arises from the fact that he sees here the furtherest advance in the legitimate sphere of Democracy. He sees here a Republic which is at the same time a rebuke to the despotisms of the past and a protest to the Red Republicanism of France. He sees here the Church and State occupying the best positions which under existing circumstances could be ex-

pected. He loves America and his children here. He
has shown that he has no fears of the Democracy of the
age. . . .

While Keane's rhetoric unquestionably pushed the Pope into a
devotion for American democracy that the latter did not himself feel, the speech was quite harmless; but this did not prevent Archbishop Corrigan of New York from sending it to his
Roman agent, Ella B. Edes,[1] who in turn brought the letter
to the Holy Office. This was but the first of many of Keane's
battles to explain what his statements had meant. He was informed by Cardinal Zigliara that "there was nothing in the
lecture that could be condemned or need be changed . . . but
if I issue another edition of it, it would be well to add a short
preface to guard against the misinterpretation of Europeans."
There would unfortunately be many repetitions of this kind of
incident. Articles and books written for American audiences
would be interpreted in a European context, and while none
of them would ever be condemned by the Holy See, they
would (through the machinations of Corrigan and his allies)
create sufficient unrest in Rome to persuade the Holy See that
some means or the other must be taken to curb the disturbances the Americanists were creating in Europe and also to
reduce the possibility that they might eventually go too far in
the United States. If Keane was more diplomatic than Ireland
and somewhat less outspoken in his rhetoric, he was not afraid
to make his position absolutely clear to Roman authorities.
When the Pope told him that he was too loud in his admiration for America, Keane is alleged to have responded,
"Please God, I will never be less loud," and he commented
himself, "During the past few years, my duty has compelled
me to cross the ocean four times and I have never visited the
old countries abroad that I haven't come back thanking God
that I am an American." There was little or no way that the
Americanists could state their enthusiasm for democracy and

[1] Miss Edes was an American journalist who by one means or
another managed to amass for herself considerable influence in the
Roman Curia and to use her position as Corrigan's agent to wage
relentless warfare against the Americanists.

freedom in the United States without antagonizing European churchmen.

Keane had been appointed rector of the Catholic University of America in 1887 and this position gave him an important platform from which to speak and he made the most of the opportunity. Unfortunately for him, each one of his statements would then be forwarded to Rome by Corrigan or McQuaid and suspicion and opposition to him grew with each passing year. He did not make many friends in Rome, one feels certain, by his address at the laying of the cornerstone of a church in Washington:

> We will not come here to abuse Episcopalians, Presbyterians, or Methodists, but will worship God according to our faith, minding our own business and expecting our neighbors to do the same. The Church is one of universal charity, and instead of abusing the neighbors that do not agree with us in matters of faith we can but say, Brothers, though you do not serve God in our way, serve Him the best you know how in your own way.

Nor was Rome reassured when Keane accepted an invitation from Charles Elliott, the president of Harvard, to preach at Appleton Chapel on the Harvard campus. Keane even anticipated the ecumenical movement of later ages by having as the opening hymn in his service "Nearer My God to Thee" and the closing hymn "Rock of Ages." One can well imagine that the suspicious Roman officials were not pleased with Keane's choice of music. Keane would be accused of being an opponent of parochial schools because of his support of John Ireland's experiments at Faribault but the charge was false and Keane for all his ecumenical bent could do battle against nativists' criticism of Catholicism and of Catholic schools when the occasion warranted. When one non-Catholic educator named Edwin D. Meade attacked the parochial schools and the Catholic Church at a National Education Association meeting in Nashville, Keane calmly refuted the accusations and then not so calmly remarked: "The American people will open their eyes and no longer be hoodwinked or duped by the 'clap-trap' of which we have heard so much this morning, clap-trap which would make men believe that by crying for an existing system they were doing all that was necessary for the public good."

Keane was also held principally responsible for the American Church's involvement in the world's parliament of religions which was held as part of the Columbian Exposition in Chicago in 1893. Even though Gibbons and other members of the hierarchy attended, Rome disapproved of American Catholics' participation in the parliament. Keane was held principally to blame for the participation, especially by his enemies such as Bishop McQuaid, who would write to Rome: "Of late years the spirit of liberalism is springing up in our body under such leaders as Monsignor Ireland and Monsignor Keane that if not checked in time will bring disaster to the church. Many a time Catholic laymen have remarked that the Catholic Church they once knew seems to be passing away so gravely shocked are they at what they see passing around them." It's worth noting that McQuaid's words are not so terribly different from the criticisms made of the changes in the church universal in the 1960s. Even more interesting is the fact that the kinds of changes McQuaid was criticizing are exactly the same changes which allegedly are shocking people in the post-Vatican era.

A decision was finally made in Rome that Keane's words and actions were not the sort of thing that one expected from the rector of a Catholic university. In 1896, Leo XIII summarily dismissed Keane from the rectorship of the Catholic University of America. Keane took it well: "This is God's will and who am I to question . . . I welcome the act of the Pope without the slightest desire to ask why it was taken or how it was brought about." Keane's dismissal was a profound shock to Americans both Catholic and non-Catholic. Though it greatly pleased Archbishop Corrigan and Bishop McQuaid, they saw it as a dramatic setback for their enemies Gibbons and Ireland. Keane never had any doubts as to who was responsible ultimately for his dismissal and he referred to the "mischief bureau" in New York which had been "founded for the manufacture and dissemination of pernicious rumors of all sorts against Christians and distinguished Catholic prelates in this country." After his dismissal, he was invited to assume a position in Rome working in the curial offices with the title of archbishop. Such an appointment served a dual purpose from the Roman viewpoint—it made his removal from the rectorship look like a promotion and it also enabled them to keep a somewhat close eye on Keane. But the appointment proved a mistake for Keane's enemies. Even though he was shabbily treated in Rome, his charm and enthusiasm managed to win for him many friends both clerical and lay. He made several prominent converts and large crowds attended his lectures. In addition, his position in Rome made it possible for him to fight the battle of the liberals through the dark days of the Americanism condemnation.

When he was appointed archbishop of Dubuque in 1900, it was in part a gesture of good will from the Pope to the American hierarchy to heal some of the wounds caused by the Americanism condemnation but it was also, one suspects, a move to get Keane out of Rome. He was too much to handle in that city.[2]

----

[2] Keane's treatment in Rome was disgraceful. He was provided with practically no income and not much in the way of occupation. Even though he was appointed as a canon of St. John Lateran, he was in this respect under the jurisdiction of Cardinal Francisco Satolli, who had been responsible in great part for his removal from the Catholic University of America. At least on one occasion, Satolli publicly ordered Keane from one of the main altars at St. John's on an occasion in which it had been announced that the Archbishop would pontificate and preach. He was also eventually ordered from his residence in the Canadian seminary in Rome on the grounds that he was exercising a "pernicious influence on the students." Furthermore, Cardinal Parocchi, the vicar of Rome, prohibited any preaching in Rome by Keane during his last days in the city. It was the same Cardinal Parocchi who was described as being "loud in his praises" of Archbishop Keane when the subject of his appointment to Dubuque was raised. One has the impression that the Romans were happy that Dubuque was such a long way from Rome and would have been even happier if it was a longer distance. However, the Curia had its revenge. When Keane's health began to fail after a decade of active service in Dubuque, he was forced to resign since the Curia would not provide him with a co-

Keane was somewhat more tactful than John Ireland but only somewhat more so. He was not afraid to take chances or to state his mind clearly and bluntly as possible. Even the shock of his removal from the rectorship of Catholic University did not seem to have notably impaired his courage. Nor did the persecution he suffered affect his loyalty to the Church. His contemporary, John Lancaster Spalding, thought that Keane was too docile and too humble in the face of persecution by his enemies in the Curia. He and Ireland made a brilliant team in the two-decade battle the Americanists were to fight. But since he was not the archbishop of a prominent see until the battle was over, Keane did not have the security necessary to be able to protect himself from his enemies. Nor was he supported strongly enough, it would seem to us, by the Cardinal Archbishop of Baltimore when the chips were down.

Keane had very little in the way of academic background required to be rector at the Catholic University and his administration of the university could not have been hailed as an immense success. On the other hand, during his years of rectorship, he had great influence not only on the Church but on the rest of American society, and his removal was a disaster. An American no matter how humble or how obedient was simply not able to protect himself from the calumnies of his enemies and the confusion of Roman officials. One can only imagine what the dimensions of Keane's influence would have been if he had served another term as the rector of the Catholic University.

---

adjutor. Keane's biographer comments: "In view of the years of splendid service which Archbishop Keane had rendered to the Church in the United States, it is not easy to explain the attitude of Roman officials and their treatment of him as an old and broken man. Many felt that he deserved to retain the security and the honor of an archiepiscopal see in his own country until his earthly sojourn was completed even though it would have been necessary to appoint someone to help him shoulder the burdens. As it turned out, he was practically forced to resign his see and to depend on the charity of his successor and of the faithful in Dubuque during his remaining seven years. Archbishop Keane himself however accepted the decision with the spirit of obedience and resignation to those superiors that had characterized all his life."

3. *John Lancaster Spalding*

While the archbishops of St. Paul and Dubuque were born in Ireland and James Gibbons spent his early years there even though he was born in Baltimore, the fourth Americanist, John Lancaster Spalding, was a descendant of a family which had been in the United States long before the Revolutionary War. Indeed the Spaldings migrated from Maryland to Kentucky in 1795, and John Lancaster at his birth in 1840 could claim to be a third-generation Kentuckian. He was far and away the most intellectually gifted of the Americanists and also the most independent thinker but there was a strange, moody streak that ran through the personality of this Kentucky aristocrat that made his behavior unpredictable, severely limited his effectiveness, and eventually destroyed his career. He is not an easy man to understand and in reading his biography one is conscious that many details are being deliberately obscured that might help us to break through the mystery of Lancaster Spalding.[3]

[3] The greatest mystery of Spalding's life was his curious relation with the Caldwell sisters. These were two young women from Kentucky whom Spalding came to know when they were in school in New York and he was living in the same city in temporary exile. In his sermon on the Catholic University at the council of Baltimore, Spalding concluded with a glowing tribute to Mary Gwendolyn Caldwell, who at the age of twenty-one had expressed her willingness to contribute $300,000 to the foundation of a Catholic University. Spalding's friendship with Mary Gwendolyn and her sister Mary Elizabeth continued through the years and it was at the invitation of Mary Gwendolyn, now the Marquise des Monstiers-Merindille, that Spalding went to Europe for his visit in 1900. During part of this visit, Spalding traveled through Europe with the Marquise. However, for some reason not recorded, the friendship ended after Spalding's return to the United States and the Marquise sent Spalding's portrait to Monsignor Denis O'Connell, Gibbons' agent in Rome, with the remark that she had no more room for it in her house. Two years later when Spalding seemed very likely to become archbishop of Chicago, Mary Gwendolyn's sister, now the Baroness von Zedtwitz, wrote letters to Rome leveling what Spalding's biographer calls "serious accusations" against the bishop of Peoria. Spalding's closest friend, Archbishop Riordan of San Fran-

Spalding was educated at Louvain, where he developed a fondness for culture and science which was to influence the rest of his life. He returned to Louisville just at the time that his uncle, Martin John Spalding, was made archbishop of Baltimore. After the elder Spalding's death, John Lancaster went to New York to work on the preparation of a biography of his uncle and then remained in New York since the new bishop of Louisville was not particularly well disposed to anyone in the Spalding family. In 1876, he was made bishop of Peoria in Illinois where he remained until his death forty years later. Part of the mystery of his life is why he did not accept the many other appointments that were offered him, for he could apparently quite easily have been archbishop of Milwaukee or San Francisco or bishop of Newark. He was also the obvious appointment as first rector of the Catholic University of America both because it was on account of his inspiration and dogged prodding that the university was founded and also because his cultural and scientific interests as well as his stay in Louvain would have made him the most qualified choice for the university. However, he adamantly declined the rectorship and indeed for a number of years had little or nothing to do with the university. After the Third

---

cisco, was in Rome at the time and was asked by Roman authorities to investigate the charges. Riordan at first did not believe them since in the forty-two years he had known Spalding, he thought him a man of "irreproachable character without stain." However, after investigating the charges, he concluded that "though it is most painful, I feel bound in conscience to prevent his promotion to the See of Chicago." Five years later, the Baroness's threats of publishing a book against his "personal probity" was a decisive factor in the apostolic delegate's request to John Ireland that he persuade Spalding to resign his see. The Caldwell sisters left the Church and apparently died (both of them in their forties) estranged from Catholicism, continuing their vendetta against Spalding, implying very strongly that in the middle years of his life, he had lost his faith. The whole matter is clouded in great mystery but if one is to understand why the talents of this most brilliant of the Americanists were wasted to a considerable extent during his life, one simply must know more of the details of the strange relationship with the Caldwell sisters. One is tempted to say that either the historians should tell the whole story or they should not have told any of it.

Council of Baltimore when Ireland and Keane were busy
fighting the battles of the time, Spalding was sitting gloomily
in Peoria declining promotion, refusing to become involved,
criticizing his friends, and writing poetry. He would observe
himself of these years, "In looking back, we see that after
much toil we have accomplished little. What we had hoped to
do, we have not or having done have ceased to care for. How
shall we grow old or take up the old tasks with the old ardor.
And surely the brave must lose heart when onto these difficulties there is added the loss of mental composure which
misunderstandings, conflicts, and contentions involve."

Ireland would at times sympathize with this: "The Church,
humanly speaking, is stuck fast in the grooves and he loses his
time who strives to move her out. Bishop Spalding is about
right. Each one to his own shanty and write poetry or save
his soul." But Ireland didn't believe it and didn't mean it,
while Spalding apparently did. His deep friendship with Ireland based on their association in colonization projects grew
cool when Spalding violently disagreed with his friend both
on the school controversy and the Cahenslyism crisis. Of the
parish school question he said, "Without parish schools, there
is no hope that the Church will be able to maintain itself in
America and opposition unites all true Catholics in a more
invincible determination to maintain at whatever cost the
cause of religious education." And of the nationalities controversy he observed that the immigrants from whatever part
of the world they came had the right to maintain their customs, languages, religious practices. It was only necessary to
be a true American to be a good man who loved liberty and a
foe of injustice. Spalding dismissed the controversy over
Cahenslyism as being unjust and laughable and he would have
no part in the campaign against the German Catholics
launched in opposition to Cahenslyism. He did not hesitate to
proclaim that the Catholic University of America was a failure; but when the Pope fired Bishop Keane, he was highly
incensed, and even more incensed at Keane's docile acceptance of his dismissal: "If the Pope had him down on all fours
kicking him each time he lifted his foot, the enthusiastic bishop
would shout, 'See how the Holy Father honors me,' " and he

added later on, "Archbishop Keane, I see, is to get eighty dollars a month and with that I suppose he is to hire his apartment and live. Archbishop Ireland, I think, is a hoodoo. Whatever he touches seems to go wrong." He viewed the archbishop of St. Paul as a perpetual "storm center and a big drum" banging away throughout the American Church where the only question seemed to be whether he was falling or rising in favor with Rome, "and if we could only hear nothing more of him it matters little whether he fall or rise." By this time, Spalding was clearly a moody and disheartened man and he could not forgive John Ireland his support for the apostolic delegation when Satolli first came to the United States. Spalding's own opposition to the delegation was unmistakable:

There is, and has been for years, in the Catholic Church of the United States a deep feeling of opposition to the appointment of a permanent Delegate for this country. This opposition arises in part from a fixed and strongly-rooted desire, which exists throughout the whole English speaking world to manage as far as possible one's own affairs. The firm determination of the American people to permit no needless foreign interference is shown in the Monroe Doctrine, and it was more practically demonstrated by the overthrow and death of Maximillian. Catholics who live here, and who, wherever they were born, are true American citizens, feel the impulse of this desire and wish to manage as far as possible their own affairs. They are devoted to the Church; they recognize in the Pope Christ's Vicar, and gladly receive from him the doctrines of faith and morals; but for the rest, they ask him to interfere as little as may be.

When the Satolli appointment was made official, Spalding wrote an article in which he strongly implied that the foundation of the apostolic delegation was playing into the hands of the A.P.A. bigotry that was raging at that time in the United States. Satolli himself was no little upset by Spalding's opposition and wrote to him a stern letter of rebuke:

Time and again, from its very inception, you have been so bold in speech, not only here, but even at Rome, as to overstep the limits of prudent moderation which a Bishop, above all, ought to have in matters pertaining to the decrees and decisions of the Holy See. Your personal reproach upon me for my ignorance of the idiom and customs of this land was easy enough to bear, but your direct attack upon the action of the Supreme Pastor . . . Leo XIII . . . appears to me to be absolutely intolerable, and coming from a Bishop, a great and monstrous scandal. Not content with your past efforts, you have now written an article . . . in which (omitting whatever would be seeming contradiction to a more sound kind of theology) you re-echo those same critical observations. These are untimely, harmful, not consistent with the truth; they also smack of a brashness towards the Roman Pontiff to the extent that you take it upon yourself to repeat that from the time the Apostolic Delegation was founded, the APA has launched a more vigorous attack against the Catholic Church.

Spalding therefore was not a part of most of the battles that raged between 1885 and 1900 and yet after the Americanism condemnation when Spalding returned to Europe and when there was nothing to gain and much to lose by espousing the Americanism cause, he fearlessly rose up in pulpits of Europe and pleaded the case of the Americanists, apparently with tremendous effect. If he had become archbishop of Chicago when that see fell open in 1902 (and for the first time he was apparently willing to accept promotion out of Peoria), it is possible that Spalding's new lease on life would have become permanent and his eloquence and intelligence would not have been as sadly wasted as they had been in the previous fifteen years. But such fantasy is at best dubious because Spalding would probably have remained until his death under any set of circumstances an erratic and unpredictable man.

For all his erratic moods and behavior, Spalding was a brilliant writer and came closer to providing a theoretical base for the Americanists than any of his colleagues. While he could on occasion be much more critical of the United States than either Ireland or Keane, his dedication to American principles was unshakable:

> . . . we have shown that respect for law is compatible with civil and religious liberty; that a free people can become prosperous and strong . . . ; that the State and the Church can move in separate orbits and still cooperate for the common welfare; that men of different races and beliefs may live together in peace . . . that the government of the majority where men put their trust in God and in knowledge, in the end the government of the good and the wise.

He was also quite open to the spirit of the time and the need for scientific and cultural advance. He insisted that the Church should be part of the best of the scientific and cultural progress of its time and emphasized the need for a Catholic university that would teach "the best that is known and encourage research. It will be at once a scientific institute, a school of culture and a training ground for the business of life. It will educate the minds that give direction to the age, it will be a nursery of ideas." And he also affirmed:

> Whatever we may think of the past, whatever we may fear or hope for the future, if we would make an impression on the world around us, we must understand the thoughts, the purposes, and the methods of those with whom we live; and we must at the same time recognize that though the truth of religion be unchangeable, the mind of man is not so, and that the point of view varies not only from people to people, and from age to age, but from year to year in the growing thought of the individual and of the world.

There was no reason in Spalding's judgment for the Church to be tied to a philosophy of the past:

> Aristotle is a great mind, but his learning is crude and his ideas of Nature are frequently grotesque. Saint Thomas is a powerful intellect; but his point of view in all that concerns natural knowledge has long since vanished from sight. What a poverty of learning does but the early medieval scheme of education reveal; and when in the twelfth cen-

tury the idea of a university rises in the best minds, how imcomplete and vague it is.

In his pleas for a Catholic university, Spalding could be powerfully eloquent:

> Let there be, then [he concluded], an American Catholic university, where our young men, in the atmosphere of faith and purity, of high thinking and plain living, shall become more intimately conscious of the truth of their religion and of the genius of their country, where they shall learn repose and dignity which belong to their ancient Catholic descent, and yet not lose the fire which flows in the blood of a new people; to which from every part of the land our eyes may turn for guidance and encouragement, seeking light and self-confidence from men in whom intellectual power is not separate from more purpose; who look to God and his universe from bending knees of prayer. . . .

Spalding's admiration of America did not blind him to its faults (as on occasion such admiration seems to have blinded his other colleagues). He bitterly denounced the imperialism of the Spanish-American War and asked:

> Should we go to the ends of the earth to take forcible possession of islands lying on remote oceans under tropical skies, inhabited by barbarous or savage tribes where both race and climate preclude the hope of ever attaining to any high degree of culture? Why should we own Cuba? We do not need it, its population is undesirable, and to hold it we must increase our army and navy and gradually drift into a militarism which must threaten our most cherished institutions. What can imperialism bring us except the menace of ruin and military rule?

He further wanted no part of the alliance between conservative businessmen and government officials which he thought had stolen the election of 1898. "In the silver campaign the bimetallists would have won had it not been for Hanna's millions and the terrorism exercised by the employers of labor."

But if Spalding during his lonely and moody middle years broke with the other Americanists and saw faults in American democracy that others had missed, the Americanism controversy for some peculiar reason seems to have recalled much of his previous brilliance. When he encountered Leo XIII in an audience on February 2, 1900, the Pope asked him about Americanism. Spalding replied by saying that such heresy had never been taught in the United States. The Pope was quoted as saying in reply, "That is what many American bishops have written to me but there was that poor Hecker. He taught the guidance of the Holy Spirit without the Sacraments." To this Spalding was claimed to have responded, "Holy Father, I knew Father Hecker well and immediately and he was a holy, disinterested, zealous and enlightened priest. I am certain he never believed or taught what they accused him of." The Holy Father continued to criticize Hecker and Spalding said quite bluntly, "Holy Father, did you know Hecker?" When the Pope admitted that he did not, Spalding replied, "Well then, I did and a better Catholic we've never had."

The following month Spalding rose in the Church of the Gesù in Rome to speak on the subject of education and the future of religion and delivered what was easily his most brilliant sermon and in the opinion of a friendly reporter "the pure essence of Americanist ideas." Spalding began by repeating his position on the higher education of women.[4] According to Spalding if the Church was to live and prosper in the modern world, it had to recognize that man's mind was free and had the right to inquire into and learn whatever might be investigated and known. If Catholicism hoped to present its supernatural beliefs in an age of civilization and culture, it must not neglect science, philosophy, culture. He contended, "We find it necessary to abandon positions which are no longer defensible, to assume new attitudes in the face of new conditions. We must remember that though the Church is a divine institution it is nonetheless subject to the law which

---

[4] Spalding could not see why women's education should be any different from that of men and insisted that a woman had every bit as much right to develop her intellect as did her husband or brother.

makes human things mutable, that though truth must remain the same it is capable of receiving fresh illustration, and that if it is to be life giving, it must be wrought anew into the constitution of each individual and of each age." What was needed, he said, was not new devotions and new shrines but rather "a new spirit, newness of life, a revivification of faith, hope and love, fresh courage and will to lay hold on the source of power." To do this the freedom to criticize even the Church was absolutely essential. "How shall we ever be vigilant if we are forbidden to criticize ourselves and the environment by which Catholic life is nourished and protected?"

It was further necessary that the Church recognize that it must reconcile itself with principles of freedom and democracy. "In the ever widening domain of the British Empire and the ever growing territory of the American Republic, Democracy is triumphant, and in all these vast regions with the exception of the Anglican and Scottish establishment there is a separation of church and state, a separation which those who are competent to judge recognize as permanent. There is everywhere freedom to write, to publish, to discuss, to organize; and there is no subject of thought, no sphere of action, no interest which it is possible to fence about and shut in from the all-searching breath of liberty."

Spalding was apparently quite pleased with the strong favorable reactions to his talk and proceeded to Paris where he and the unfortunate Abbé Klein became close friends. Klein published a collection of Spalding's essays with an article of introduction that was almost as enthusiastic as his description of Hecker, which had originated the Americanism controversy. Spalding had almost overnight become the same kind of sensation in Europe that John Ireland had.

But the European episode was short-lived. Spalding returned gloomily to Peoria and the European excitement became a thing of the past. There is something admirable in the cool defiance with which Spalding defended the Americanist position after his enemies claimed it had been condemned. He seemed more willing to fight the Americanist battle after it was for all practical purposes concluded than when it was still raging. But while his defense of true Americanism when it had apparently lost the battle was admirable, one wonders if it might not have been more effective if Spalding had chosen to do battle before the papal encyclical condemning false Americanism had been written.

The whole story of John Lancaster Spalding is not known, but even on the basis of what we do know his career was obviously a tragic one, tragic not only for himself personally but also for the American Church. If Spalding's realism had been able to restrain both the aggressive enthusiasm of Ireland and the enthusiastic docility and obedience of Keane, the outcome of the Americanism battle might have been somewhat different.

4. *James Cardinal Gibbons*

It is easy to sympathize with the role of James Cardinal Gibbons, archbishop of Baltimore, during the crises in the waning years of the nineteenth century. Gibbons' sympathies were of course with the Americanists. Ireland was a close friend whom he admired greatly. Keane was a priest of his own diocese whose ecclesiastical career Gibbons had sponsored. Denis O'Connell, who was rector of the North American College and Gibbons' agent in Rome, was the young man whom Gibbons had recruited as a priest for the diocese of Richmond and who was one of his closest friends. O'Connell's dismissal from the rectorship of the North American College was a deep disappointment to Gibbons just as his eventual appointment to the Catholic University was a great victory. Gibbons' own alliance to the cause of the Americanists was unquestioned. But as archbishop of Baltimore, president of the Third Plenary Council in 1884, and acknowledged leader of the American Church in fact if not in theory, Gibbons had the responsibility of holding the American Church together through the critical years of controversy. He could not accept the machinations of some German-Catholics for a separate and distinct German-Catholic Church in the United States, yet he was sensitive to the needs of the Germans and did not wish to unduly antagonize them. He approved of Ireland's experiments in merging Catholic education with public education but understood the need for protecting Catholic schools. He sympathized with the Americanists' desire to become fully integrated in American society and yet he knew that he had to maintain unity in the hierarchy, which included not only Ireland and Keane but also the extremely conservative, not to say reactionary archbishop of New York and bishop of Rochester as well as the fence-straddling Archbishops Patrick J. Ryan of Philadelphia and John J. Williams of Boston. He supported the Catholic University and the Knights of Labor and did his best to oppose the condemnation of Henry George's book *Progress and Poverty*. On the other hand, his desires to maintain unity and peace as well as to be docilely obedient to Rome led him to hesitate about involvement in such controversial issues until his more passionate colleagues had forced him into it. It is easy enough to be critical of Gibbons for failing to oppose more vigorously the establishment of an apostolic delegation or for failing to defend more vigorously his young colleagues Keane and O'Connell when they were dismissed from their positions. It is also easy to be critical of him for not responding with greater vigor and determination to the condemnation of Americanism.

But Gibbons had an extremely difficult responsibility to exercise and his leadership of the American Church from 1877 to 1920 was, if not always brilliant and imaginative, at least dedicated and effective. His patience, gentle charm, dignity, and kindness won him the respect not only of the Catholic population but of all Americans. There can be no doubt that for twenty or thirty years in the eyes of the American republic James Gibbons *was* the American Church. If his leadership was not more successful, if he was not able to preside over the kind of Americanization that Ireland and Keane so eagerly sought and to which he himself was committed at least in theory, the reason may well have been that Gibbons saw more clearly than did his colleagues that the time was not yet ready for the church universal to understand the implications of the American experience. Ireland would say on one occasion that he himself was ahead of his time but it is doubtful that he really believed it, and when he went through France and Italy preaching that the rest of the world ought to learn about religion from the United States, Ireland thought of himself as a prophet for his own time. Gibbons may have understood much more clearly how novel the Americanists' notions were and how slowly the Church would have to proceed if it was to be able to assimilate such novelty.

James Gibbons was born in Baltimore in 1834; however, his family moved to Ireland in 1837 and did not return to the United States (New Orleans) until 1853. Gibbons was ordained in 1860 in the archdiocese of Baltimore and then served in the city of Baltimore during the troubled times of the Civil War. In 1868 he was made vicar apostolic for North Carolina and as such was the youngest bishop at the Vatican Council. In 1872 he became bishop of Richmond and in 1877 archbishop of Baltimore. In 1886, after the successful conclusion of the Third Plenary Council of Baltimore, over which he presided, Gibbons became a cardinal and continued to lead the Church in America until his death thirty-four years later. As the years went on, Gibbons would become one of the first citizens of the United States—the friend and confidant of presidents from Grover Cleveland up to but not including Woodrow Wilson, the adviser to government officials, and the respected friend of many important non-Catholics. Even though he was the second American to become a cardinal (Archbishop John McCloskey of New York had preceded him in the red robes), Gibbons was in most peoples' minds *the* American cardinal and by anybody's standards was the most important ecclesiastical figure since the time of John Carroll.

Gibbons was not either an original thinker or an innovative administrator. His involvement in the controversies of the last fifteen years of the nineteenth century was in reaction to the promptings of his more militant friends. Yet in the midst of the controversies that we will discuss later on in this chapter, Gibbons was always the leader, the man trying simultaneously to maintain some sort of consensus and to move the American Church down the path desired by the Americanizers. His writings are free of the rhetoric of Ireland or intense intellectualism of Spalding but there was no doubt where he stood despite all his cautions and his discretions. In a sermon delivered in March of 1887 in Rome in gratitude for his being elevated to the cardinalate, Gibbons stated as clearly as anyone the essential principle that motivated the Americanists through all their controversies:

> For myself, as a citizen of the United States, without closing my eyes to our defects as a nation, I proclaim, with a deep sense of pride and gratitude, and in this great capital of Christendom, that I belong to a country where the civil government holds over us the aegis of its protection without interfering in the legitimate exercise of our sublime mission as ministers of the Gospel of Jesus Christ.
>
> Our country has liberty without license, authority without despotism. Hers is no spirit of exclusiveness. She has no frowning fortifications to repel the invader, for we are at peace with all the world! In the consciousness of her strength and of her good will to all nations she rests secure. Her harbors are open in the Atlantic and Pacific to welcome the honest immigrant who comes to advance his temporal interest and to find a peaceful home.
>
> But, while we are acknowledged to have a free government, we do not, perhaps receive due credit for possessing also a strong government. Yes, our nation is strong, and her strength lies, under Providence, in the majesty and supremacy of the law, in the loyalty of her citizens to that law, and in the affection of our people for their free institutions.
>
> There are, indeed, grave social problems which are engaging the earnest attention of the citizens of the United States. But I have no doubt that, with God's blessings, these problems will be solved without violence, or revolution, or injury to individual right.

It would seem to be very difficult for anyone to disagree with such noble sentiments and surely most of those who opposed Gibbons and the other Americanists would have hardly rejected Gibbons' profession of loyalty to American political democracy. But the enemies of the Americanists strongly objected to the practical programs which Gibbons and his allies contended were appropriate for the Catholic Church in the American environment. We must, therefore, say something about the enemies of the Americanists.

Archbishop Michael A. Corrigan of New York, unlike his Americanist opponents, had been trained in the North American College in Rome and took a profoundly conservative view of progress and also entertained grave suspicions about American society. Robert Dougherty Cross says of Corrigan, "A cautious even timid man, Corrigan had been sheltered by his affluent family from acquiring intimate experience with American life that might have altered his stereotyped projections of its basic characteristics . . . even had his professional disposition been more liberal, Corrigan would necessarily have to shape policy to accord with the traditionalism and conservatism of his immigrant charges. At the same time he was so readily deferred to by the New York Tammany machine that he felt no need to seek working alliances with non-Catholic elements. While courteous and charitable towards those outside the Church, he did not wish his priests to spend a large share of their energies in seeking converts and he forthrightly opposed all suggestions that the Church would modify its teachings or behavior for that purpose."

Corrigan was not given much to public controversy and would even indicate by silence at meetings of the archbishops of the country that he agreed with a course of action to which he was opposed. His predilection rather was for controversy through planted newspaper stories and secret accusations to Rome made through his Roman agent, Ella Edes. He was a secretive, devious man and as time went on the Americanists, including even the gentle Gibbons, made no secret of their dislike for him. Quite the opposite was Corrigan's doughty suffragan bishop, Bernard McQuaid of Rochester. McQuaid was a vigorous, outspoken, opinionated man who had opposed the definition of papal infallibility at the Vatican Council but seemed to be an enthusiastic supporter of the Syllabus of Errors. He denounced John Ireland from his pulpit and chortled with glee when Keane was dismissed from the Catholic University: "The news from Rome is astounding. The failure of the university is known in Rome at least and the blame is thrown on Keane. Much of it is due to him but other causes are there. These causes are irremediable now. The failure implicated the Holy Father who was made to father the undertaking from the beginning. What collapses on every side! Gibbons! Ireland! and Keane! They were the cock of the walk for a while and dictated a country and thought to run our dioceses for us. They may change their policy and repent. They can never repair the harm done in the past."

When the Americanist condemnation finally took place, McQuaid did not hesitate for a moment to name the people and the events the Pope was condemning; the parliament of religions, the disobedience to the papal ban on membership in secret societies, Keane's speeches at non-Catholic universities, and the liberals' attitudes toward the public schools. McQuaid overlooked the fact that none of these things had been either explicitly or implicitly condemned in the papal document and that the Pope had not affirmed even that any Americans held the doctrines that he condemned. For McQuaid it was quite enough that he could tar his opponents with the charge of Americanism and claim that Americanism was something that was worthy of papal condemnation. Corrigan's mischief was secretive, McQuaid's mischief was public; but ultimately they did succeed in bringing their Americanist opponents to a dead halt and casting a cloud on much of the liberal activities between 1885 and 1900. McQuaid was quite capable himself of being liberal in other matters, however, especially in the training of priests. He was strongly opposed to the traditional measures of clerical education that he thought would sap the independence and initiative of young men. He opposed boarding-school preparatory seminaries, arguing that young men would be much better off under the supervision of their parents. He was against rigid discipline in the seminary lest it ill fit the young priest for "a life of self-reliance young priests have to face almost immediately after leaving the seminary." Seminarians should be free "from constant watching" and the seminary should not be confused with a reformatory. He refused to ban women domestics from seminary grounds, for "if in the seminary the presence of women is suggestive of evil, it will be so after he leaves the seminary. Such young men should avoid the priesthood or withdraw to a Trappist monastery."

Some writers suggest that McQuaid's intransigence was not so much an idological one as based on his resentment of John Ireland and his loyalty to the archbishop of New York. However, a vigorous opponent McQuaid was, and the public debates between him and John Ireland represented "an open dialogue" the like of which the American Church has not seen since.

The religious orders were split on the Americanism issue with the Paulists, the Baltimore Sulpicians, and the Holy Cross priests of Notre Dame under the direction of their provincial Father John A. Zahm (whose book on evolution was barely saved from public condemnation) supporting the Americanists and the Jesuits in stern opposition. Curiously enough in our time the position of the Jesuits would be rather the reverse, with some of the leading liberals of the contemporary American Church being members of the Society of Jesus. But in the 1880s and 1890s the ultra-papalism of the Roman Jesuit publication *Civilta Cattolica* and the perceived threat to Catholic education in the Faribault experiment as well as the obvious threat to Jesuit higher education represented by the Catholic University of America aligned Jesuits on the side of the conservatives.

Finally, most but not all of the Germans in the clergy and the hierarchy were opposed to everything that John Ireland and John Keane stood for. By the nature of things, Germans would not necessarily have been against programs for social progress and surely not against intellectual and cultural development, but in their minority position they felt themselves extremely threatened, especially by the aggressive Americanism of John Ireland. In addition, they were heavily committed to the Catholic schools as a means of preserving German culture in American society. While the First World War brought a definitive end to the attempt, many if not most German immigrants believed until this time that it was possible in the New World to preserve a distinctive German cultural community which would at the same time be thoroughly American. And even those who were committed in theory to a process of Americanization thought the process must necessarily be a very slow one. The pace demanded by Ireland seemed to them to be dangerously rapid.

Before we turn to the battles that the Americanists fought, it would be well to summarize their position. Any attempt at synthesis of the perspective from which the Americanists viewed the role of the Church in late nineteenth-century America would have to take into account the following points:

1 With the exception of Lancaster Spalding in his more moody moments, they were incurable optimists, as befits any American of the late nineteenth century. They were first of all optimistic about the United States. They were convinced that American democracy was the most noble work of polity that man has ever devised and that eventually the whole world would come to imitate this form of government. They were optimistic about the Catholic Church, which they felt was coming out from behind the walls with which it imprisoned itself and was about to provide all of the answers for which the age was looking simply by becoming part of the age. They were optimistic about the Church in the United States—perhaps not quite so optimistic as Isaac Hecker had been, but still terribly optimistic about the Church's growth and about its future possibilities in American society. They were optimistic about the spirit of the age. The modern world from their viewpoint was a good place and it was getting better and the scientific and cultural achievements of the world were something which Catholics ought to admire and embrace.

They were confident, expansive men and did not seem in either their ideology or their behavior to know the meaning of uncertainty and fear. They had lived through the misery of the Civil War and seen America recover from this tragedy and grow stronger and richer. They had little doubt that the Church and the republic and probably the whole world had seen its worst days and that the future was filled with boundless hope.

It can readily be understood how foreign such optimism was to the European Church, still very much on the defensive against the liberalism and the secularism of the nineteenth century which Pius IX had condemned, still very much threatened by the hostile reaction to the First Vatican Council, still very suspicious and distrustful of the modern world. Those American clerics who were in sympathy with the European perspective viewed the optimism of the Americanists as naïveté; and Roman officials, quite honestly and frankly puzzled by the bounce and vitality of the Americanists, were not sure but what the naïveté had within it the seeds of heresy.

2 The Americanists were democrats; at least they were committed to the American political system. They believed in freedom and democracy and in the separation of church and state. They thought that a situation of religious freedom, at least in the modern world, provided the best possible atmosphere for Catholicism to flourish in. They were perhaps less likely than John England or even than John Carroll to introduce the democratic practices in their governance of the Church. Keane could be quite autocratic with faculty opposition at the Catholic University. Ireland in dealing with the priests of his diocese (even the young priest named John Ryan who was to become the great social actionist of the twentieth century) was anything but permissive. Gibbons' style of administration was quite traditional. And Lancaster Spalding's moody brilliance apparently was quite a trial to the priests of Peoria. Their enthusiasm for American culture and political organization and for the American virtues convinced apparently none of them that the internal organization of the Church could benefit from Americanization.

3 They were all intensely socially conscious. Keane and Ireland were supporters of the temperance movement. Ireland and Spalding backed the colonization project, which they viewed as a means of improving the social lot of the immigrant. Keane, Ireland, and Gibbons vigorously defended the Knights of Labor and successfully headed off the condemnation of the writings of Henry George. All of them vigorously denounced exploitation of labor and applauded Leo XIII's encyclical *Rerum novarum*. Their understanding of social problems was superficial, but by contemporary standards and even by our own their hearts were in the right place.

4   They were eager for friendship and amity in relations with non-Catholics. Keane's speech at Harvard, the world parliament of religion, the personal friendship all the Americanists had with non-Catholics were one side of the coin. On the other side of the coin the defense of the Knights of Labor, hesitancy to condemn the secret societies, and fear of an apostolic delegation were all based at least in part on fear of what mistakes in these matters might do with non-Catholics' attitudes toward the Church. They certainly were not inclined to water down Catholic doctrine but neither were they of a mind to state Catholic doctrine in such a fashion that it would be offensive to Americans who were not Catholic.

5   The Americanists were proud of the American Church. They believed quite correctly that it had successfully overcome immense obstacles to become the most vigorous and healthy manifestation of Catholicism in the whole world. They believed that the answers that Catholicism in the United States had forged to the problems of the Church in the nineteenth century could be generalized beyond the American environment and would provide a model that the Church in the rest of the world ought to imitate. Ireland and to a lesser extent Keane and Spalding traveled through Europe as evangelists, bringing the good news of the American way to the backward churches of the Old World. While they received enthusiastic welcome from those Europeans who were in favor of modernization, their behavior was deeply offensive to more traditionally European Catholics.

6   The Americanists were assimilationists culturally. They believed that the immigrants ought to become American in every way as quickly as possible, which often seemed to the immigrants to mean that they must become Irish Catholics as quickly as possible. It never occurred to them that the Irish reaction to Brownson's Catholic nativism was not so terribly dissimilar to the German reaction to what they thought was John Ireland's nativism. They were quite conscious that the Lucerne memorial of Peter Paul Cahensly would offend non-Catholic Americans but they were much less conscious of how their own policies of forced draft assimilation would be offensive to German-Americans and Polish-Americans. At the

time of the Spanish-American War, their Americanism would
lead them to positions on international problems which can
only be described as imperialist and at times even jingoist.

7   As befits Americans of any era, the Americanists were
concerned about education, and two of the most critical battles
they fought had to do with matters of educational policy—
the foundation of the Catholic University of America and
Ireland's experiment in cooperation between public and parochial schools. In the European Church, where educational
concern was much less serious, these controversies could never
have occurred. And the Europeans probably could not comprehend why the American Catholics were so excited about the
question of schools. Nevertheless it is interesting that the
Roman officials who insisted on Catholic schools in every
parish could hardly claim that Italian parishes had much in the
way of a parochial school system. For a cultivated man like
Lancaster Spalding, the interest in education also meant an interest in science and culture and philosophy and poetry.
Ireland probably would have agreed though it's dubious that
he read much poetry and it was even less likely that he wrote
any. Keane was acutely conscious that he did know much
about university administration and with characteristic American efficiency visited the European universities after his appointment to learn how a university ought to be run. It was
hardly likely that the Catholic University would become a
great intellectual center when American Catholicism, especially the Irish variety, was anything but intellectual. If the
Americanists, however, were not intellectuals according to
their lights, they respected the things of the intellect and did
their best to promote intellectual development.

8   The Americanists were activists. They would certainly
not deny the importance of the contemplative virtues, and the
charge that along with Father Hecker they had denied the
importance of contemplation was terribly disturbing to them.
Nonetheless in their own personal lives they were doers, not
contemplators, and their restless energies hardly furnished any
of them with time to ponder the profound meaning of what
they were about. If they were ever so tempted, they could
always look to their colleague, Lancaster Spalding, to see what

too much thought and too much contemplation would do to a man.

9 The Americanists were at all times loyal to Rome. The understandable curial concern about the strange happenings across the Atlantic ought not to have deceived Roman officials into thinking that they need fear either schism or heresy in the American Church. Even though the Americanists were impatient with what they took to be Rome's lack of comprehension of what they were doing and even though they were anything but eager to have an apostolic delegate in their midst (John Ireland lived to regret his eagerness), they were most eager to be considered loyal sons of the Church, and even the slightest hint that they were not (as in the formal condemnation of "Americanism") hurt them deeply. The vigor with which they denied ever holding the doctrines condemned was an indication of how serious the hurt was. It is quite safe to say that whatever its advanced notions about the relationship between Church and society were in the late nineteenth century, the American hierarchy was much more loyal to Rome than either the French or German hierarchies. Unfortunately the Roman officials could not be certain about this.

The controversies of the last fifteen years of the nineteenth century can be arranged around five headings: (1) the Catholic University; (2) Cahenslyism; (3) the school question and the apostolic delegation; (4) the secret societies and the Knights of Labor; and (5) the "Americanist" heresy.

The Catholic University of America. There was some talk at the Second Plenary Council of Baltimore in 1866 about a national Catholic university but the opponents of such a plan became insistent only in the years immediately preceding the Third Council of Baltimore. Spalding, who could remember with joy his years at the great European university in Louvain, began to agitate in the early 1880s and suggested that financial embarrassment of Mount St. Mary's Seminary in Cincinnati might provide an occasion that the seminary be taken over by the national hierarchy and serve as the nucleus for a university. At the Council of Baltimore itself Mary Gwendolyn Caldwell made her famous offer of $300,000 for the beginning of a university, followed three days later by Spalding's appeal from the pulpit of the Baltimore cathedral for such a university. A committee composed of Corrigan of New York, Kenrick of St. Louis, Allemeny of San Francisco, Ryan of Philadelphia, and Spalding studied the possibilities of a university and reported back to the main body of the council recommending that a university indeed be founded. There followed a period of vacillation and negotiation in which Miss Caldwell with a great deal of spirit refused to transfer the money for the university to the hierarchy until more definite plans had taken shape. There was discussion of converting Seton Hall College at South Orange, New Jersey, but Miss Caldwell was none too enthusiastic about that and Gibbons dreaded the thought of the "terrible Jersey mosquitoes." Finally it was decided that the university would be built in Washington though the Jesuits, who already had a university at Georgetown, were not happy about the scheme.

In the meantime even though Rome had approved in principle the idea of a university, Denis O'Connell, Gibbons' agent in Rome, reported that there was some considerable skepticism in Rome about the prospect. Gibbons pursued a policy of masterly inactivity for some time and on May 12, 1886, Keane was appointed rector of the university after Spalding had refused the unanimous choice. In the meantime opposition to the idea of a university was growing. Archbishop Michael Heiss of Milwaukee resigned from the university committee on the grounds that he would have to travel too far from Milwaukee to Washington, though O'Connell thought that Heiss's resignation was an "ominous" sign in Rome. In the meantime Archbishop Corrigan began to connive against the university since his notion was that a Jesuit university in New York would be a much better scheme than a national university in Washington.

Keane set off to Rome to get definitive Roman approval for the project and was joined by John Ireland, who was making his ad limina visit. The opposition to the university mounted on both sides of the Atlantic and Corrigan and McQuaid managed to persuade some of the Roman officials that a number of American bishops had signed a petition for the university against their will. This was one of Corrigan's favorite techniques in dealings with Rome, to plant suspicions. When a document seemed to go against his policies he would plant suspicions that the document lacked total validity. Gibbons himself finally arrived in Rome to do battle on the subject of the Knights of Labor and was quite discouraged by the amount of opposition he encountered. Both Keane and Gibbons were almost persuaded to drop the whole prospect of the university and let the responsibility for blocking it fall where it ought, that is to say on the shoulders of the archbishop of New York and his suffragan in Rochester. John Ireland, however, would have none of this "cowardly surrender to so unworthy an opposition." And a letter from Gibbons to the Pope finally won approval from the Holy See for the foundation of the university.

But the university was not to have an easy time of it. Raising of funds proved extremely difficult, especially since collectors were banned from the archdiocese of New York. The whole problem of funds would continue to plague the university into the twentieth century when Denis O'Connell, the third rector, would discover that the university's trusted financial adviser had misappropriated close to one million dollars of university funds. The sniping at the university by the New York conservatives and the German bishops as well as by the Jesuits made life on the campus uneasy and there seemed to be a constant warfare among various faculty factions, a warfare which was to proceed for many years to come and indeed even to the present. Spalding quickly lost interest in the university when it became clear to him that its status as a football in ecclesiastical politics and the inability of the university's supporters to raise enough money would doom it at least for a time to a level not much above mediocrity. The Americanists had indeed won the battle for the university though it had been a difficult one to win. But their victory would not be complete at any time and would seem very empty when Keane was dismissed as rector.

The whole history of the Catholic University of America has yet to be written, though volumes covering the first three rectorships have been published. But it is quite clear that Spalding's dream of an American Louvain has not even to the present time become a reality. Some of the departments of the Catholic University are respectable. Others are only average and others are quite poor. The financial problems have been continuous, intra-faculty feuding has flared up frequently, not all of the rectors were academically or administratively competent, and support from the hierarchy has been unpredictable. Located in the nation's capital and with the theoretical support of the whole American Church, the Catholic University has always had great potential but in the almost eight decades of its existence the potential has not come close to full realization. The confusion and the struggles of its early years seem to have set the tone for the succeeding decades. The Americanists had their university, only it turned frequently to be more of a burden than a help, and it has yet to accomplish what Lancaster Spalding had in mind when he first proposed it. Roman suspicions and opposition from the Germans and the New York hierarchy had effectively checkmated the plans of the Americanists. But even in the absence of such opposition, it is not clear that the American Catholic population at the turn of the century was able to support a great university or indeed was capable of understanding what a great university was.

Cahenslyism. There were two basic reasons for the Irish-German strife which raged from the 1880s until the beginning of the First World War. The Irish hierarchy was committed to a thoroughgoing Americanization of the Catholic population. Thus it was very difficult for them to accept the principle of separate German (and later Polish) cultural enclaves within the Church. Although they would permit the establishment of national parishes of one sort or another, these parishes would often be dependent on predominantly Irish territorial parishes. They also felt that it was their duty to protect the minority within the German-American contingent who were in favor of rapid Americanization. Finally they felt the German separateness would play into the hands of the nativists and A.P.A. bigots. The separatism of German-American Catholics was from the point of view of the Irish hierarchy suspicious and quite possibly dangerous.

On the other hand, the Germans were quite conscious of the intellectual superiority of their own cultural tradition and saw no reason why it should be replaced by what they took to be an inferior tradition. Further, they thought it was possible to be German and American—to be loyal to the new nation and still maintain their own separate cultural enclaves. They resented the meddling of the Irish hierarchy in their affairs and also resented the fact that they did not have an adequate representation on the bench of bishops. Thus when Ireland and Gibbons attempted to have an Irish bishop appointed to the traditionally German see of Milwaukee, the Germans were highly offended. They were also convinced that the rapid Americanization policies of the Irish leadership of the hierarchy led them to neglect the spiritual needs of the immigrants and did not hesitate to claim that millions of immigrants had lost the faith. Obviously there was not much room for compromise between the two stands.

The problem began to grow more serious when a priest from the Milwaukee archdiocese, Peter M. Abbelen, went to Rome to plead for the full rights of German-American Catholics. A copy of Abbelen's memorial fell into the hands of Keane and Ireland who were in Rome at the time on the affairs of the Catholic University. Keane described it as a villainous tissue of misstatements criticizing the decrees of the Council of Baltimore insofar as they related to the Germans. He also expressed his suspicion that Abbelen was a secret emissary of a clique of German bishops. After meeting with several other archbishops, Gibbons dispatched a letter to Rome deploring the division that the Abbelen memorial was threatening to produce in the Catholic Church in the United States and said, "The only way to correct the evil is at the beginning to absolutely refuse to recognize any distinctions in our governance of the Church for if any one nationality is accorded special privileges, other nationalities will thereafter demand the same."

When Gibbons later went to Rome, he was prepared to concede some of Abbelen's requests though he still bitterly resented the rather secret and underhanded way that the Germans in the hierarchy had used to protest to Rome. National

parishes were to be established and children of families of
foreign nationalities were restricted to this nationality's parish
so long as they lived in their parents' home. But demands for
separate vicar-generals for the foreign and a stern warning to
the bishops to make provision for the German language were
rejected. It was a notable victory for the Americanists though
their anger at the Germans for a secretive method of register-
ing a protest was to some extent unjustified. The Irish argued
that there was but one hierarchy in the United States and that
the Germans by operating outside of the decisions of that hierarchy had violated the spirit of the council of Baltimore and
were disloyal to the American Church. The Germans could
easily have replied that they were underrepresented in the
national hierarchy and that since they were unable to make
their opinions felt in national meetings, they had no choice but
to proceed through unusual channels. Both sides were completely convinced that justice was on their side and neither
was prepared to compromise. The stage was set for the major
battles to be initiated by the good intentions of Peter Paul
Cahensly.

Peter Paul Cahensly was a German Catholic layman and a
member of the Reichstag who devoted his entire life to extraordinarily unselfish service of the immigrants in the ports
of embarkation, on the high seas, and in the New World. Any
careful reading of his career leaves no doubt that Cahensly
was altruistic and extremely generous. Attempts to cast him
as one of the major villains of American Catholic history are
quite unjust.

The trouble began when Cahensly and other leaders of the
St. Rafael Society journeyed to Lucerne, Switzerland, in 1890
for a congress on immigration problems. The Lucerne conference produced a memorial of eight recommendations to
the Holy See for the protection of immigrants in the United
States. The Holy See was urged to establish separate parishes
for each nationality and to appoint to these churches priests
of the same nationality as the faithful. If there were not
enough people for a national parish, then it was urged that
the territorial parish have priests who understood the language
of the immigrants. Parochial schools were to be set up every-

where and should be separate as far as possible for each nationality, with the language of the country of origin included in the curriculum of the school as well as the language and history of the adopted country. Priests of every nationality should have equal rights with native priests, and Catholics should be organized into societies and mutual-aid unions to keep out of the Freemasons and related organizations. The Holy See was requested to sponsor mission seminaries in which priests could be trained for the United States. Finally it was asked that "the Catholics of each nationality . . . have in the episcopate of the country where they immigrate several bishops who are of the same origin. It seems that in this way the organization of the Church would be perfect for in the assemblies of the bishops every immigrant race would be represented and its interests and needs would be protected."

Their suggestions were all relatively harmless, at least on their face value, but it was possible to misinterpret or misunderstand them as a direct attack on the American Church. When he was informed of the memorial by the Associated Press, John Ireland did not hesitate to make a strong statement: "What is the most strange feature in this whole Lucerne movement is the impudence of the men in undertaking to meddle under any pretext in the Catholic affairs of America. This is simply unpardonable and all American Catholics will treasure up the affront for future action. . . . The inspiration of the work in Europe comes from a clique in America. The great mass of German-speaking Catholics, laymen and priests, are totally opposed to all plots and intrigue to retain foreign ascendancy."

Some of the dispatches of the Associated Press from Rome apparently planted by Denis O'Connell gave what Colman Barry, author of the definitive study of the Cahensly controversy, considers to be wildly distorted accounts of the implications of the Lucerne memorial. Indeed, Barry goes so far as to suggest that the battle would not have been nearly so fierce if the dispatches from Rome had not been slanted to make the Cahensly proposal look more insidious than it was. The proposal could be interpreted as requesting the establishment of separate national churches within American Catholicism but it did not say so in so many words and could also be interpreted as much more moderate in its demands.

Perhaps more serious than the requests of the Lucerne memorial, however, was the way the requests were made. From the Irish-American viewpoint and indeed from the viewpoint of non-Catholic Americans, Cahensly and his colleagues were foreigners interfering in American affairs. They had not dealt directly with the American hierarchy, they were spreading wild rumors about the large number of immigrants lost to the faith, and they were impugning the intelligence and efficiency of the American Church to the Holy See. The usually gentle Gibbons would say, "We cannot view without astonishment and indignation a number of self-constituted critics and officious gentlemen in Europe complaining of the alleged inattention which is paid to the spiritual wants of the foreign population and the means of redress which they have thought proper to submit to the Holy See." The Cahensly memorial occasioned no action by the Holy See though the ill feelings stirred up when the controversy raged around it were to remain within the American Church for many years to come. Gibbons journeyed to Milwaukee for the installation of Archbishop Frederic Katzer in that see in the late summer of 1890 and delivered stirring words against what he thought was false nationalism within the American Church:

Woe to him my brethren, who would destroy or impair this blessed harmony that reigns among us! Woe to him who would sow tares of discord in the fair fields of the Church in America! Woe to him who would breed dissension among the leaders of Israel by introducing a spirit of nationalism into the camps of the Lord! Brothers we are, whatever may be our nationality, and brothers we shall remain. We will prove to our countrymen that the ties formed by grace and faith are stronger than flesh and blood. God and our country!—this is our watchword. Loyalty to God's Church and to our country!—this our religious and political faith.

The Germans were impressed with Gibbons' rhetoric but it is unlikely that they were willing to forgive his support for those who had attacked them over the Cahensly memorial.

The ill feelings would persist for years to come. The American-ists had won the day once again. Both Abbelen's and Cahen-sly's complaints to the Holy See had been sidetracked. Yet the Germans were not converted and would continue to be stanch opponents of everything that the Americanists stood for.

The problem of the nationalities would remain well into the twentieth century and even to the present. The First World War would eliminate most of the German problem, but Polish, French, and Italian Catholics would continue to resent the domination of the Church by the Irish hierarchy, and the Irish hierarchy, clergy, and laity would continue to resent the sepa-ratism and what they took to be the anti-Americanism of the immigrants. The problem was insoluble in the 1890s; it is insoluble apparently even today. Although it may perhaps be possible to develop some theory in which ethnic pluralism and national unity can both be protected, the practical application of such a theory escaped the Church in the 1890s and still escapes it.

If the traditional view of Cahensly as a villain is exag-gerated, however, so one should not be too harsh in judging the violence of the Americanist reaction to the Cahensly me-morial. The signers of the Lucerne propositions should have realized that the American hierarchy would react violently to what they thought was the officious meddling of foreign busy-bodies. Cahensly and Ireland later became friends and de-veloped great respect for one another, though both of them would be older and more mellow than they were in 1890. Even then it is to be doubted that Cahensly could understand why the American hierarchy would have been so incensed by the implications that it had failed to provide for the immigrant. On that subject it must be said that Ireland was right and Cahensly was wrong. The immigrant had not lost faith in the United States; for reasons of which neither of them were aware, the immigration experience, if anything, reinforced the faith of those who came to the New World. But it would take a much more sophisticated understanding of social theory be-fore American Catholics could cope with this rather astonish-ing fact.

Secret Societies, the Knights of Labor, and Henry George.
The American Church was always at something of a loss as to
how to handle the problem of secret societies. The Masons
never seemed quite the threat to Catholicism in this country
that they were in Europe and a number of the Carrolls saw no
conflict between being Masons and being practicing Catholics.
As the years went on into the nineteenth century, it became
clear that Catholics could not be Masons, but the rise of a
number of other secret societies puzzled the bishops no little
bit. The Ancient Order of Hibernians, the Grand Army of the
Republic, the Fenians, the Odd Fellows, the Knights of
Pythias, the Clan-na-Gael, the Sons of Temperance, the Modern Woodmen, the Knights of the Maccabees, and the Improved Order of Redmen were but some of the manifestations
of the nineteenth-century American predilection for societies
with strange names, mysterious robes, and secret rituals. Rome
had condemned secret societies consistently, and some of
them, like the Fenians, by name. From the Roman viewpoint,
secret societies were usually religious sects and frequently violently anti-Catholic; but the American organizations were usually relatively harmless fraternal groups (though some of the
branches of the Ancient Order of the Hibernians became the
murderous Molly Maguires of the Pennsylvania coal fields).
None of the American bishops particularly liked the secret
societies, and while they were able to accept with ease the
Ancient Order of Hibernians and the Grand Army of the Republic, the other organizations presented more serious problems. The position of Gibbons and the other liberals was that
there was no certainty of any positive evil in the societies and
hence no reason for a general mandate forbidding them, while
on the other hand if such a mandate was given, a great deal
of offense would be taken by non-Catholic Americans.

Gibbons successfully procrastinated until 1894, when the
Holy Office condemned the Odd Fellows, the Knights of Pythias, and the Sons of Temperance and directed that the American bishops be notified to warn their people against such
societies, adding that if Catholic members persisted after being
warned, they were to be deprived of the sacraments. Gibbons,
usually a very obedient servant of Rome, persuaded the arch-

bishops of the country to decide that the promulgation of the decree was inopportune largely because of the bitter campaign that the American Protective Association was waging. However, the archdiocese of New York and the diocese of Brooklyn promptly promulgated the decree and eventually the Holy See insisted that the other bishops do the same. Gibbons reluctantly agreed.

Seventy years later the struggle over organizations such as the Knights of Pythias may seem minor. But Gibbons and his colleagues were not eager to needlessly offend the American public, especially in the midst of the A.P.A. campaign. However, the battle over the secret societies is important because it provided the context for what was perhaps Gibbons' greatest effort, the protection of the Knights of Labor. The Knights were founded in 1869 by one Uriah Stephens who was a Mason, an Odd Fellow, and a member of the Knights of Pythias, all of whose rituals had some influence on the development of the Knights of Labor. In 1880 a Catholic, Terence Powderly, was elected president and since large numbers of the working class in America were Catholic, Powderly began to campaign for an approval of the Knights of Labor from the Catholic bishops. He succeeded in removing some of the objectionable sections from the ritual and the operation of the Knights; and at the council of Baltimore in 1884, Archbishop Gibbons and Archbishop Patrick A. Feehan of Chicago succeeded in excepting bona fide labor unions from the condemnation aimed at secret societies.

Shortly thereafter the Holy Office, in response to a plea from the archbishop of Quebec, responded by stating that the Knights of Labor was a society that "ought to be considered among those prohibited by the Holy See." Conservative American bishops led by Bishop James A. Healey of Portland, Maine (the only Negro bishop in the nineteenth century), began to agitate for an extension of the decree to the United States.

Gibbons continued to be sympathetic to the cause of the trade unions in general and to the Knights of Labor in particular. But he was in no rush to take action to clarify the question of the precise canonical standing of the Knights.

Rather he said, that as far as he could see, the Knights existed merely to defend the members from "the tyranny with which many rich corporations, especially those controlling the railroads, inhumanly oppressed the poor workers." However, Gibbons' inactivity could not continue, because as Denis O'Connell, his Roman agent, noted, there was every reason to think that Archbishop Corrigan was quietly working behind the scenes to have the Knights in the United States condemned, that and his clever agent in Rome, Ella Edes, was busy planting stories critical of the Knights.

Keane and Ireland were in Rome arranging matters for the university and Gibbons instructed them to stall against an extension of the decree of the Holy Office until he could arrive in Rome in the early winter of 1887 to receive the red hat. The very best in Gibbons' personality emerged in his battle in Rome for the Knights. He told Vincenzo Sallua, the commissary of the Holy Office, that he would hold him responsible for the losses in the United States if the Knights were condemned. He then prepared a memorial defending the Knights from the accusations made against them and warning of the danger of losing the support of the people, particularly the working people, if the Knights were condemned. The memorial was a very tough document. Gibbons concluded by noting that only five of the seventy-five bishops in the United States desired the condemnation of the Knights. He added, "To speak with the most profound respect but also with the frankness which duty requires of me, seems to me that prudence suggests, and even the dignity of the Church demands, that we should not offer to America ecclesiastical protection for which she does not ask and of which she believes she has no need."

The memorial was of course leaked to the press and Gibbons' popularity with the labor unions soared. On the other hand, the editorial writer in the *New York Times* regretted that Gibbons had spoken about "hard and obstinate monopolies" and added of Gibbons "that he is a man of weak judgment, and the Church would make a terrible blunder if it permits him to persuade [it] into taking the side of an organization which was trying to substitute brute force, intimidation, for law, reason, equity and the precepts of the Christian religion."

Gibbons' intervention had saved the Knights from condemnation and the workingmen hailed him as a hero. The Knights themselves were in deep trouble already, both because of unsuccessful strikes and apparent misuse of funds. McQuaid was able to write gleefully to Corrigan, "How does His Eminence feel now about his pets, the Knights of Labor? They are evidently breaking to pieces and are getting many more kicks than kisses. For the countenance His Eminence gave them, he will have to suffer. He exceeded his instruction and must bear his burden." However, it was not a burden for Gibbons because the workingmen were convinced that he was a hero, and he surely was. Four years later when the encyclical *Rerum novarum* was published defending the rights of workers to form unions, Gibbons felt that his attitude had been justified.

There was one other controversy on social problems that involved the progressives and conservatives within the American Church. A New York priest named Edward McGlynn became a disciple of Henry George, the author of *Progress and Poverty* (McGlynn had previously championed public schools against parochial schools). When McGlynn supported Henry George in 1886 in his campaign for mayor of New York, Archbishop Corrigan ordered him to cease such support, which he refused to do, and was promptly suspended for two weeks by the Archbishop. McGlynn continued to preach in support of George's single-tax theory even after George was defeated in the election, and Corrigan in January of 1887 removed him from his parish.

When he was in Rome to get the red hat, Gibbons attempted to persuade McGlynn to come to Rome and explain his case to ecclesiastical authorities, and Corrigan held such interferences in the affairs of his diocese to be one more example of the archbishop of Baltimore's presumptions. In addition, Gibbons did his best to prevent George's book from being put on the Index. He argued that George was not the originator of his theories about private property and that if Rome was to condemn George, "a humble American artisan," it should also condemn Spencer and Mill who had expressed the same idea. He also contended that whatever George's theories were, he was not a socialist and concluded that since the matters were before the American electorate in political controversy, and since there was no possibility that Americans would adopt George's theories, prudence suggested that the fallacies and absurdities be allowed to perish in and of themselves and that the tribunals of the Church ought not to run the risk of giving them an artificial life of importance.

After his return to the United States, Gibbons continued to campaign against the condemnation of the book, but Corrigan was opposing him every step of the way. The solution was an ironic compromise. The book was condemned but the American hierarchy was advised that the condemnation need not be published. Gibbons was reasonably satisfied that he had slowed down what would have been an unfortunate condemnation of a social theory that was no threat to the faith of American Catholics, but Corrigan and McQuaid were disappointed. As McQuaid observed, "What is the use of it if you can't publish it?" McGlynn was excommunicated but in 1892 Archbishop Satolli, the apostolic delegate, lifted the ban of excommunication and McGlynn proceeded to Florida where he served until 1895, when he returned to New York and was appointed by Corrigan as a pastor of St. Mary's Church. Two years later he gave the funeral eulogy for his friend Henry George. The matter was settled with Gibbons once more persuading Rome that American problems ought not to be solved by harsh decisions from the Holy See. Yet he had paid a heavy price for his success, because Corrigan's animosity was now so fierce that no amount of explaining on Gibbons' part could end it. Corrigan would wait for the day when he could get revenge.

The Americanists had again won a victory in the battle over the Knights of Labor and Henry George. For many decades to come, the Catholic workingmen could remain convinced that their ecclesiastical leaders were on the side of the unions. But for a wide variety of reasons the advantage was not followed up. As we will notice in the next chapter, Gibbons, Keane, Spalding, and Ireland were the founders of American Catholic social action, and while the tradition they began would prove to be a strong one, its influence on American society was not very great. The vast majority of American Catholics would for at least another half century be quite uninformed about the social doctrines of the Church. Indeed the attitude of Corrigan and McQuaid, who viewed the unions as dangerous socialist organizations, would have the support of many priests and bishops for years to come. The Americanists had their victory, but they failed to bring the Church completely and enthusiastically behind the cause of the workingman.

The School Question and the Apostolic Delegation. From the perspective of the middle of the twentieth century, the conflict over John Ireland's school experiments seems very much a tempest in a teapot. The experiments he had proposed would not upset any Catholic educators today, though they might seriously disturb the members of the American Jewish Committee or the American Civil Liberties Union. It is not at all clear, especially in retrospect, how two experiments at combining public and Catholic education in Minnesota could possibly have been viewed by anybody as a threat to the parochial school system, especially since John Ireland himself had a vast network of parochial schools in his own diocese. But even his sometime friend Lancaster Spalding took deep offense at Ireland's experimentation and the rhetoric with which he described it. The only possible explanation for the bitterness with which the school controversy was fought and the Roman intervention it made necessary was that the education issue had become the focal point for many of the other grievances which the liberal and conservative wings of the hierarchy felt against each other.

The roots of the so-called Faribault controversy could be found in past experiences. In 1870, Bishop Verot of Savannah worked on an agreement with the school board of the city in which the board assumed ownership of the parochial schools and was given responsibility for the buildings, the hiring and testing of teachers, the selection of textbooks, and other such functions. Several years later a similar arrangement was worked out at St. Peter's Church in Poughkeepsie, New York, in which the Catholic school was rented to the school board for one dollar and religious education took place after the regular school hours. The appearances of Gibbons and Keane at the National Education Association meeting in 1889 and John Ireland's dramatic speech in which he suggested that the hand that was raised in sign of destruction of the public schools ought to be withered was the prelude to another attempt to work out a *modus vivendi* between Catholic and public education.

In 1891 in two parishes in Ireland's diocese—Faribault and Stillwater, Minnesota—arrangements similar to the Poughkeepsie plan were worked out. At this point all hell broke loose around John Ireland's pugnacious Irish head. Rome wanted to see the text of the Ireland speech at the N.E.A. meeting. Catholic newspapers in the country, particularly those edited by Germans, labeled Ireland an enemy of the parochial schools. Even those who were pro-Ireland were somewhat upset by his apparent romance with public education. Gibbons dispatched a letter to Rome in defense of his friend, pointing out that Ireland had said nothing unusual, that he was a stanch promoter of Catholic schools in his diocese, and that American Catholics had to learn to live with the public school system. In November of 1891, Father Thomas Bouquillon of the faculty of the Catholic University of America issued a pamphlet entitled *Education: To Whom Does It Belong?* The Bouquillon pamphlet was not an extraordinary document by contemporary standards but his insistence that the state had a vast area of rights and jurisdiction in the matter of education incensed the conservatives who with Archbishop Ryan of Philadelphia would concede to the state compulsion only with regard to the three R's since they seemed necessary to qualify a citizen to vote intelligently. Shortly afterward Father René I. Holaind, a New York Jesuit, wrote a pamphlet in reply called *The Parent First* which sought to refute Bouquillon's stand with Catholic philosophy and theology. Corrigan, McQuaid, and the German hierarchy were as usual in such matters sending a steady stream of letters to Rome denouncing Ireland and all his experiments.

The controversy spread to Italy where *Civilta Cattolica* also joined in the attack on Ireland, but Ireland himself promptly

sailed to Rome, where he persuaded the Pope that there was
nothing dangerous in the Faribault experiment. The Roman
decision was that while the legislation of the council of Baltimore was still in effect, all circumstances considered, the
Faribault and Stillwater experiments could be tolerated. By
Ireland's standards this was a vindication though his enemies
insisted that the experiment was only a tolerated exception
and not to become a general practice. The controversy raged
on even though nativist opposition in Minnesota had forced
the cancellation of both experiments within two years. The
battle therefore was academic and would remain to be settled
in theory by the new apostolic delegate.

Rome had for many years desired to have a representative
in the United States so that a curial official would be closer to
the problem and perhaps be able to more accurately judge
what was going on in the strange land beyond the sea. The
American hierarchy had consistently resisted the appointment
of such an envoy on the grounds that American public opinion
simply would not be sympathetic to a foreign churchman on
American soil supervising the work of American Catholicism.
The disturbances at the time that Archbishop Bedini came to
the United States (his tour of the United States as papal legate
occasioned widespread outbreaks of nativist riots) were cited
as an example of the opposition of Americans to such an emissary. Another and perhaps more important reason was that
the American bishops felt that they were quite capable of
governing the Church in the United States by themselves without any foreign interference.

On the occasion of the four-hundredth anniversary of Columbus' discovery of America, the Holy See decided to send
Francisco Satolli to the United States as a representative of
the Holy See for the celebration. Satolli was taken to be a
liberal and John Ireland and his friend in Rome, Denis O'Connell, were delighted at the prospect that Satolli might also
bring with him a papal statement settling the school controversy. Other American bishops including Spalding were quite
upset by the prospect of even a temporary visit from a papal
legate, especially since the American Protective Association

was engaging in a violent anti-Catholic campaign and seized upon the Satolli mission as a pretext for even more furious attacks on the Catholic Church.

It developed after Satolli's arrival that he also had faculties from the Pope for settling disputes between bishops and priests, and rumors of the establishment of a permanent papal delegation grew more intense. The archbishops of the United States sent a letter to Rome arguing against the establishment of a delegation, contending that American non-Catholics would be greatly antagonized by it; but, before the letter could be presented to the Pope, Rome announced the appointment of Satolli as the apostolic delegate and the American hierarchy instructed O'Connell not to submit the letter. Instead Gibbons wrote to the Pope thanking him for the appointment of a delegate and saying that everywhere in the United States public sentiment of satisfaction and gratitude had been expressed. John Tracy Ellis, Gibbons' friendly biographer, admits that this was perhaps going a bit too far and it proved quite embarrassing to Gibbons when the press obtained copies of his earlier letter. Spalding and Bishop James Ryan of Alton, Illinois, continued their opposition to the delegation but Rome had spoken and the matter was closed.

Satolli issued a series of fourteen propositions which were intended to compose the difficulties of the parochial schools. The propositions were generally quite favorable to the Ireland position, and Ireland's confidence that he could control the apostolic delegate and influence even more directly the development of American Catholicism seemed confirmed. After some hesitation, Rome sustained the fourteen propositions of Satolli and the Americanists had won another victory. Public education was not to be condemned, Catholics were permitted to go to public schools if there were no parochial schools available, sacraments were not to be forbidden to parents who sent their children to public schools, the kinds of experiments that John Ireland had tried (unsuccessfully, as it turned out) were to be permitted. But like many of their other victories, the school victory was a particularly hollow one and John Ireland was to regret to his dying day his support of the Satolli mission. Within two years, Satolli's friendship with the liberals cooled decidedly and in 1895 he gave a speech in Pottsville, Pennsylvania, which was vigorously in support of the German position and against the Americanizers. Satolli would return to Rome to be succeeded by another delegate in 1896 and for reasons that are not yet clear, he returned to Rome the bitter enemy of all the Americanists. He was suspected of being instrumental in the condemnation of the so-called Americanist heresy as well as in the removal of both O'Connell and Keane from their respective rectorships in Rome and at the Catholic University even though O'Connell, at least, was removed before Satolli's return to Rome. Ireland's friends also blamed Satolli for blocking the elevation of the archbishop of St. Paul to the cardinalate.

The history of the relationship between Catholic and public schools since the 1890s has not been a particularly happy one. In some instances there has been open animosity, especially as the officials of the N.E.A. have done everything in their power to prevent any sort of state aid for Catholic schools. It has been difficult to escape the impression that public educators would rather like to have a monopoly on education and resent the presence of a massive Catholic system as a threat to their monopoly. On the other hand, many Catholic educators have felt compelled to make a case for the inadequacy of public education to justify their own existence. Where animosity has not flared into the open, the normal state of the relationship between the two school systems is one of somewhat suspicious but peaceful coexistence. Even in the 1960s, cooperation between Catholic and public schools is extremely rare. John Ireland's attempt to work out both in theory and in practice a *modus vivendi* between the public school and the Catholic school could only be termed an abject failure.

The confident expectation of non-Catholic Americans that the Catholic schools would fade away as the Catholic population became more Americanized does not seem to have been substantiated. Seven per cent of the school children in the country were in Catholic schools in 1940 and close to 14 per cent in 1960. In addition there was a direct relationship between Catholic education and social class so that it was precisely the more successful and the better-educated Catholics who are the most likely to send their children to parochial schools. In very recent years a good many non-Catholics have changed their position on the parochial schools and have begun to argue that since the schools are certainly going to continue to exist it ought to be the concern of all Americans to see that they do the best possible job educationally. It was impossible during the Kennedy Administration for any national compromise on the school question to be arranged, though the educational act of the Johnson Administration certainly can be taken to represent the beginning of such compromise. Influential publications such as the *New Republic* have dramatically shifted their stand in favor of aid to Catholic schools and national public opinion polls also show rather marked increase in the proportion of the American public who could live with such assistance. At the same time, however, a liberal elite within the Catholic Church has grown increasingly critical of the schools as being divisive and as absorbing practically all of the money, personnel, and effort of the American Church. In these circles it has become a mark of one's liberalism to withdraw one's children from Catholic schools and the schools have also been a useful scapegoat into which one can project all one's frustrations against the organized structure of the American Church. The National Opinion Research Center studies of Catholic education show that parochial schools are doing a better than adequate job academically, that they are not having any detectable divisive effect on American society, and that they are indeed producing a graduate who is somewhat more devout and somewhat more enlightened than the Catholic who attends public schools. But the climate of opinion within the Church is slowly shifting against the parochial school. While the short-run future of Catholic education is still somewhat bright, unless an ideological thrust can be recaptured in the next few years, it is doubtful that Catholic education in the United States can perdure into the twenty-first century.

What the situation would be today if John Ireland's experiments had been successful and been imitated elsewhere in the country is difficult to judge. It ought to be clear for the record that the failure of the Faribault and Stillwater experiments cannot be blamed on the Vatican but must rather be blamed on nativist opposition in the United States. It is highly doubtful that the American public then or now would be willing to sit still for a vast expansion of Ireland's experiments and their constitutionality in view of the Supreme Court decisions of the last two decades. Whether or not the Canadian system of state aid for denominational school systems would have been more satisfactory in American society is an open question. Surely it seems to work very well in Canada, and might, in some theoretical set of circumstances, have been very satisfactory in the United States. However the climate of American public opinion has been and continues to be such that the Canadian method would be totally unacceptable in this country.

From the perspective of history, therefore, Ireland's plan was doomed to failure from the beginning. This was most unfortunate for if conservative Catholics and non-Catholic Americans could have been persuaded to seek a *modus vivendi* on the school questions in the 1890s, a good deal of bitter religious controversy might have been avoided. However, a compromise was no more feasible in the 1890s than it is in the 1960s and the school question will very likely continue to be an occasion for considerable animosity for many decades to come. John Ireland, supported by Gibbons and Keane, had played for high stakes against great odds. Even though they won the gamble within the Church, they were to pay a very high price for it in years to come. But as far as non-Catholic American society was concerned, the gamble was a waste of time.

The "Americanism" Heresy

As the nineteenth century drew to a close, it became clear that the Americanists were in trouble. Satolli had turned against them and then returned to Rome to occupy a key place in the Curia. The Jesuits were angry because of their defeats on the school question and on the issue of the Catholic University. The Germans had not forgotten the humiliation of the Cahensly controversy nor for all of Archbishop Katzer's words were they willing to forgive what they took to be the arrogance of John Ireland. Corrigan, backed up by the irascible McQuaid, was deluging Rome with letters of protest over the brave risks that were being run and Miss Edes was doing everything in her power to poison the minds of Roman officials against Ireland and his friends. O'Connell was removed from his rectorship of the North American College though Gibbons kept him on in Rome as the vicar of his Roman church and as his own personal delegate to the Holy See. Keane was summarily dismissed from the Catholic University and summoned to Rome where he was submitted to a number of what could only be described as carefully planned humiliations. The spirits of Denis O'Connell and John Ireland rose and fell with each new Roman rumor but the handwriting was on the wall for those who cared to read it. Rome was growing daily more suspicious of the strange doings in the United States. The suspicions were aggravated by the beginning of the Spanish-American War, which John Ireland had confidently hoped that he personally could prevent. The Roman officials were not at all pleased that an aggressive young Protestant nation like the United States was dismantling the empire of an ancient and loyal Spanish kingdom, and were perhaps inclined to blame American bishops for the conduct of their national leaders.

The Roman viewpoint is of course quite understandable. America was a strange country and whatever Archbishop Satolli said when he came back, it was quite clear that the net result of his years as apostolic delegate was suspicion and distrust for everything that the American liberals stood for. It was evident that men like Ireland and Keane were not only arousing suspicions in Europe but were also proving deeply offensive to American Catholics such as the Germans and the bishops in New York whose loyalty to the Holy See was unquestioned. No one of course could doubt Gibbons, but was he not after all a bit too much under the influence of his good friend John Ireland? And Ireland was certainly a gifted speaker and probably orthodox on most important matters. Keane was a pious man and though less outspoken than Ireland could be quite blunt on occasion. The two of them

seemed to lack the delicacy and tact that the Roman officials
thought most appropriate in a prince of the Church. It would
be a mistake to condemn these men, because they were certainly sincere and no definite errors or heterodoxies could be
charged against them. What was needed rather than a condemnation was an admonition which would dampen their
enthusiasm somewhat while not pushing them so far that
Rome might have a messy situation on its hands and possible
schism. Perhaps Cardinal Satolli assured his confreres that
there was little need to fear that a mild slap on the knuckles
would create a violently adverse reaction in the United States.
Had not, after all, the American bishops submitted quite
quickly and even with the appearance of enthusiasm when
an apostolic delegation was established? Furthermore they
had not uttered a word of protest when Keane had been
fired from the rectorship of the Catholic University. They
were good men and one certainly did not intend to break
their spirit but they needed to be slowed down and taught
a little moderation and discretion.

It is hardly my intention to suggest that Roman officials
were explicitly looking for an occasion to dampen the spirits
of the Americanists. However, it does seem to be a mistake
to make too much of the details of the "Americanism" controversy. Even if Isaac Hecker had never lived, even if Walter
Elliott had never written a life of Hecker, even if this biography had not in a French translation stirred up a violent
controversy between monarchists and republicans in France,
it was only a matter of time before the Roman officials would
have decided that something had to be done about the
Americanists.

Elliott's life of Hecker is a dull if relatively harmless book.
It had never been terribly popular in the United States. But
in 1897, a French edition was published which was inaccurate
at least in some respects; to this translation was added a preface by Abbé Félix Klein of the Catholic Institute of Paris
which according to one observer out-Heckered Hecker "precisely on those points for which it was possible for a critic
bent on fault-finding to attach to his words a meaning of doubtful orthodoxy." Klein argued that it was to the United States

and to the active democratic virtues preached by Father Hecker that Europe must look for leadership if Catholicism was to adjust to the modern world. The Elliott book was a sensation in France and Klein's introduction was even more of a sensation. Controversy immediately broke out in the French journals with the monarchists joining forces against Klein and Hecker and so-called "Americanism" while the Catholic republicans spoke out vigorously in favor of them. The "Americanism" which was under discussion was several steps removed from anything that Ireland, Keane, or Gibbons were preaching and practicing. The French controversy in fact had nothing to do with the United States nor with Hecker nor even with Elliott's life of Hecker but rather with the exaggerations in Abbé Klein's introduction, exaggerations which themselves were never so unorthodox as to have the French translation put on the Index.

A French priest, Charles Maignen, published a book called *Studies on Americanism: Father Hecker, Is He a Saint?* which was a vicious attack on Klein, Hecker, and the American republic. The controversy could not stay limited to France but quickly traveled to Rome, and rumors of a condemnation of many of the Americans spread rapidly. Leo XIII set up a special commission to investigate the problem and Cardinal Rampolla, a champion of the Americanists, assured Keane that nothing would be done hurtful to the American interests. Ireland made a hurried trip to Rome either to stop the encyclical, or if he could not stop it, at least to influence its contents. Apparently the commission which put together the encyclical draft was headed by Cardinal Mazzella, a Jesuit and vigorous opponent of all things American, and Cardinal Satolli, who had become disillusioned with the United States during his tour of duty as apostolic delegate. Apparently too Leo XIII rewrote the document taking much of the sting out of it. Rampolla confided to John Ireland that he would not be disappointed in the letter. Despite last-minute attempts to stop the sending of the encyclical on the part of Ireland and Keane, it was sent and quickly thereafter leaked to the press. Keane wrote, "We have done our utmost to hinder its publication but all signs indicate that they will be obstinate and we will fail. We have the consolation of knowing that we did our full duty. The blow I fear will be a sad one for the Paulists and for the memory of Hecker and a blow to the Cardinal and Ireland who wrote in their behalf. We must simply make the best of it and carry on our game of explaining to the American people the administrative blunders of our superiors." The encyclical was signed on January 22, and a month later the full text was published in the United States.

Read today the encyclical seems inoffensive. It does not condemn the *Life of Hecker* and only notes that through the action of those who had undertaken to publish it and interpret in a foreign language a certain amount of controversy had arisen. Among the opinions the Pope censured was one which held that Christian doctrine ought to be softened in such a way as not to have the same meaning which it previously had held, that there was no need of spiritual direction, that natural and active virtues were superior to the supernatural and that passive virtues of the religious life and vows were not pertinent to the modern world, and that the Church's authority and discipline ought to be reduced in the modern world.

The Pope in the concluding paragraphs was quite clear about distinguishing between three different kinds of Americanism. Those characteristic qualities that reflect on the honor of the people of America and the laws and customs which prevail in the United States the Pope did not find blameworthy. But if the term "Americanism" was used to describe the doctrines that he had previously rejected, then the Pope noted he was sure that the American bishops would be the first to repudiate and condemn such Americanism.

At no point in the encyclical did the Pope affirm that the condemned doctrines were in fact held in the United States or that they were contained in the writings of Isaac Hecker. Indeed it was not even claimed that the French translation of Hecker's book or Abbé Klein's introduction to it contained these ideas. Klein himself denied that he believed such doctrines and a reading of the English edition of Elliott's *Life of Hecker* would indicate to the impartial reader that only by taking statements completely out of context could Hecker be accused of holding anything even faintly resembling the condemned "Americanism." There has been some controversy in Catholic historical circles as to whether Leo XIII personally felt that there were Americans who held the ideas he reprobated. From later remarks to Keane and Spalding and Ireland, it seems likely that the Pope was inclined to suspect that some Americans did or that there was a danger that such doctrines would become popular in the United States if he did not head them off. But the important point is not what Leo XIII personally thought but what his encyclical said. The encyclical at no point said or even implied that the Americanism which was condemned was actually professed by Catholics in the United States. Apparently the Pope was of a mind to give a general warning to American Catholics that they should not begin to think the ideas which some French conservatives accused them of having. If indeed the Pope had toned down the work of Mazzella and Satolli, which was intended to be a vigorous and forthright condemnation of the American Church, he had done the Americans a favor. He would have done them even more of a favor if he had never written the encyclical.

Ireland was furious. In a letter to the Paulist superior, he wrote, "Read the letter carefully and you will see that the Americanism condemned is Maignen's nightmare. Whoever preferred natural to supernatural virtues? Whoever taught that the practice of natural virtues was not to be vitalized and supernaturalized by divine grace? Whoever thought that in harkening to the Holy Ghost the Christian was not to be constantly guided by the visible magisterium of the Church?

"Their antics conjured up Americanism and put such before the Pope. Lepidi and Mazzella wrote the body of the letter. I cannot pray that God forgive them." And to the Pope, Ireland wrote:

. . . New Light has come; misunderstandings are no more. Now we can even define the errors which "certain ones" have wished to cloak with the name of "Americanism" and define the truth which alone Americans call "Americanism." . . . I repudiate and condemn those opinions without any exception, literally as Your Holiness repudiates and condemns them, and I repudiate and condemn them with all the greater readiness and heartfelt joy because my Catholic faith and my understanding of the teachings and practices of the Holy Church never for a single instant permitted me to open my soul to such extravagances. . . .

Gibbons himself reacted much as Ireland did, though with somewhat more moderate language: "This extravagant and absurd doctrine as I would willingly call it, this Americanism as they have chosen to call it, has nothing in common with the views, the aspirations, the doctrines and conduct of Americans. I do not think that in the whole country could be found a single priest or bishop or even a well instructed layman who has ever put forward such an extravagance. No, this is not and never has been and never will be our Americanism. I am deeply grateful to your Holiness for having yourself made this distinction in your apostolic letter."

But the Americanists were not to get off that easily. Archbishop Corrigan wrote a self-congratulatory letter to the Holy Father strongly implying that the false Americanism had indeed been held by many Catholics and the papal letter had saved the American Church from disaster. Apparently, he then signed the names of his suffragan bishops without first bothering to check with them. Similarly the German bishops of the Milwaukee province also wrote the Pope not only welcoming the encyclical but condemning those Americans who denied the doctrine had ever been professed in this country and accusing them of dishonesty in their denial. A conservative Catholic press also hailed the letter as a defeat and quite probably a condemnation of John Ireland and everything he stood for.

At the meeting of American archbishops in October of 1899, Patrick W. Riordan of San Francisco, who had been a fellow traveler of the Americanists, called the attention of his colleagues to the letter from the Milwaukee province, acknowledging that Americanism had in fact been professed by people in the United States. Archbishops Ireland and John J. Kain of St. Louis agreed and urged that the entire hierarchy be asked to answer two questions—whether the errors existed in their diocese or other parts of the country, and if they did, to specify where they existed and by whom they were held. Corrigan of course opposed such a poll and Ireland's motion was defeated by a vote of five to four, with Gibbons casting the decisive vote against Ireland's proposal. Ireland was quite upset: "Baltimore cried peace, peace, death even for the sake of peace, and nothing was effected." But as far as Gibbons was concerned, nothing was to be gained by keeping the issue alive.

Perhaps he was right. The Americanists would soon recover much of their optimism. Ireland would tour Europe, preach a great sermon in honor of St. Joan of Arc, and once again be hailed as a great prophet out of the West. Keane would shortly become archbishop of Dubuque and in 1903 Denis O'Connell would become the second rector of the Catholic University of America, an appointment which would lead John Ireland to exclaim, "O'Connell in Washington. Simply impossible. Well he is here. *Viva sempre l'Americanissmo.*"

But John Ireland was wrong. Even though none of the Americanists were officially condemned and several of them were later rewarded in one way or another, even though the encyclical letter did not contend that any Americans actually professed the condemned doctrines, even though the doctrines that were in fact discussed by the encyclical were not even on subjects that were essential to the thinking of men like Ireland and Keane, and finally even though the encyclical did not address itself directly to any of the controversies of the previous decade and a half, it nonetheless effectively brought to an end the controversies that had raged since the end of the council of Baltimore. The Germans and Corrigan and his allies could claim that their enemies had been condemned and would thus be able to withdraw from the field of battle with a sense of triumph. Gibbons, Ireland, and Keane, even though they argued with some conviction that they had not been condemned, were deeply hurt by the letter and some of the joy and verve went out of their lives. All of them were now in their sixties and had little stomach for further controversy. If the intention of the Holy See had been to restrain the enthusiasm of the Americanists without stirring up too violent and adverse a reaction, then *Testem benevolentiae* had been an extremely successful encyclical.

Nonetheless the American Church had been humiliated. Rome had condemned under the name of "Americanism" a doctrine that was a blatant distortion of the Americanists' ideas, concocted by a rabid French monarchist to suit the needs of political controversy in France. A letter to Cardinal Gibbons about a controversy that was essentially French was certainly a curious way of doing business. It is simply astonishing that there was not much more American resentment over the encyclical. The Roman officials were uninformed about the situation of the Church in America and a condemnation of "Americanism" was an unintended insult to the United States. The encyclical has cast a cloud over the American Church which has persisted even until our time.

Robert D. Cross in his book on the controversy suggests that in the twentieth century a liberal Catholicism emerged in the United States. But the truth of the matter is rather just the opposite, it seems to us. The condemnation of "Americanism" represented not the emergence of a liberal Catholicism but rather its submergence. The shock and the hurt of the condemnation would persist for a long time, especially since in the minds of many "Americanism" would be viewed as a forerunner of Modernism, whose condemnation in the next decade was to be such a traumatic experience for the Catholic Church. If American churchmen did not hold the "Americanism" that was condemned by the encyclical, they were even less inclined to hold or for that matter to understand the Modernist heresy which Pius X was to condemn. But while Modernism was not a problem in the United States, at least some American seminary professors were removed in the intellectual reign of terror that followed the Modernist condemnation, and the fears and suspicions of innovation that were part of the anti-Modernist reaction simply reinforced the caution that American bishops were inclined to exercise after *Testem benevolentiae.*

We know precious little about the history of the American Church in the twentieth century but some observers list four reasons for the failure of leaders of the stature of John Ireland, James Gibbons, and John Keane to emerge: the establishment of an apostolic delegation, the training of future bishops at the American College in Rome, the Modernist controversy, and the condemnation of "Americanism." Such reasons must of course be merely hypotheses until more careful research is done. But there can be no doubt that the vigor and enthusiasm of the closing years of the nineteenth century have yet to be duplicated.

There have been great bishops in the twentieth century, many of them more democratic in their personal behavior and in the governance of their dioceses than was John Ireland, who for all his democratic beliefs was quite a bit of an autocrat within the boundaries of St. Paul. There have also been some bishops whose intellectual and scholarly capacities certainly excelled those of all the Americanists save perhaps Lancaster Spalding. There have been bishops who have been far better informed on social questions and at least as concerned about social problems as were the Americanists. What the twentieth century has failed to produce in church leadership is not democratic inclinations, social concern, or intellectual competence. All of these have existed and at least on occasion in abundance. What is missing is the style, the flair, the charismatic enthusiasm which could move the minds and hearts of men as they have not seemed to have been moved in the years since 1900. It can be argued that the Americanists were ahead of their time, that they would have been giants of the Second Vatican Council if they had lived to attend it. This argument is probably quite correct, but where the American Church might be today if their intuitions, which antedated the Vatican Council by seven decades, had been given an opportunity to develop and flourish is a question that points up one of the great tragedies of ecclasiastical history. It isn't wise to lament too long about those things that might have been; but a great Catholic University, a *modus vivendi* with the public schools, a solution to the ethnic problem, a more intense commitment to question of social justice, and more vigorous experimentation with implications of American democracy for the life of the Church could have given to the vigorous American

Church a depth, a richness which it does not have and which lack is increasingly becoming a serious defect.

The odds, however, were against the Americanists. They had strong and at times unscrupulous opponents within the American Church. The Roman officials did not understand the Church in the United States and were growing more deeply suspicious of it. The church universal was still in an era when problems were to be treated by condemning evil rather than by attempting to understand its occasions and change evil to error. The American Protestants were not yet ready to accept Catholics as full-fledged partners in a national enterprise. The enthusiasm and the optimism of the Americanists must in that respect be judged as a mistake. Yet one cannot help but wish that they had been right.

VII

RYAN AND COUGHLIN
Two Reformers of the 1930s

The rich, mellow voice with the faint touch of the Irish brogue raged onward. His adversary was a right reverend spokesman for the New Deal, a right reverend Democratic politician, a right reverend New Dealer. He was a Democratic stooge, a dupe of the Communists, and his economic theories were no better and probably worse than that of the speaker. The voice raved on and on and the stout, balding priest with the long nose stared moodily at the radio, smiling only at the epithet of "right reverend New Dealer." The two great Catholic social reformers of the New Deal era, John Augustine Ryan and Charles E. Coughlin, had joined battle. Ryan was a doctor of theology, a specialist on labor legislation, a friend of government officials, the acknowledged spokesman of the Catholic Church on matters social, the director of the social action department of the National Catholic Welfare Conference. Charles E. Coughlin was the radio priest of Royal Oak, Michigan, with no credentials other than his compelling radio voice and five million followers. Ryan had all of the best of the argument but he was no match either for Coughlin's rhetoric or for his mass of followers. The right reverend New Dealer represented a tradition that would last and the radio priest a tradition which would eventually die out. But in 1936 it was not at all clear which side would win. And for a few terrible weeks, it seemed to many Americans that Charles E.

Coughlin had seized control not only of the Catholic Church
but quite possibly could seize control of the whole nation. The
right reverend New Dealer did not seriously weaken the
thrust of Coughlin's drive for power but at least he persuaded
many non-Catholics in the country that there were Catholic
prelates who were quite capable of standing up to the radio
priest from Royal Oak, Michigan.

The confrontation between John Ryan and Charles Coughlin emphasized the fact that in the midst of the Depression the
Roman Catholic Church did indeed have a social doctrine,
although it was not clear in 1936 who were its valid expo-
nents. The social doctrine went back a long time, more than
fifty years at the very least. James Hastings Nichols, no friend
of Roman Catholicism, would describe it as the best social
action doctrine of any church in America. It would inspire
hundreds and perhaps even thousands of young Catholic
progressives, reformers, liberals, and radicals in the first half
of the twentieth century. It would have no difficulty reconcil-
ing itself with some elements in the mainstream of American
social reform. Its thought and action would represent one of
the happier marriages between the Catholic Church and
American society. But, for a vast variety of reasons, the
social doctrine would have substantially less influence at the
grass-roots level than it might have had, so that in the 1930s
when American Catholics like all other Americans were suffering from the monstrosity of the Great Depression, a man
whose friends would call confused and his enemies would
call a demagogue could usurp that tradition and twist it eventually into something that was surely anti-Semitic and quite
close to fascist. If John Ryan symbolized by his life and teaching the intimate relationship between American reform and
Catholic social action, so Charles Coughlin in the 1930s would
demonstrate how weak was the popular understanding and
popular support for the official "Catholic Social Action" and
how readily it could be replaced by a counterfeit, a counterfeit which curiously enough had its own roots in a deviant
variety of the American social reform ethos.

In 1960, it was fashionable to moan the absence of much
authentic liberalism within the American Catholic Church.

Even such a distinguished observer as Daniel Patrick Moynihan has pointed out that while the Irish voted Democratic, their version of democracy was a conservative one. Before the argument could be settled as to whether Irish Catholic Democrats were liberal or not, one would have to define what one meant by liberal and also establish that the "authentic" liberals of the *New Republic–Nation* variety are very frequent in the Protestant population. Insofar as any statistical data are available, there is no evidence at all that Catholic Democrats are any less liberal on the standardized measures of liberalism than are Protestant Democrats; nor despite all self-criticism to the contrary is there any evidence that the graduates of Catholic colleges are any less likely to describe themselves as liberal Democrats than Protestants or Catholics who attend non-Catholic colleges. There are certainly some forms of doctrinaire liberalism that are not attractive to Catholics in general and to the Irish in particular, especially since the latter tend to be much more pragmatic in their political approach (the lack of enthusiasm for the Irish pragmatism of John Kennedy on the part of doctrinaire American liberals has conveniently been forgotten).

Catholics could be pardoned for being less than enthusiastic about the reforming instinct of the Populist movement since the Populists were frequently also bitter nativists and virulently anti-Catholic. Tom Watson, Georgia's remote ancestor of Lester Maddox, managed to maintain his political career for ten or fifteen years at the end of his life solely on the basis of attacking the Roman Church.[1] Nor were the Catholics in the early part of the twentieth century terribly enthused about the good-government approach of Woodrow Wilson and the Progressives because it often seemed to them that the Progressive movement was a supercilious Anglo-

---

[1] In a little-known facet of American Catholic history, a brilliantly planned and executed campaign by "The Catholic Laymen's Association of Georgia" kept Watson at bay and ultimately contributed to his defeat. The story of this strange and fascinating battle is told in an unpublished doctoral dissertation from Fordham University by Brother Edward Cashin of Marist College, Poughkeepsie, New York.

Saxon attempt to deprive the immigrants and their children
of their hard-earned political power. Finally the philosophical
assumptions of Catholic social reform, rooted as they are in
Thomistic philosophy and the memory of the medieval
guilds, are usually very different from the philosophical
assumptions of the American liberal reform tradition. But
all these qualifications having been made, it is still true that
Catholic social teaching and practice in the United States,
particularly as summarized in the career of John A. Ryan,
is remarkably liberal with a small "l" if not a capital "L," and
distinctively American.

Ryan and the other greats of Catholic social reform succeeded in capturing the best elements of the Populist, Progressive, and New Deal philosophies and merging them with
the traditional wisdom. Unfortunately this highly successful
American gambit attracted relatively little grass-roots support,
made only small impact on Catholic education, and at no
time could command wide universal enthusiasm in the Catholic press. The Catholic workingman would overwhelmingly
join unions whenever it was possible and indeed would be
led by Catholics such as Terence Powderly, first Grand
Master Workman of the Knights of Labor, and "Black John"
Mitchell, president of the United Mine Workers of America.
But only a few of these Catholic unionists would realize that
there was much connection between their trade union activity
and their Church; on the contrary, they frequently would be
informed from their parish pulpit on Sunday morning that
union activities (which seemed to them to be necessary for
physical survival) were dangerously tainted with socialist or
communist influences. Under these circumstances, many
Roman Catholics were readily swayed by the hypnotic appeal
of Charles Coughlin.

The roots of American Catholic social tradition date back
even before the publication of the encyclical letter *Rerum
novarum* in 1891. Cardinal Gibbons' defense of the Knights
of Labor antedated the papal encyclical by four years and
committed the American hierarchy to the defense of the labor
movement and its goals before the church universal was committed to it. The Boston diocese led the way in the Catholic

press with the extraordinarily astute and vigorous labor columnist who wrote under the pseudonym of Phineas. William J. Onahan, leading Catholic layman in Chicago, with Bishops Spalding and Ireland a promoter of the Irish Catholic Colonization Society, was a vigorous supporter of unions. Spalding himself pulled no punches. Speaking of unions, he said, "They exist and the ends for which they exist in spite of incidental abuses connected with their working are praiseworthy and there is no power that can put them down. If the trade unions shall succeed in forcing politicians to recognize that financial interests are not the only or the principally human interests, they will have conferred a benefit on the whole nation."

Ireland did not hesitate to make his support for the labor movement known, and defend Catholic immigrants against the charge of socialism or radicalism. Bishop George Montgomery of Los Angeles wrote an open letter to the American workingman urging him to set the labor cause on a religious pedestal, arguing that since capital possessed "an undue purchasing power" in courts and legislatures, his only hope of securing justice lay in the emergence of honest and conscientious representatives and public servants; so long "as gold can buy votes and legislation, the laboring man will be the victim of capital and gold will have that power wherever religious principles do not form and control man's consciences." Montgomery was quite willing to argue for income taxes, municipal socialism, and nationalization of the railroads as early as 1901. Patrick J. Conway, the vicar general of the archdiocese of Chicago, encouraged labor organizations because they were necessary for the protection of the rights of workingmen. James E. Quigley, who was later to become archbishop of the same diocese, was against the formation of Catholic trade unions in the United States (an idea of German social reformers who tended to be much more conservative and suspicious of non-Catholic organizations than did their Irish counterparts). Quigley wrote, "We do not tell you to leave the unions. The enemies of religion in society would be glad if you were out for then they could play their nefarious business unchallenged. We want you to stay there to guard the unions against the influences of the enemies of Christian labor."

When *Rerum novarum* did appear on the scene, the reaction to it among the small band of Catholic reformers was vigorous. Bishop Spalding pointed out that the "deep import of the encyclical lay in its pronouncement [that] . . . the mission of the Church is not only to save souls but also to save society." Bishop Keane of the newly formed Catholic University wrote sensitive commentaries on the encyclical for several journals in which he insisted among other things that "the majority of workers for social reform have been convinced that all volunteer efforts would fall short unless aided by legislative reform wisely framed and gradually applied." Since "the wealthy cannot be trusted to see to the amelioration for the past, it must be accomplished by organized endeavor on the part of the laboring classes but when this falls short by legislative enactments prompted by humanity and justice." Father Zahm from Notre Dame jumped on the bandwagon by insisting that Leo XIII was calling for industrial peace, a new kind of truce of God.

Despite the enthusiasm of the social reformers for *Rerum novarum,* and despite the fact that Onahan and his colleagues were able to make *Rerum novarum* one of the principal topics at the Columbian Catholic Congress of the world's Columbian Exposition in 1893, *Rerum novarum* had little impact on the vast majority of American Catholics. It is to be feared that most of the laity, many of the clergy, and some of the hierarchy were quite unaware that there was any relationship between the encyclical and the social problems of the United States. Even such a dedicated social reformer as John Ryan would only discover *Rerum novarum* when he got to college. Father William J. Kerby and Professor Neil of the Catholic University of America would do their best, but by and large the Catholic schools were in the 1890s, and continued to be for another fifty years, quite unconcerned about the social teachings of the Church. Peter Dietz became one of the first "labor priests," and founded "The Militia of Christ for Social Service" in 1910 as a Catholic auxiliary for the trade union movement, but only a handful of Catholic workingmen belonged to the Militia. Nevertheless Dietz would have many friends among the trade union leaders and great influence in the movement. But while Dietz was successful, two of his predecessors as labor priests, Fathers Thomas McGrady and Thomas J. Hagerty, both were forced out of the Church when they insisted too strongly on the need for concerns about problems of the workingman. Frederick Kenkel would turn the concerns of the *Centralverein* to the questions of social reform in the United States as a new development in the quest for a uniquely German contribution to the American Church. As Philip Gleason, professor of American Church history at Notre Dame and an authority on the *Centralverein,* has pointed out, the *Centralverein* was essentially a conservative social action organization but while its publication *Central Blatt and Social Justice* would have considerable influence among some German-American Catholics, the vast majority of German Catholics were no more won over to the social reformers than were their Irish coreligionists.

The Catholic Social Service Commission founded in 1911 with Dietz as its secretary and Bishop Peter Muldoon of Rockford, Father John Cavanaugh of Notre Dame, Professor James Hagerty of Ohio State, and Charles A. Denechaud of New Orleans as members, would keep up the drumbeat of pronouncements on social problems. But while their work did contribute substantially to the formation under Muldoon's leadership of the Social Action Department of the National Catholic Welfare Conference after the end of the First World War, it did not win over substantial numbers of the clergy to the position that social reform and social problems were legitimate concerns of organized religion. Thus when the Social Action Department was established,[2] there was already existing a tradition well over thirty years old of official and quasi-official Catholic concern about social reform, but a tradition which unfortunately lacked much in the way of popular

[2] After Bishop Muldoon and Bishop Schrembs succeeded in persuading Rome that the NCWC was not an attempt to set up an independent American Church, a notion strange indeed in this age of canonically established national hierarchies.

support. For the next quarter of a century the continuation of this tradition was the task of John Augustine Ryan.

Ryan came by his commitment to social action legitimately. He was born on the prairies of Minnesota south of Minneapolis in the heart of the country where Populism has always been strong and where even in our own time the Farmer Labor Party is a power to be reckoned with. Ryan's early years were influenced by the writings of Patrick Ford in a journal called *Irish World and Industrial Liberator* which, even though it was essentially conservative, supported the Knights of Labor and the American Federation of Labor with great vigor and even invective. Furthermore his father was a member of the National Farmers Alliance which in the last years of the nineteenth century waged a vigorous Populist war against big business and particularly against the railroad system. Being born on the prairies of Minnesota in 1869 was almost a guarantee that one would be exposed to Populism and also to the oratory of the great Populist theoretician Ignatius Donnelly who was elected to the House of Representatives from the very district in which John Ryan lived.

Another major influence in John Ryan's life was Bishop John Lancaster Spalding, whose *Education in the Higher Life* he discovered while preparing a valedictory address in 1892. Fifty years later Ryan would describe Spalding as the "greatest literary artist produced by the American hierarchy." It was only two years later at the age of twenty-five when Ryan was in the seminary that he discovered the encyclical letter *Rerum novarum* (three years after it was written). This was the most decisive event in John Ryan's whole life. His previous political and social concerns suddenly came into meaningful focus and through the reading of *Rerum novarum* John Ryan could see his whole career stretching out in front of him. The merger between American Populism and Catholic social philosophy had been accomplished and the rest of his career would consist simply in developing the basic insights of 1894. After ordination in St. Paul Seminary, Ryan would go on to the Catholic University of America to obtain a doctorate in moral theology with a classic treatise on *The*

Living Wage which defended man's right to a decent living from the nature of his dignity as a human person. For the rest of his career, Ryan would be essentially a social ethician who could back up his ethical arguments with a reasonable amount of sophistication in economics and sociology. While he was on the faculty of the St. Paul Seminary after his graduation from the Catholic University, Ryan prepared two lists of the labor legislation which he thought was absolutely essential for American society. On the first list were the following reforms: (1) legal minimum wage; (2) eight-hour day; (3) protective legislation for women and children; (4) legislative protection for peaceful picketing and boycotting; (5) unemployment insurance and employment bureaus; (6) provision against accident, illness, and old age; (7) municipal housing. The second list was equally advanced for 1909: (1) public ownership of public utilities; (2) public ownership of mines and forests; (3) control of monopolies either by breaking them up or by fixing their prices; (4) progressive income and inheritance taxes; (5) taxation on future increase in land values[3]; (6) prohibition of speculation on the stock and commodity exchanges.

These thirteen suggestions were revolutionary to most Americans in 1909 even though ten of them have been adopted in some way or another in the ensuing years. One can hardly claim credit for Ryan as being a major influence in the promotion of such legislation. But at least as the years went on he would put the Catholic Church officially in support of such social reforms. Whatever mistakes and blunders might be made at the grass roots, Ryan saw to it that the upper levels of the ecclesiastical structure of the Church were thoroughly committed to intelligent social reform.

Ryan's interest was in social reform through legislation, and his own personal style was to exercise influence through articles, lectures, and committee memberships. His lectures got him into trouble very early in the game when a speech in Ford Hall in Boston in 1913 occasioned the ire of William

[3] Here Ryan shows his sympathy with Henry George and George's ecclesiastical supporter in New York's Father McGlynn.

Cardinal O'Connell, archbishop of Boston. Ryan held the socialists at Ford Hall at bay with ease but earned the suspicion of Cardinal O'Connell, who felt he was too ready to compromise with socialism, a suspicion which was to plague Ryan for the rest of his career. In the meantime, he continued to push for minimum-wage legislation for women and children in Minnesota and other states in the Middle West and was an active member of the committees that forced several such laws through state legislatures before the Supreme Court struck them down.

Ryan's forthright stand on controversial issues was not calculated to win him many friends in a good number of ecclesiastical quarters. He did not spend very much time condemning socialism (though he did condemn it) and many of the reforms he suggested seemed to be pretty much the same things the socialists were suggesting. *The Wanderer,* a German-language newspaper in St. Paul, had attacked Ryan as being suspect of socialism; a Catholic layman named Edward F. McSweeny denounced him as a supporter of pagan and socialistic quackeries. But while the label "socialist" was hurled at Ryan, it did not stick. As his biography by Francis L. Broderick notes, the general opinion of Ryan up until the New Deal days was that he was "not technically enough of a socialist to draw the formal censure of his ecclesiastical superiors but too radical for most of his co-religionists. Ryan's view was simpler. He was about as radical as Leo XIII."

When the minimum-wage law was passed in Minnesota, Ryan became chairman of the advisory board that was to preside over its enforcement, the first of a long list of such assignments he would receive in his life. Three years later after the publication of his most serious socio-ethical tract, *Distributive Justice,* Ryan was appointed to the Catholic University of America, where he would send out lightning bolts in support of social reform for most of the rest of his life. Four years later when the NCWC was founded, Ryan was the only logical choice to be the first director of its Social Action Department, while retaining his chair at the Catholic University of America.

But before the official establishment of the NCWC, Ryan almost by accident composed a statement for the American bishops on social reform at the request of Bishop Muldoon of the Administrative Committee of the National Catholic War Council. Apparently Father John O'Grady, one of Muldoon's assistants, noticed an unfinished fragment on Ryan's desk and insisted that Ryan finish it and turn it in to the bishops as a statement on the problems of postwar reconstruction. The bishops' program for "social reconstruction" was typed in five hours and even though it was not the world's best-organized statement, it was easily the most progressive document yet issued by any American denomination. The bishops urged the government to maintain the United States Employment Service, the National War Labor Board, and to promote the principles of the family living wage, the right of labor to organize and to bargain collectively, and the prohibition of coercion of union members. They called for the prevention of monopolistic control of commodities "from prevention on, adequate government regulation of public service monopolies as well as those under private operation, and heavy taxation of incomes, excess profits and inheritances." If antitrust laws proved ineffective, they were willing to endorse direct governmental competition with private industry. They urged a wider distribution of ownership of stock by workers and of shop committees of workers to serve in management of industries. Women were entitled to equal pay for equal work. Labor was acting legitimately when it resisted general wage reductions. The living wage was not the full measure of justice, only the minimum of justice. Good morals and sound economics demanded that the workers be paid above this level. The bishops observed that "there is no longer any serious objection urged by impartial persons against the legal minimum wage." Therefore the state should enact such laws gradually raising the level of pay so that individuals could protect their families against sickness, accident, invalidism, and old age. At the same time, the state should undertake housing projects and comprehensive insurance programs for their citizens, and cities should make themselves responsible for health clinics.

It was by the standards of 1918 a revolutionary document. And it was not surprising that the president of the National Association of Manufacturers would complain to Cardinal Gibbons that the document was "partisan, pro-labor, union socialistic propaganda." The editor of the *National Civic Federation Review* would insist that the bishops had been deceived by radicals whose program "would overthrow our present institutions and inaugurate a reign of chaos." Upton Sinclair, the socialist, was so astonished that he referred to the program as a "Catholic miracle." Whether all the bishops fully understood what they had agreed to under the auspices of Ryan and Muldoon seems dubious. Surely there were not many episcopal pronouncements through the 1920s backing up the recommendations of the so-called Bishops' Program. But the official stand had been taken and the American Church was committed more or less irrevocably to social reform. The Bishops' Program would be the charter that would sustain John Ryan through the 1920s until the appearance in 1931 of the Pope Pius XI encyclical *Quadragesimo anno*.

At the end of the 1930s, Ryan and his colleagues at the NCWC would prepare another and even more advanced episcopal statement entitled *The Church and the Social Order* which would update the 1918–1919 effort. This document was a much better organized effort and endorsed every major reform that Ryan had promoted for the last two decades (except the Child Labor amendment). It warned about industry's abuse of power, reaffirmed the legitimacy of unions and the right to strike, insisted that industry and government should provide not merely a living wage for the moment but "also a saving wage for the future against sickness, old age, death, and unemployment." The bishops also commented: "Heartening indeed are the beginnings towards the greater security of the people that have already been made through legislative enactment and public policy." Between the extremes of socialism and individualism, they pointed to the "*via media* which will bind men together in the society according to their respective occupations thus creating more unity." Again not all the bishops who signed the document may have realized its implications, but for John Ryan and his colleagues *The Church and the Social Order* was an official ratification by the American hierarchy of most of the social reforms of the New Deal.

Between 1919 and 1939, Ryan was to have more than his share of problems, especially in the first decade. The World War had destroyed most of the thrust and energy of the reform movement and the conservative administrations and the Supreme Court of the 1920s upset many of the reforms of the previous years. The Child Labor amendment never had much of a chance from the beginning, but the determination by the *Centralverein* and by Cardinal O'Connell of Boston that somehow or other the amendment was a threat to the sanctity of the family cinched its demise. Cardinal O'Connell was not happy about Ryan's support of the amendment and even less happy when Ryan's newsletters of support poured into Boston. The Cardinal could not see how an NCWC staff member could support "a nefarious and Bolshevik amendment" and pointed out that unless something was done quickly to change the stance of those in Washington so close to the "dangerous influence of the Capitol"[4] Rome would be asking for an explanation. In a handwritten note to Archbishop Curley of Baltimore, O'Connell demanded, "Why are all these people busying themselves attending dinners, making dubious addresses, talking before committees, etc. It is all wrong and all hurting the university and the Catholic position which is certainly not theirs. Something ought to be done soon. I know Your Grace will not hesitate."

Before Curley could get around to replying (and he was in no particular hurry), a hundred thousand reprints of a labor magazine appeared in Boston with a pro-Amendment article by Ryan. O'Connell, who was one of the less pleasant characters the American Church has produced in the last century, fired off another letter to Curley:

> Yesterday the city was flooded with the nefarious and false views of the amendment, supposed falsely to be in the interest of the child, sent out from Washington by sly methods in which he seems to be an expert, by the Reverend

[4] Who in the world in the Capitol would be dangerous in 1924 is indeed a mystery.

J. A. Ryan, professor at the University. In this malicious propaganda, it is made to appear that we Catholics who oppose this Soviet legislation are incapable of reading plain English and making correct, logical conclusions, a thing which it would appear is the special privilege of J. A. Ryan, Jane Addams, and a few more socialist teachers and writers. These same views are again neatly summarized in the pink slip distributed broadcast among our people. Again the clear crooked view of J. A. Ryan who undoubtedly knew that his doctrines and his radical point of view would be made use of to offset the position taken by me and all my priests here during these trying days before the voting. Your Grace, there is only one thing left for us to do—either abandon weakly our duty and turn it over to the hands of the Ryans, the Kerbys, and the Reagans, who undoubtedly have been inoculated with the radical by too close affiliation with bureaucrats and jobbers that are in Washington or demand that these servants of the University and paid agents of the NCWC either cease their crooked and false activities or leave the University and the offices of the NCWC.

For a long time this weak sort of thing by which the authority of the hierarchy has been too liberally and unwarrantedly entrusted to hands and brains unfit to be entrusted with so sacred a duty as that of the hierarchy alone has been all too evident. In the strongest possible terms, I protest against it. Evidently the rector is either powerless or supine else long ago this would have been put in its place. Therefore with the fullest confidence in Your Grace, I now repeat my request that these professors and paid agents be firmly reminded of their duties as Catholics.

It is worth remembering of course that what was under consideration was an Amendment to the American Constitution which prohibited paid labor by children under a given age. Such a reaction to so mild a proposal would make one wonder exactly what was troubling the good cardinal archbishop of Boston whose rhetoric was as violent if not as graceful as that of John Hughes seventy-five years before. However, Archbishop Curley did not back off and no action was taken against Ryan. O'Connell was not about to forgive Ryan and neither, for that matter, was Ryan about to forgive O'Connell. However, for all the condemnations that were aimed at him, Ryan was only in trouble with Rome once in his life—when someone complained, of all things, about his giving a talk at a YMCA meeting. Archbishop Curley reassured the Holy Office and there was no further problem. It was curious that Ryan could take the many strong positions he took and still encounter suspicion from Rome on something so minor as the YMCA. In any event, the secret of Ryan's continued freedom was the firm support of Archbishop Curley. Curley would eventually turn his bitterly sarcastic tongue against Ryan when in his (Curley's) judgment Ryan became too closely identified with Franklin Roosevelt. But by that time, Ryan's position was so secure that he did not need Curley's support nearly as much as he had a decade before. Before their deaths, however, these two stubborn but vigorous men were reconciled.

During the 1920s, Ryan became a member of the board of directors of the American Civil Liberties Union and deepened and widened his contact with the liberal remnant in the country. The liberals always respected him and he them, but he was not hesitant about disagreeing with them and even violently on certain matters. He was not at all afraid of denouncing Walter Lippmann, and Norman Thomas for overlooking the persecutions of the Church in Mexico. But if the liberals at times were uncomfortable with Ryan and he at times uncomfortable with them, they held so many common positions that there was little question of the relationship coming to an end, and they would fight together with him through the bitter and frustrating Al Smith battle which was one of the most unpleasant experiences of Ryan's life. How traumatic the 1928 disaster was for him is clear from an article written a month after the election:

> As a Catholic, I cannot be expected to rejoice that some millions of my countrymen would put upon me and my coreligionists the brand of civic inferiority. As an American, I cannot feel proud that the spirit of the Sixth Amendment to the Constitution is thus flouted and violated. As a believer in personal freedom and political honesty, I cannot feel cheerful over the prospect of four more years of the ele-

gant, despotic, and hypocritical domination from which we are suffering by the grace of the anti-saloon league. As a Democrat and a lover of justice, I cannot look with complacency upon a president-elect who, judged by his campaign addresses, believes the economic welfare of the masses should be confided practically without reservation to the care of corporate business in the naive faith that corporate business will dispense and hand down universal justice. This is industrial feudalism. Possibly it may turn out to be benevolent. In any case, it will do violence to the most fundamental and valuable traditions of the America we have known and loved.

John Ryan was a very angry man and he would have four more angry years before his day would dawn once again.

But dawn it did in March of 1933. Even though Ryan was considerably less than enthusiastic about Franklin Roosevelt and was inclined to suspend judgment, it did not take him too long to warm to the new Administration and then he became, in very short order, the foremost Catholic apologist for the social reforms of the New Deal, a man who could claim legitimately the title that Father Coughlin bestowed upon him as an insult—right reverend New Dealer.

Despite the mythology at the Catholic University to the contrary, the black limousines to the White House did not appear at two and three in the morning to bring Ryan to private consultations with the President. His role in the New Deal was strictly a fringe one and as far as his biographer could determine, he only saw the President personally four times during the course of Roosevelt's years in office. He did serve on a number of somewhat lesser New Deal committees such as the National Advisory Committee of the Subsistence Homestead Division of the Interior Department and the Advisory Council of the United States Employment Service. Ryan's close friends in the Administration were Frances Perkins, Felix Frankfurter, and Hugo Black, but Ryan had no close contacts in the White House and his correspondence with Roosevelt was polite and noncommittal on both sides. His service to the New Deal was one rather of legitimations on the outside than active cooperation within. Presumably, though, President Roosevelt was anything but unhappy when Ryan took on Coughlin in 1936.

And he minced no words. "In the light of this experience [of forty-five years of publishing articles on economic questions, carrying him back even before Father Coughlin was born] I say deliberately to the laboring men and women of America that Father Coughlin's explanation of our economic maladies is at least fifty per cent wrong and that his monetary remedies are at least ninety per cent wrong. If the latter were enacted into law, they would prove disastrous to the great majority of the American people, particularly to the wage earners. Moreover Father Coughlin's monetary theories and proposals find no support in the encyclicals of either Pope Leo XIII or Pius XI." He went on to beg the toilers of America not to abandon Roosevelt and any of the others who were "your tried and competent champions in public life." The reaction to Ryan's speech was divided. Twelve hundred letters descended upon him of which he noted only twenty-five were in courteous language. Some of the more moderate ones charged him with munching at the Democratic pie counter while yearning to bask in the sunshine of hypocritical smiles. Archbishop Curley's paper *The Catholic Review* of Baltimore commented, "If both the reverend gentlemen would retire for some time to the Carthusian Order where professional silence is observed, they would do a great favor to the Church and the country at large." On the other hand, much of the secular press hailed Ryan's speech as the proof that the Catholic Church was not committed to the Coughlin program. When Coughlin turned anti-Semitic in 1938, Ryan once again went on the radio (after Cardinal George William Mundelein of Chicago had explicitly disowned Coughlin's stand) and warned American Catholics that Coughlin's weapons against the Jews were no different than those that could be used in the future in any anti-Catholic campaign. Again, one suspects that Ryan's influence was negligible with Coughlin's followers, but it may have been considerable with non-Catholics who wondered where the Church stood on anti-Semitism.

Through the New Deal years, Ryan lived to see most of the plans of his lifetime come true. Labor unions were legalized with the Wagner Act, old-age insurance was set up with the Social Security Act, minimum wage and hour legislation became reality with the Fair Labor Standards Act. The core of the New Deal reform was also the core of Ryan's own program; and even though he had little direct influence on its enactment, New Deal reforms represented a culmination of decades of agitation of which Ryan had been a fairly important part. Under such circumstances, he certainly had no patience with those (including Archbishop Curley) who viewed the New Deal as a Communist plot. He replied, "America is in far less dangers from the preachings of the Communists than from certain professionally anti-Catholic propaganda which is really directed against social justice." He pointed out that in Europe the Church had lost the working-man because it failed to identify itself with his legitimate aspirations. To what extent the Catholic social reformers in the United States prevented such an occurrence in this country is difficult to ascertain. In all likelihood there are other and more powerful social forces which prevented the alienation of the working class (particularly the identification of the working-class ethnic groups with their Church) but at least it would have been difficult for Socialists and Communists to persuade those elite Catholic workingmen who would be interested in such matters that the Church was against the working class. Furthermore, Ryan could have certainly argued that the American Church had done far more than any of the European churches to identify itself with the cause of social reform.

Ryan also did battle with Mayor Frank Hague of Jersey City who had prevented CIO organizers from entering the city and blocked attempts by Norman Thomas to speak there in protest. He was not eager to offend the archbishop of Newark and he knew that he was less than popular with Archbishop Curley, who had said of Ryan's invocation at the Roosevelt second inaugural, "Here is the old man from Minnesota at it again. I wonder if he will not throw off the purple soon and put on a red shirt. It would be a little going up in color anyhow." Nonetheless when the fourth of July of 1937 rolled around, even though he turned down an invitation to speak in Jersey City, Ryan denounced Hague from Duluth, Minnesota (while speaking for B'nai B'rith). He described Hague's acts as illegal and arbitrary and lamented the fact that Catholics could be taken in by charges of atheism and communism against those who insisted on the CIO's right to organize and every American's right to speak in their defense. "The real conflict was between American civil rights as against the subserviency of city officials to selfish employers who seek to prevent the organization of labor." It is unlikely that Mayor Hague was convinced but at least the CIO and the members of the Civil Liberties Union realized that there was one Catholic priest on their side.

Ryan's life was drawing to a close but he still persisted in his loyalty to the New Deal through the isolationist period immediately before Pearl Harbor when, despite his position in the Catholic Association for International Peace, Ryan nonetheless supported the Roosevelt foreign policy. In 1939, he was retired from the Catholic University (much against his will) and even worse summarily ejected from his residence on the Catholic University campus. Nor were he and John Courtney Murray welcome to speak at the Institute for Religious Studies in New York City. Cardinal James McIntyre of Los Angeles, then Monsignor McIntyre and chancellor of the New York archdiocese, vetoed that idea quite emphatically. One of his Ryan's friends was led to comment, "These people would have forbidden St. Paul to preach to the Athenians."

Ryan died in September of 1945, living to see victory in the Second World War but not the beginning of the postwar prosperity which would eliminate many if not most of the social problems against which he had crusaded all his life.

Ryan's direct influence on the New Deal was marginal. He was respected by leaders of labor unions but was not on the same friendly, intimate terms with them as was Father Dietz before him and his successor Monsignor George Hig-

gins after him.[5] He was admired by the intellectual liberals of
the Civil Liberties Union and *New Republic* variety. He could
be hailed by editorial writers as an outstanding Catholic social
reformer. He was a constant proof to those workingmen who
cared that their Church was officially committed to social
reform and he was a patriarch and a prophet to the younger
Catholic liberals who went through their high school and
college years during the New Deal. He was living evidence
that Catholic social philosophy and American social reform
could readily be harmonized. But despite this unquestioned
accomplishment, Ryan's influence on much of the American
Church was negligible and it is doubtful whether one-tenth
or even one-hundredth of the people that knew who Father
Coughlin was had ever heard of John Ryan. So much the
worse for them.

The Coughlin story was a very different one. Just as Ryan
had become much more Progressive than Populist in his
approach to social reform, so Coughlin was far more Populist
than he was Progressive. The isolationism, the anti-Semitism,
and the nativism that found their way into Coughlin's teachings before the end of the 1930s were an important if a
somewhat deviant part of the Populist tradition. Not a few
observers have suggested that Charles Coughlin was the link
between the older Populists and the more recent forms of
extremism represented by the late Senator Joseph McCarthy
and by the John Birch Society. To say that Coughlin was an
out-and-out fascist would certainly be unfair, but his mixture
of Catholic social teaching and far-out Populist monetary
theories eventually brought him to a position where he would
be violently anti-Semitic and so opposed to the war against
Nazism that his magazine would be suppressed and the Detroit
chancery office would be forced to silence him. However,
between 1930 and 1942, Charles Coughlin had immense in-

[5] Higgins also would bring to the social reform position and to
the social action department a flair and a color that Ryan lacked.
The good Monsignor (Higgins), who was recently denounced by a
conservative columnist as the Hubert Humphrey of the American
Church, was the product of the Chicago liberal clergy, which we
will discuss in the next chapter.

fluence in the United States. And the hundreds of thousands of letters that poured into his Royal Oak, Michigan, parish every week were proof, if anyone needed it, of how great was the radio priest's power.

Born in Canada, educated by the Basilian Fathers, and a professor at their college in Windsor, Ontario, Coughlin became a part of the diocese of Detroit in the 1920s; in 1926, he began broadcasts over a Detroit radio station to support his new parish in Royal Oak, Michigan. For those who have never heard Coughlin's voice on the radio and even for those of us who can but dimly remember it, it is difficult to believe the immense influence that his rich, melodious voice was able to command. But by 1931, at the age of forty, he had a huge audience for his weekly sermon. It was in that year that he turned to politics with an attack on Herbert Hoover's promise that prosperity was "just around the corner." Coughlin observed, "It appears to have been a circular corner to which they referred, a corner which if we could turn, we would not be willing to negotiate if it foreshadows a repetition of those recent occurrences for the children a generation to come." He then went on to denounce the international bankers on whom he blamed the Depression and said that the world had grown weary of their attempts to "perpetuate their gambling and gold-seeking at the expense of a torture more refined than was ever excogitated by the trickery of the Roman or the heartlessness of the slave owners."

The die was cast and for ten years Coughlin would continue to attack all those whom he thought were the enemies of the people. He jumped early on the Roosevelt bandwagon and would later claim credit for turning Hoover out of office and putting Roosevelt into office. The bitterness of his denunciation of Roosevelt in the late 1930s could probably be explained by the fact that he felt Roosevelt never showed any gratitude for Coughlin's great favor of having elected him President. During the banking crisis in Detroit, he issued statements as though he were part of the Roosevelt team and embarrassed the Administration. Marvin McIntyre, one of the Roosevelt staff, in a memo to Louis Howell on March 27, 1933, said of this performance, "Confidentially I think the reverend father took considerable liberties with the fact and most certainly misquoted me and misstated the case in saying that the request for him to go on the radio and to answer the commissioner came from the administration."

Roosevelt was too shrewd a politician to be taken in by Coughlin but also feared his vast audience and so played a devious waiting game with the radio priest, permitting him to think that up to a point he had influence with the Administration, but never really encouraging him, while at the same time not denouncing him either. It was the old act of giving somebody enough rope so he could hang himself, an act which Franklin Roosevelt could play with more calculating coldness than most American politicians. Coughlin would, in his letters to the White House staffers, refer to the President as "the boss" and would even be invited to the White House. But Roosevelt never took Coughlin's advice, a curious blend of simple-minded monetary reform proposals and quotations from papal encyclicals, very seriously. He recognized Coughlin's power, especially when the radio priest marshaled his supporters to deluge Congress with letters against the United States entering the World Court. Coughlin's remarks on this occasion were characteristic: "If I am properly informed, Tuesday, January 29, will be remembered by our offspring as a day which overshadows July 4, the one date we associate with our independence, the other with our stupid betrayal." The truth of the matter, according to Coughlin, was that the World Court and the League of Nations were both organized by international bankers to exploit world resources and to deprive individual nations of their freedom. The World Court program was in trouble anyhow and it may not have passed even without Coughlin's opposition, but Coughlin's campaign against it provided a rallying point for its foes.

At least from his point of view, Coughlin was forbearing and patient with the Administration, but by 1935, his patience had run thin and he observed, "The first two years of the New Deal shall be remembered as two years of compromise, two years of social planning, two years of endeavoring to mix bad with the good, two years of surrender, two years of matching the puerile, puny brains of idealists against the virile viciousness of business and finance." Even though Roosevelt was not ready to fight back, the same could not be said of some of the other members of his Administration. General Hugh Johnson condemned Coughlin and Huey Long together, saying of Coughlin, "There comes burring over the air the dripping brogue of the Irish-Canadian priest," and "these two men are raging up and down this land preaching not construction but destruction, not reform but revolution, not peace but a sword." And Harold Ickes said that Coughlin was "the cloistered individual whose rich but undisciplined imagination has reduced politics, sociology and banking to charming poetry which was disposed mellifluously into the ether for the entrancement of mankind."

Franklin Roosevelt was not pleased with this and told Jim Farley that Ickes' reference to Coughlin was very unwise. As he himself said, "People tired of seeing the same name day after day in the important headlines of the paper and the same voice night after night over the radio . . . individual psychology cannot be attuned for long periods of time to a constant repetition of the highest note in the scale." However, Coughlin was continually on the highest note of the scale and was moving more and more rapidly toward a complete break with Roosevelt, a break which was to come finally in 1936 when Coughlin's National Union for Social Justice would run its own candidate for the presidency—Congressman William Lemke—against Roosevelt and Landon. Lemke was the hand-picked choice of Coughlin, who announced that if he could not deliver nine million votes for his choice, he would go off the radio. Even though the National Union for Social Justice had five million members, less than a million votes were cast for Lemke. Coughlin's radio personality was powerful indeed, but as it turned out, Franklin Roosevelt's was much more powerful.

In retrospect, the whole Coughlin interlude has about it an aura of unreality. One wonders how a priest could have so deceived himself into believing that he could take on the President of the United States and beat him or at least substantially weaken his power. More than anything else, it would

appear that Coughlin's head was turned by the huge mountains of mail that poured into Royal Oak, Michigan, each
week. Even though he lacked any formal training and indeed
any sophistication in the understanding of economic problems
and even though his solutions were almost universally extreme
or oversimplified, nonetheless it was very easy for him to stare
at the seemingly endless piles of letters and conclude that the
common man agreed with him. Furthermore, despite the
criticism from ecclesiastics such as Cardinal Hayes and Cardinal O'Connell and Cardinal Mundelein, Coughlin's own
bishop, Michael Gallagher, supported him to the hilt even
after a rebuke by the Vatican paper *Osservatore Romano*.
With his bishop supporting him and five million followers,
with a triumph in the World Court battle, and a number of
seeming triumphs for candidates endorsed by the National
Union for Social Justice in the 1936 primaries, Coughlin was
willing to lead his followers (without ever bothering to question or consult them) in a battle against Roosevelt in 1936. He
did not expect the Union Party, as he called it, to defeat Roosevelt but thought it would develop sufficient strength so that
by 1940 it could be a serious challenge to the two existing
political parties. It was an incredible display of self-deception,
but if Coughlin permitted himself to be deceived on the extent
of his power, at least his fantastic popularity with the radio
audience provided some basis for the deception. Coughlin did
not realize that it was one thing for a man to write a letter
approving a radio broadcast and quite another to go into a
voting booth and cast a vote against Franklin D. Roosevelt,
especially when such a vote would be wasted on a candidate
who never had much of a chance of winning anyhow. American voters are notoriously disinclined to cast protest votes.

Coughlin went off the radio after the crushing defeat of
the Union Party but not without scaring the living daylights
out of a number of Americans, including TRB, the weekly
columnist in the *New Republic* who argued that the Union
Party marked the entrance of the Catholic Church into
American politics. He observed that (1) Coughlin was the
logical choice to organize Christian socialism in America,
(2) the Vatican was losing influence all over the world and

was relying more and more on the United States, and (3) many American Catholics opposed Roosevelt on religious grounds; his sons' divorces and his wife's support of birth control, and his appointment of the supposed anti-Catholic Josephus Daniels as ambassador to Mexico, had alienated many Catholics.[6] Even though the three leading cardinals of the American Church had publicly disavowed Coughlin, and even though John Ryan had denounced him during the campaign, and even though *Osservatore Romano* had openly criticized Coughlin's attacks on the Administration, it was still possible for the more narrowly anti-Catholic observer of the American scene to see Coughlin not as an embarrassment to the Church but as part of a deliberate scheme. The embarrassment would become acute as Coughlin would begin to denounce Roosevelt as a Communist. "As I was instrumental in removing Herbert Hoover from the White House, so help me God, I will be an instrument in taking a communist out of the chair once occupied by Washington."

The attack on the New Deal grew even more violent during the election campaign when such New Deal agencies as the NRA, WPA, AAA, and PWA were denounced as Communist and a number of people around Roosevelt such as David Dubinsky were also accused of being Communists. But if the attacks on the New Deal embarrassed the Church, when Coughlin turned anti-Semitic during the second Roosevelt Administration, it was even more embarrassing. In 1938, he resurrected the ancient fake called "the protocols of the wise men of Zion" and described them as pre-eminently a communistic program to destroy Christian civilization. Archbishop Mooney, Bishop Gallagher's successor, had apparently attempted to exercise censorship over what Coughlin said on

[6] The various writers who have occupied the TRB position have periodically displayed their nativist biases. Thus almost thirty years later when the Kennedy education bill was blocked by the House Rules Committee, TRB informed his readers that it was a victory for Cardinal Spellman even though the effective opposition to the bill was not from Catholics but from Southern Democrats and two of the three Catholics on the Rules Committee had voted in favor of the bill.

the radio (Coughlin having returned to the air after Gallagher's death on the grounds that this was the bishop's dying
request, a statement that the bishop was in no position to
confirm or deny), but the outpouring of pro-Coughlin mail
apparently led the archbishop to believe that he, like Franklin
Roosevelt, must play a waiting game. It must have been hard
to play the game when Coughlin, commenting on the protocols of the elders of Zion said, among other things, "Is it not
true that some unseen force is taking Christ out of government, business, industry and, to a large degree, education? Is
it not true that a force over which we Christians seem to have
no control has gained control of journalism, motion pictures,
theaters, and radio? Is it not true that some unseen force has
woven the threads of international banking to the detriment
of civilization, that a godless force is dominating industry,
has monopolized controls of industrial activities, has used
governments as their servants, and has been instrumental in
flinging one nation against another's throat?" It was easy for
John Ryan and others to point out that the protocols were a
fake, but Coughlin was not to be stopped. The question in his
mind was not whether articles were really written by the wise
men of Zion but the "factuality of their content," a factuality
which he argued was evident all around. By this time there
was no stopping Coughlin and he proceeded to announce that
Kuhn, Loeb and Company, the Jewish New York banking
firm, was responsible for financing the Russian revolution.
Denials from Kuhn, Loeb, and from Alexander Kerensky and
Leon Trotsky did not stop him either.

Most Catholic reactions to Coughlin's journal *Social Justice*
and the Christian Front, an organization which had replaced
the National Union for Social Justice, were unfavorable.
America, Commonweal, his own diocesan paper the *Michigan
Catholic,* Cardinal Mundelein of Chicago, and many other
church leaders wanted no part of anti-Semitism. And yet there
was support for him. The *Brooklyn Tablet* under the editor-
ship of Patrick Scanlon did not hesitate to join in the anti-
Semitism: "The feeling is abroad that in the present crisis in
Germany, the Jews in America have overreached themselves.

They have corraled everyone from the President down to plead their case but they have shown no sympathy for the persecuted in other lands."

It can be easily understood that under such circumstances Coughlin would bitterly oppose the New Deal's aid to Britain before Pearl Harbor: "The lend-lease bill is not substantially concerned with lending or leasing or giving materials to Britain. It is concerned however with scuttling the last vestige of democracy in the world—American democracy. The lend-lease bill will substitute Karl Marx for George Washington." And then *Social Justice* asked the rhetorical question, "Will *Social Justice* join in this world's greatest sellout of a mesmerized people, mesmerized by British gold and Jewish propaganda? Not as long as a printing press can be found to spread the truth as we see it. We will not oppose Mr. Roosevelt physically but by the Eternal God we will not acclaim his radicalism, his crackpotism, his un-Americanism. *Social Justice* is honored in having been singled out to become the leading victim of dictatorial censorship."[7]

After Pearl Harbor, Coughlin very quickly began to expect that it was a plot on the part of Roosevelt to entrap America in the war, and in March of 1942, *Social Justice* discovered "who started the sacred war," and stated, "Soon nine years was elapsed since the worldwide sacred war was declared on Germany not by the United States, not by Great Britain, not by France, not by any nation, but by the race of Jews. America was under the impression that this was a war to save democracy, a war to guarantee the lastingness of the four liberties." To Coughlin it was anything but this. It was part of a Communist and Jewish plot. Responding to the charge that he was pro-Nazi and un-American, *Social Justice* declared, "If pro-Americanism consists in boycotting a suffering forty million Germans upon whose neck there rests the yoke of the Nazi Party, if pro-Americanism consists in casting the entire civilized world into a seething cauldron of bloody war for the protection of 600,000 racialists or religionists as you

[7] This after the Army banned *Social Justice* in March of 1941 from all military posts, hardly a particularly intelligent thing to do.

care to call them, if pro-Americanism is identified with the
secret economics at Amsterdam and dictatorial forces emanating from Prague which nullifies the peaceful progress of our
country, then Americanism under that interpretation is not
worth fighting for."

Even though Attorney General Francis Biddle did not want
to repeat the harsh governmental action of censorship during
the First World War, the pressures of public opinion and of
presidential opinion made it difficult for him to continually
ignore Coughlin and *Social Justice;* the postmaster of Detroit,
Michigan, was instructed not to handle *Social Justice* in the
mails. However, the Administration was not eager to haul the
problem before a grand jury since under such circumstances
Coughlin could easily play a martyr's role and perhaps attract
many Catholics to his defense and interfere with the war effort. As Biddle put it, "The point was to win the war not to
indict a priest for sedition." So Postmaster General Frank
Walker and Leo T. Crowley, the chairman of the board of
the Federal Deposit Insurance Corporation, apparently persuaded Archbishop Mooney to silence Coughlin and thus to
prevent the demoralizing effects of a sedition trial. Mooney
was happy to cooperate. The rope he had given Coughlin
came to an end. Roosevelt did not know of the strategy until
afterward but was delighted with the smooth handling of a
troublesome nuisance. One of the writers who has analyzed
the Coughlin phenomenon claims that Mooney confirmed the
deal in a brief letter to Roosevelt but reports that apparently
the letter was destroyed. It is to Coughlin's credit that when
the chips were down he proved himself a loyal and obedient
priest and has since the 1942 compact between Crowley and
Archbishop Mooney spoken not at all (save for one recent
and obscure television interview) on the problems about
which he was so eloquent during the 1930s.

It is possible to see Coughlin as a fascist and quite easy to
think of him as an anti-Semite. It is also convincing to analyze
him as the link between Populism and McCarthyism. It may
be more charitable, however, to see him as a sincere and
well-meaning social reformer without much scholarly or intellectual understanding of economic problems and social

problems, whose head was turned by the immense popularity of his radio broadcasts. Disillusioned by the New Deal's failure to take him seriously, he turned more and more against it and his anger and frustration carried him down the path that ended in the worst sort of demagoguery. If John Ryan represented a merger between Catholic social philosophy and part of the American reform tradition, then Charles Coughlin represented a similar merger. Both in their own ways represented a victory for the Americanizing elements in the Catholic Church since both would array themselves with strands of the American reform tradition. Unfortunately the deviant strand of extreme Populism which Coughlin chose seemed to many Americans a threat to their nation's freedom when it was on the lips of a Catholic priest.

Apparently Coughlin's basic support came from the lower middle class and upper-working-class Irish and German Catholics. These groups were particularly hard hit by the Depression and perhaps were still smarting from the hurt of the Al Smith campaign; not yet fully accepted by American society and caught in severe economic stress, they were easy victims for an eloquent but simplistic analysis of the ills of society, especially when such analysis blamed the problems on the traditional enemies of the groups involved—bankers, the British, the Jews, and Communists. Careful analysts, such as Seymour Martin Lipset, have pointed out that it was the same groups that rallied to the cause of Senator Joseph McCarthy in the 1950s although at this time economic misery had been replaced by social misery of those groups who had made it economically and had yet to become fully accepted socially in American society. By the late 1950s and early 1960s, however, the picture had substantially changed and what was left of the Coughlin tradition as manifested in the John Birch Society had no more attraction for Catholics than for any other Americans. The economic distress of the 1930s and the social distress of the 1940s and 1950s were no longer enough part of the Catholic experience that Catholic Americans would be overrepresented in extremist movements. In addition, it was very difficult for Irish and German Catholics to be seriously persuaded that John Fitzgerald Kennedy was a Communist. Extreme right wing Populism had lost its appeal for American Catholics. But the crucial question from the viewpoint of this study is not why Coughlinesque Populism would have an appeal or why that appeal should wane; it is rather why the more legitimate social doctrine of the Church as manifested by John Ryan was virtually unknown to most American Catholics.

Several different reasons can be advanced. First of all, the abiding fear of many priests and bishops of socialism and Communism made them suspicious of most social reform movements and caused some of them to place at the root of social sufferings demon rum. In retrospect the popularity of the total abstinence movement among clerics such as John Ireland seems a bit quaint, but at one time it was a major element in the social concerns of many prominent ecclesiastics. Secondly, the social reform movement both inside and outside the Church seemed unaware of the basic urban political realities, and its opposition to the big city machines ignored the major service these machines were rendering to the immigrant population. John Ryan in Washington was a very poor competitor to the local precinct captain, especially when those good-government enthusiasts in the city were often well-to-do Protestants whose major concern in reform seemed to be aimed at taking political power away from the immigrant and his ethnic political organization. The immigrant Catholic and the immigrant Catholic politician simply did not trust most of the reformers, and to this day the skepticism of doctrinaire reform persists in the Catholic population.

The paternalistic leadership of a number of Catholic bishops (such as Cardinal O'Connell on the Child Labor Amendment) prevented the social doctrine as propounded by Ryan from filtering down to the parish level; when it did, the paternalism of the pastor frequently prevented it from getting to the rank-and-file Catholics. The bishop and the priests would often argue they knew the needs and problems of their people and did not require the advice of scholars or intellectuals at the Catholic University of America. As long as the Sunday collections were not dwindling and the Sunday church attendance was not threatened, many an urban pastor and bishop felt that all concern over social reform could easily be dangerous radical agitation.

The Catholic press did not jump enthusiastically on the reform bandwagon, particularly diocesan newspapers.[8] In addition, Catholic education until after the Second World War (when the matter was no longer of such great importance) found only minor room in its curriculum for teaching of un-Catholic social doctrine. Sunday church attendance, loyalty to the Church, belief in the primacy of the Pope, and sexual morality were the principal areas in which Catholic education was affected. Social teachings were not completely ignored but they were not given very powerful emphasis either.

Finally, there was not much practical competence in the American Church at the time of the great social reform movements. Ryan was not an economist, he was a social ethician who knew a fair amount of economics and something about social reform legislation. The Catholic colleges and universities had economics and sociology departments but there was virtually no research being done at these schools on the root causes of social ills. Whether the "official" social teaching of the American Church would have had more influence if it showed a deeper grasp of economic technicalities is questionable but it was perhaps difficult for technicians in government, industry, and labor to take the Catholic social doctrine seriously even when they came from such a respected man as John Ryan in the absence of anything but the most naïve notions of how the economy functions.

The social reforms of the New Deal and the great economic boom brought on by the Second World War solved most of the economic problems of the Catholic population; and if the overwhelming majority of the Catholics were not capable of rising beyond bread-and-butter trade unionism when they themselves were affected, it is most unlikely that they would become terribly concerned about the misery and injustices encountered by other groups especially when these

[8] Although there were some very notable exceptions. Ryan and his followers were not altogether safe men and many of the diocesan papers were disinclined to give much publicity to anyone but the safe.

other groups had skins of a different color. The social action tradition persisted after Ryan's death and continues even to the present, but even though some of its leaders like Monsignor Higgins are able and even brilliant men it seems that the social action movements are seeking none too successfully for new goals and new reforms on which to embark. In this quest for a new mission they are not so terribly different from most other American liberals who have seen the New Deal enact most of the social reforms they had expected without producing much in the way of gratitude from the general population toward the reformers who had pressed for so many years for the New Deal legislation. In their present confusion (as well as in their present unfriendliness with many of the civil rights radicals), Catholic social reformers are being once again distinctively American.

It is perhaps expecting too much to wonder why an essentially elite concept of social reform could not be effectively communicated to a large and only moderately well-educated population. Perhaps it would have been impossible in any case for the social doctrine tradition represented by John Ryan to compete effectively with the splendid rhetoric of Charles Coughlin. Nevertheless the failure of the American Church to make more than it did out of its own quite impressive social reform tradition must be evaluated as a major failure of the Americanizing element in the history of the Catholic Church in the United States.

VIII

THE CHICAGO EXPERIENCE

In the late 1930s there began in the archdiocese of Chicago a series of experiments that would anticipate in many respects the spirit and teachings of the Vatican Council. These experiments in lay action, social action, catechetics, liturgy, and marriage education would be imitated all over the United States, and the men who began them would become national figures and the heroes of many of the progressive Catholics of the country. How important their contribution in the historical development of the American Church really was can only be determined in the future. But one can still speak of the "Chicago experience" as an illustration of elements in the genius of American Catholicism, an illustration which might point toward one of the possible areas of future development. Furthermore, the strengths and the weaknesses, the success and the failures of the Chicago liberals embody in miniature the strengths and weaknesses of American Catholicism through much of its history.

It is difficult to write contemporary history. It is even more difficult to do so when one is writing about one's friends, and it is most difficult to attempt such an account when one has had a part, albeit a very minor one, in making the history that is being discussed. Nevertheless this volume has already departed so far from the canons of impartial historical reporting that there seems no reason not to depart a bit further and

talk about the adventures of the Chicago liberals in the last
two and a half decades.

For young Catholics with social awareness and some familiarity with the papal encyclicals on social issues, the 1930s
were stirring and challenging times as the era of the Spanish
Civil War, the New Deal, the NRA, the Wagner Act, the CIO,
John L. Lewis, Philip Murray, the Battle of the Overpass, and
the Republic Steel Massacre. Franklin Roosevelt was giving
fireside addresses and John Ryan was refuting Father Coughlin. *Commonweal* was moving to the left and the spirit of social reform was abroad in the land. The Great Depression
hung like a dreadful pall over the nation, but at least one
knew who the enemies were and one had clear blueprints
on how the enemies were to be defeated and the new social
structure was to be built. If the ideology of Marxism had a
wide appeal among young intellectuals, so for a relatively
small group of the younger Catholics the "social teachings of
the Church" offered a promise for a brighter and better
future.

There were several different influences at work in Chicago
in the 1930s to serve to focus this social enthusiasm. *The
New World,* the Chicago archdiocese newspaper, at that time
took a consistently liberal stand on political and social questions. Bishop Bernard Sheil became identified as a great patron of liberal causes, particularly the organization of labor
unions and community organizations. A charismatic Jesuit, Martin Carrabine, had important influence among the
younger generation through an organization called CISCA.[1]
Among those whose social awareness was reinforced and directed by Carrabine were men like Edward Marciniak, who
later went on to edit *Work,* and now is director of the Chicago
Commission on Human Relations; James O'Gara and John
Cogley, who would found the Catholic Worker Movement in
Chicago, *Today Magazine,* and later join the staff of the *Commonweal;* and John Egan, who would go to the seminary and
become one of the key priests in the developments of the next

1 The initials stood for Chicago Inter-Student Catholic Action.

two decades. But besides the more famous products of the Carrabine efforts, there were a large number of other young Catholics who were part of CISCA in the 1930s and would provide enthusiastic support for the new movements that developed in the early forties.

On a different level, the Jesuit priest Edward Dowling would prove most effective in working with well-to-do Catholic families in the North Shore suburbs on the kinds of problems which would then be called "family renewal" but which would come to be known in the 1940s as the Cana movement. Professor Jerome Kerwin of the political science department of the University of Chicago was, for many years, "the unofficial Catholic chaplain" at the university (since the archdiocese would not permit the appointment of a Catholic priest as a chaplain to the students). Kerwin and his followers interjected into the developing Chicago ferment a touch of intellectualism through contact with European Catholic philosophy. In addition, Father Daniel Lord, a Jesuit priest from the Institute of Social Order in St. Louis, made a tremendous impression on adolescents, and also contributed to the ferment through his summer schools of Catholic action. Dorothy Day and Peter Maurin of the Catholic Worker Movement in New York paid periodic visits to Chicago, and the House of Hospitality founded by Cogley, O'Gara, and Marciniak brought to the city the concern about poverty, social reform and charity (but not pacificism) that was characteristic of the Catholic Worker Movement. Finally, many of the German parishes in the archdiocese under the influence of St. John's Abbey in Collegeville, Minnesota, were deeply involved in the beginnings of the liturgical revival. The social actionists were by and large Irish and not terribly concerned about liturgy. And liturgists were, by and large, German and not terribly concerned about social action. Furthermore, those who were putting emphasis on family renewal were generally upper middle class and not nearly so deeply committed to social reform as were Cogley, O'Gara, and Marciniak. What was needed, then, at the end of the 1930s in Chicago was a catalyst which would bring all the fermenting factors together and produce a powerful surge of enthusiasm. Fortunately for Chicago, such a catalyst was readily available.

The most important person in developing the Chicago liberal movement was Monsignor Reynold Hillenbrand. He was appointed rector at the Chicago Archdiocesan Seminary at Mundelein College in 1935 while he was still in his early thirties. His graduate training was in theology and he also had a deep interest in poetry, literature, and art. His German background and his theological studies had made him a dedicated liturgist. His wide range of reading had brought him familiarity with the social encyclicals. From these diverse interests, Hillenbrand was able to compose a powerful synthesis which offered for the young priests and the laity of Chicago a vision of the Church's role in the modern world. The Christian community would be formed through liturgy and the members of the Christian community would be committed to correcting social ills through the inspiration of the teachings of the social encyclicals. They would return periodically to the liturgy in the community to gain the strength and vigor they needed and then once more depart for the social battle in the world needed to be reformed. In later years many would come to believe that Hillenbrand's vision was much too simple, not to say simplistic, and that his use of the papal encyclicals as a blueprint for practical social reconstruction was much too a prioristic. Others would resent what they felt was a high-handed, authoritarian leadership that Hillenbrand provided. But whatever is to be said in later years, there can be no doubt that in the 1930s and 1940s Hillenbrand was a giant who exercised tremendous influence on the seminarians, the young priests, and the laity of Chicago. Those who came to know him for the first time after he had been removed as seminary rector and after an automobile accident shattered his health, frequently could not understand the awe and reverence in which he was held by his early followers. Reynold Hillenbrand's charisma was, and in some ways still is, a powerful one. Without his synthesis and vision, the Chicago movement would never have begun, nor if begun would it have ever continued.

Hillenbrand was hardly an ivory-tower liberal. He and the coterie of young priests around him first of all became engaged in the network labor schools in Chicago at the time when Catholic social actionists were persuaded that the education of Catholic trade unionists in labor schools was to be a major means of social reform. However, as the 1930s turned into the 1940s, Hillenbrand through John Egan, still a seminarian, became acquainted with a North Shore attorney, James O'Shaughnessy; the two men, having discovered through the influence of an Oklahoma priest, Donald Kanaly, the tremendous impact of the specialized Catholic action movements such as the JOC (Jeunesse Ouvrière Chrétienne) in France, were determined to develop Americanized versions of these movements. The turn of Hillenbrand's interests from the labor schools to Catholic action could well mark the beginning of seven years of tremendous ferment in Chicago.

During the years of the Second World War, the Catholic action organizations in Chicago began to flourish. Under the influence of Father Daniel Cantwell, a member of Monsignor Hillenbrand's faculty at Mundelein, the Catholic Labor Alliance and the Catholic Interracial Council were formed, and *Work,* the publication of the former edited by Edward Marciniak, proved to be a lively and influential journal. Catholic action groups, at first somewhat secretive in their approach, began to appear in Catholic high schools and colleges as well as among Catholic businessmen, the businessmen's wives, and also young working people. The young clergy around Hillenbrand—Egan, John Quinn, James Voss, William Quinn, Julius Marhoffer, James Kilgallen, Gerard Weber, Donald Runkle, Romeo Blanchette,[2] and others[3]—became deeply involved as moderators for these groups.

[2] Presently the bishop of Joliet.

[3] Two of Hillenbrand's disciples exercised immense influence on the national level: George Higgins in the social action department of the NCWC, and William Rooney (professor of English at the Catholic University) as secretary for the Catholic Commission on Intellectual and Cultural Affairs—the organization that stimulated the self-critical works of O'Day, Ellis, Weigel, and Donovan.

Monsignor Hillenbrand and Johanna Doniat moderated an extremely important Catholic action group at Senn High School, a leader of which, the late George Sullivan, was eventually to become an effective national president of the Young Christian Workers. In the meantime, the first Cana Conference was given in Chicago and a skeleton Cana organization was established in 1944. Friendship House was opened under the direction of Baroness Katherine De Hueck Dougherty, the Grail made its first foundation in the United States near Libertyville, Illinois, and the Sheil School of Social Studies provided some of the intellectual stimulus that was needed in the midst of so much activity.[4]

Immediately after the end of the war, developments both on the University of Chicago campus and at the University of Notre Dame added to the ferment of ideas and activity. While not directly a part of the Hillenbrand activity, the so-called Greenwood community of Catholics at the University of Chicago was closely related to it and some of its members would later have great influence, principally through their friendship with John Egan. In the meantime, at the University of Notre Dame, Father Louis Putz, C.S.C., had a flourishing young Christian student group from which came the magazine *Concord* and eventually the Fides Publishing Company. In the midst of all these different ventures and operations, there was a great deal of talk in Chicago, especially at the various headquarters—the Calvert Club at the University, the apartment on Greenwood, "3 East" Chicago Avenue (the original headquarters of the Catholic Labor Alliance), Friendship House, and for a time the seminary at Mundelein.

Hillenbrand believed in seminars, study weeks, retreats, and training programs. Indeed, during 1938 and 1939, he had month-long summer schools on the seminary campus to which the leaders of Catholic social action as well as a number of prominent union officials were invited. It was through these meetings that the participants from the various organizations came to know each other. Eventually, as they began to at-

---

[4] Bishop Sheil himself was not in any real sense part of the ferment.

tend national meetings, they became aware of influences beyond the United States. The international meeting of the Young Christian Workers at Montreal in 1947 was a turning point in many ways for the younger Catholic action organizations who now began to drop their own names and assume translations of the European names such as Young Christian Workers (YCW) and Young Christian Students (YCS). The English Catholic action leaders, in particular Father John Fitzsimons and Patrick Keagan (a *peritus* at Vatican II) spent lengthy periods of time in Chicago and provided the links in the communication network by which the Chicago movements were plugged in to what was going on in the rest of the world.

It should be stressed that most of these organizations and movements had only unofficial sanction. The archdiocese did not approve of them but neither did it disapprove. When Cardinal Mundelein was alive, the activities of Reynold Hillenbrand were unquestionable since he was Mundelein's hand-picked seminary rector. Samuel Stritch, Mundelein's successor in Chicago, was not inclined to interfere in the work that was going on and the protection of the late Monsignor Joseph Morrison, then the rector of Holy Name Cathedral, and later Monsignor Edward Burke, the chancellor of the diocese, was to prove indispensable to the liberals.

In 1944, however, they suffered a major setback when Hillenbrand was removed as seminary rector and appointed pastor of a suburban parish on the North Shore. The reasons why Archbishop Stritch removed Hillenbrand have never been clear. Some argued that the Jesuit faculty at the seminary objected to what they thought was Hillenbrand's social radicalism and the many "distractions" which he was bringing on the seminary grounds. Powerful pastors in the city were alleged to have complained that the assistants ordained during the Hillenbrand years were more interested in Catholic action than they were in obedience, and apparently a few assistants did behave somewhat indiscreetly. Still other critics of Hillenbrand argued that he was involved in so many things outside of the seminary that he was not able to give adequate attention to the development of the seminarians. Even some

of Hillenbrand's friends admitted that he was little concerned
with building a network of friendships among the pastors of
the city,[5] and other friendly critics argued that for all of
Hillenbrand's enthusiasm and vision, for all the power of his
Sunday homilies at the seminary, he was neither a tactful nor
an adroit diplomat.

His successor at the seminary was committed to none of
the things for which Monsignor Hillenbrand stood, and in the
minds of many of the seminarians at the time seemed dedicated to reinstituting the nineteenth century at Mundelein.
Three years after Hillenbrand's dismissal, many of the young
diocesan faculty at the seminary who had been his close supporters were also removed. While the younger clergy who
would be ordained after 1947 would be sympathetic to the
Hillenbrand movements, they had not been exposed to his
charismatic power. They were not part of the group of clergy
who had, under Hillenbrand's inspiration, begun most of the
activity in Chicago. Even though this group periodically went
through the motions of trying to attract younger members, it
never did so with much vigor. For all practical purposes, by
1947 it had cut itself off from the possibility of being rein-
vigorated by younger blood.

Even though Hillenbrand's removal would ultimately prove
to be disastrous for the Chicago liberals, the middle forties
were still highly successful years for the liberals (as we shall
call the Hillenbrand group henceforth, resisting the notion
to dub them the Liberal Establishment). In 1946, a committee
of prominent North Shore business and professional men approached Cardinal Stritch and suggested that it was time that
at least some of the activities of the last several years be more
formally integrated into the work of the Church. It was spe-
cifically requested that an official chaplain be appointed to the
Catholic action organizations and to the Cana Conference.
Following the suggestions of Monsignors Burke and Hillenbrand, the Archbishop in October, 1946, appointed John

[5] One such friendly critic said that if Hillenbrand had attended
more wakes and funerals, he would have been in a much better
position to defend himself from the criticisms of his pastoral opponents.

Egan as chaplain of the Cana Conference and William Quinn as secretary for Catholic action. The following year after he had been removed from the seminary faculty, Daniel Cantwell became the chaplain of the Catholic Labor Alliance, and for all practical purposes, social action director of the diocese. With these two appointments the period of great growth and consolidation was to begin.

About the time of the appointment of Quinn and Egan, another extraordinarily important development occurred. For a number of years a group of Catholic business and professional men had been meeting in the Catholic action group, concerned with the implications of their faith in their working life. Simultaneously the wives of these men had a Catholic action group of their own. By 1947 a number of people, particularly the wives, were beginning to ask whether it made any sense for husbands and wives to be separated and whether it would not be much more appropriate for the two groups to merge. There was considerable debate and controversy over the subject, with some chaplains threatening to resign if the groups were merged, but the merger nevertheless took place and the Christian Family Movement was formed. Under the dedicated leadership of Mr. and Mrs. Patrick Crowley, the movement grew at a fantastic rate, first in the archdiocese of Chicago, then in the United States, and then in the entire world. Beyond any doubt, the CFM has been the largest and most impressive and indeed the most uniquely American contribution of Chicago to the development of the Church in the 1940s and the 1950s. Along with the Cana Conference (with which it worked, at least in Chicago, quite closely though not without tension), it fit in perfectly with the great emphasis on family life in the postwar world, and was also easily legitimated with ecclesiastical authorities as being a response to the soaring divorce rate in the late 1940s.

The Christian Family Movement was not without its critics. Some charged that the merger of the husbands' group and the wives' group destroyed any possibility for there to be an effective Catholic action organization concerned with the world of work and that the inevitable result of the merger was a development of a strong emphasis on problems of the home and family and indeed a suburbanization of Catholic action. Others contended that the CFM was naïvely enthusiastic in recruiting everybody in sight instead of being much more selective about the members sought, so that frequently it became a little more than a social club. Hillenbrand, who became the national chaplain of the CFM, attempted to focus its interests on the world beyond the family with annual programs concerned not only with family or school, but also with race, social justice, and international problems. But most of these programs were quite unsuccessful and did not appeal to the rather narrowly familial interests of most of the CFM membership. There were other critics who argued that Hillenbrand's autocratic and simplistic approach to establishing the yearly programs precluded their having any effectiveness since it was contended that the Monsignor was more interested in deriving a program from the papal encyclical than from the needs and problems of the people who were members of the organization.

But for all these criticisms, the CFM flourished and had considerable influence in the lives of thousands of people. It does not seem to have lost either its vigor or its flexibility at the present moment and it is now deeply engaged in ecumenical activities. It is too early to say how much influence the CFM really has. Thousands of couples have joined it only to abandon it through waning of interest or personality conflicts. Other couples left it to become more deeply involved in specialized efforts such as racial justice or political reform. The critics of the CFM state that even in Chicago it has not produced very many married couples who are particularly concerned about the problems of the inner city.[6] However,

---

[6] In the early days of the tutoring movement in Chicago, CALM, an organization of college and graduate students, came into conflict with one CFM group that was working in the inner city. The CFM couples argued that it was impossible to have the same tutor for each child during every week of the tutoring sessions because married people could not be expected to come to the tutoring center each week. The CALM members, on the other hand, pointed out that all the theories of tutoring insisted that tutoring relationship was wasted unless it was indeed a relationship between one tutor

if the CFM has made mistakes and has not lived up to all its promise, and even if it may have temporarily impaired the development of a more socially committed Catholic action movement, it would seem at the present time still to have enough health and vitality to be able to grow and to fulfill the not inconsiderable promise that it seemed to have in the 1940s and the 1950s.

In the last half of the forties and the first half of the fifties, the Chicago liberals, now with official status and rapidly growing organizations, began to settle down to the difficult task of organizing and structuring their work. Fathers Quinn and Egan (both to be elevated to the monsignorial purple in the fifties) were eminently personable men and began to visit the parishes of Chicago to acquaint pastors with the work their organizations were doing. While they were not warmly received everywhere, their charm and the reasonableness of their message made for them many friends. Having learned from Hillenbrand's mistake, Quinn and Egan very carefully built up a vast base of popular support and friendship throughout the diocese, and the Cana Conference and the Christian Family Movement rapidly were accepted not only in the chancery office (particularly with the aid of Monsignor Edward Burke) but also in the large number of parishes in the city. Egan and Quinn were not viewed as crackpots or radicals and had managed to gain wide acceptance without watering down their program. In retrospect, this careful building of a popular-based program might be the ultimate explanation for the widespread success of the Chicago liberals in comparison with their counterparts in other dioceses.

Nor did the liberals limit their work to Chicago. Egan, and to a lesser extent Quinn, established a network of friendship relationships throughout the country, particularly by being constantly available to help other dioceses to establish Cana

---

and one pupil through the entire program. Since the CFM was able to muster eight volunteers and CALM over two hundred, there was not much doubt about who won the debate, and the CFM was very bitter about the arrogance of the young people, whom they accused of driving them out of the parish.

and Christian family programs (and in later years, even indeed to the present, Egan would respond to bishops' requests around the country for advice and help in establishing offices of urban development). New national organizations were founded, and old national organizations were infiltrated and reorganized, even though the Chicago liberals encountered opposition from national bureaucrats who resented the innovations that the CFM and Cana represented and particularly Egan's notion that each diocese should have its own program rather than receive a prefabricated program from a national office. Nevertheless, Cardinal Stritch stood by his two appointees and supported them in every one of the controversies in which they found themselves. Egan began to emerge more and more as the key man among the liberals. The three months that he spent in France in 1953 at the suggestion of some graduate students at the University of Chicago who were familiar with the postwar developments in the country, widened Egan's horizons considerably and brought him back to Chicago with a vastly expanded view of the work that the liberals could be doing.

When Bishop Sheil was removed as director of the Catholic Youth Organization and many of the organizations that had been a part of the bishop's complex operation were threatened with extinction, Egan devoted himself to picking up as many of the pieces as possible and making sure that the work continued. The Sheil School of Social Studies was replaced by the Adult Education Center which Egan was largely responsible for inspiring, though control of it was shifted to the office of the Catholic Labor Alliance (to be renamed the Catholic Council of Working Life). St. Benet's Bookstore, long an important influence in the liberal scene in Chicago, was salvaged and a separate, independent board of directors was established to guarantee the continued existence of the store. A program of pastoral counseling was begun at Loyola University. Father Charles Curran, a priest of the Columbus diocese, was invited to Chicago to direct the program, through which hundreds of Chicago priests have received basic training in the principles of Rogerian counseling. Egan was instrumental in establishing all of these activities as well as encouraging a number of others, while at the same time beginning a series of publications through the office of the Cana Conference. But there was about Egan almost nothing of the empire builder and he did not attempt to keep control of any of the projects for whose launching he was responsible.

The leadership that Egan was beginning to exercise among the Chicago liberals was based largely on an extensive network of personal friendships and a great capacity for sympathetic listening and the ability to come up almost instinctively with the right sort of advice at precisely the time it was needed. Being far different from Hillenbrand, his great flexibility left him open to charges of being without clear principles or ideology. In addition, his extraordinary diplomatic abilities would lead a few people to accuse him of deviousness. But his instinct for a good idea was unerring and his encouragement to those who had such ideas kept many such brave new notions from being lost forever.

I am obviously prejudiced in favor of Quinn and Egan since they were the heroes of my early years in the priesthood. I do not think, however, that I deceive myself about the mistakes that they have made, and as I am sure they will both be only too willing to admit, I have not concealed my opinions about those mistakes from them. Despite my friendship for them, therefore, I think I may be able to speak with at least some semblance of objectivity. During the forties and fifties these two men were the key to the success of the Chicago liberals. Their personal charm, diplomatic skills, and breadth of vision enabled the Chicago liberals to have vast local and national influence. Their consistent refusal to build empires[7] and their constant openness to new ideas and new experiments proved that it is not absolutely necessary for liberals to become authoritarian conservatives when they acquire power of their own. If Hillenbrand provided the initial impetus for the Chicago experience, Quinn and Egan kept that impetus moving.

[7] Both agreed that they would only stay in their jobs for ten years and shortly after the decade was over, departed for other work —Quinn to Latin American problems and Egan to urban affairs.

Other influences were at work in Chicago during these years too. With the coming of Dan Herr to the Thomas More Bookstore in 1948, the bookstore and its magazine *Books on Trial* (later *The Critic*) became an important part of the Chicago scene, though Herr's refusal to be serious at times and on matters which some of the more solemn liberals thought demanded seriousness prevented him from ever really becoming part of the emerging lay liberal network. His warm personality and his sharp insights, however, gave him much influence both locally and nationally. The magazine *Today,* allegedly aimed at high school students but actually having content capable of appealing to a much higher level of readership, made its impact felt on young people. Fathers Weber and Kilgallen began the publication of a series of highly innovative catechisms, at least innovative by the standards of the 1950s.[8] At the University of Chicago, Father Thomas McDonough began to serve as assistant chaplain and thereby established a direct relationship between the liberals and the university. A group of younger priests working in the Negro parishes of Chicago developed an organization and a style of their own which stressed too much the making of large numbers of converts. It soon became the most effective form of inner city work to be found anywhere in the country among Catholics or for that matter any other religious group. The liturgical movement moved ahead more slowly, though by the middle fifties it seemed reasonably evident that liturgists were not crackpots; eventually active participation, at least at some Masses, was to exist in most parishes in the

[8] The Weber-Kilgallen collaboration began at one of the Sunday night meetings in the late fifties which had been designed to re-kindle the fires of the original Hillenbrand group. Commenting on another catechism, Kilgallen proclaimed, "I could write a better catechism than that." Someone (perhaps Quinn) responded, "Why don't you?" "All right," Kilgallen shouted back. "And I'll help you," shouted Weber in the loudest voice yet. Quinn participated in the early catechetical work but as a silent partner. Even though the main purpose of the meetings was not served and they eventually came to an end, a number of projects did come out of them—and most in the highly and almost deliberately casual style of the catechism collaboration.

diocese. No one, of course, was prepared for the liturgical revolution at the Vatican Council.

The late forties and early fifties, then, were times of great expansion and consolidation for the liberals. But seeds of problems had already been sowed. In the late 1940s, Hillenbrand was almost killed in an automobile accident in Texas. He was away from Chicago for almost two years. When he finally returned, his magic did not seem to have the power of previous years, even though he continued (and still does continue) to be the national chaplain of the CFM, YCW, and YCS.[9] Secondly, the large number of new organizations and projects which had emerged were now each going in their own direction and the concerns of the priests and lay people involved in these organizations were so completely taken up with their own specific problems that communication among the various groups was declining. Even though rivalries were at a minimum, some resentments did occur. But the real problem was not rivalry or resentment, but preoccupation with one's own concerns and lack of time to communicate with others. Periodic lip service was given to the problem of communication but no steps were taken (even to the present) to deal with the problem. Finally, the vision, the ideology, the theoretical thrust that Hillenbrand had provided in the thirties had served well for almost twenty years, but it needed to be deepened and renewed; by 1955 it was highly questionable in the minds of many of us whether that renewal was going to take place. The Chicago liberals, for all their successes, were apparently running out of ideological steam.

During the last half of the 1950s, the problems mentioned in the concluding paragraph of the previous section grew more acute. For all practical purposes, Hillenbrand's group was disintegrating. Over substantial opposition Hillenbrand had authorized the merger of the young women's and young men's YCW. There followed a period of rapid growth for

[9] In the middle 1950s, he and Egan strongly disagreed on the YCW, of which Egan had been the national chaplain. Hillenbrand asked for his resignation. The breach between the two widened as the years went on.

YCW but eventually a loss of its sharpness and drive. For a yet unexplained reason, the girls' YCW had always been the stronger of the two. But in the merged group, the antifeminism which had crept into YCW ideology decreed that the male members should be the leaders. The YCW rapidly became another parish organization for young people concerned principally with mate selection. The CFM was emerging as a suburban movement concerned with suburban problems and Hillenbrand's efforts to inject extrafamilial concerns in the annual program were unsuccessful. Social action organizations were handicapped by the fact that the affluence of the 1940s and 1950s made the labor school approach to social action seem quite irrelevant. Finally, communication among the various lay and clerical members of the group was rapidly diminishing.

An attempt was made to have monthly meetings of the clergy involved, but these meetings were something less than completely successful. As young priests were brought into the group in what turned out to be a very limited attempt to attract "new blood," I found myself surprised by the resentments and frustrations just beneath the surface of the conversation. It was fairly easy to see that most of the liberals had come to resent Hillenbrand's leadership but were not ready to revolt (and to some extent are still not ready to revolt). He was still a towering prophetic figure, but the charisma did not have much impact on the generation ordained after 1950, especially since it so often seemed to get lost in the squabbles that were going on within the liberal group. While there was a great deal of talk of freedom, the Sunday evening meetings were not particularly free and one felt all kinds of inhibitions about expressing one's opinion. It soon became evident that these inhibitions and frustrations were widespread among the liberals.[10]

[10] In my years as a writer I have had only one article suppressed. It was an article critical of some aspects of the CFM and it was suppressed by the CFM national leadership on the grounds that open discussion of these problems would hurt the movement. Such was the demise of the liberals when they came into power.

A rather peculiar situation was developing in the late 1950s with regard to the three specialized Catholic action movements—the YCW, YCS, and CFM. The national organizations were still much under Hillenbrand's influence and in the case of the Christian Family Movement under the influence of Hillenbrand and Crowley, whereas the Chicago organizations presided over by Hillenbrand's clerical followers were now operating quite independently and on occasion in conflict with the national office. The battles never came into the open (perhaps it was regrettable that they did not) but the tensions were there and contributed to the aggravation of an already difficult situation.

The crisis became even more acute when Egan left the Cana Conference to become active in a vague area known as urban problems. Even though he had been involved in the essentially familial Cana Conference for more than a decade, Egan's early interests had been in more direct social action, and while these interests had been held in abeyance through the late forties and early fifties, his first love remained social reform. When the opportunity came to develop special training in Saul Alinsky's Industrial Area Foundation and Cardinal Stritch approved such training, Egan leaped at the chance. He was shortly thereafter assigned as secretary to the Cardinal's Conservation Committee, a group of clerics concerned with the problems of urban renewal in the city, although he continued, until the arrival of Cardinal Meyer, to be the nominal director of the Cana Conference.[11]

[11] Egan's early contacts with Saul Alinsky came in the middle 1950s when an assistant pastor in Woodlawn, Father Leo Mahon, and a group of graduate students at the University of Chicago became concerned about the problems of the Spanish-speaking people in the Chicago area. Mahon brought Egan into the conversations and Saul Alinsky was recommended as someone who knew much about community organizing. This was also the first contact between Alinsky and Nicholas Von Hoffman, who was later to become one of the principal organizers of the Industrial Area Foundation. Out of the Spanish-speaking work, there came an organization for the Spanish-speaking in the archdiocese which Father Mahon would direct until he resigned to become pastor of the Chicago mission in Panama.

Egan's involvement in the urban problems area was greeted with some distrust by many of the other liberals who did not trust Saul Alinsky and were suspicious of what "Egan was up to." The suspicions grew more acute at the time of the Hyde Park–Kenwood urban redevelopment controversy, which marked the definitive end of the Chicago liberals as a coherent group.

With the approval of Cardinal Stritch (who was about to leave for Rome where he would soon die), Egan and his staff (composed largely of Nicholas Von Hoffman)[12] began a campaign to substantially modify the University of Chicago's plan to redevelop the neighborhood in which it was located. The whole battle is recounted by Peter H. Rossi in his book *The Politics of Urban Renewal,* and there does not seem much doubt in retrospect that the university was in the process of demolishing and institutionalizing the neighborhood in order to prevent it from becoming part of a Negro ghetto. Egan had no intention of denying the legitimacy of the university's struggle for survival but strongly questioned the treatment accorded to the Negroes who lived in the areas to be demolished. The battle was a fierce one and Egan found himself aligned with the NAACP and the CIO and at least in some fashion with formal Protestant and Jewish groups in the city although a number of Protestant and Jewish leaders, particularly in Hyde Park–Kenwood, violently denounced Egan's intervention. The Hyde Park–Kenwood plan went through, of course, but modified to at least some extent to satisfy Egan's criticisms. Thus, Rossi has little trouble in his volume in justifying Egan's intervention.

But the Catholic liberals, or at least most of them, felt otherwise and Egan was subjected to severe criticism from many of his friends. Quinn summoned a meeting of clergy and laity who were concerned, and a final confrontation between Egan and Hillenbrand took place. It was a strained meeting, having about it many of the aspects of a heresy trial. Egan was accused of proving false to everything that the lib-

[12] Saul Alinsky also was in Europe and argues convincingly that if he had been in Chicago that he would have advised strongly against the Hyde Park–Kenwood battle.

erals had stood for and virtually read out of the group. The reading out, of course, was not successful, since at least some of us were in sympathy with Egan's position and most of us, even if we did not understand what had happened, were not about to question his sincerity. However, the emotionally charged atmosphere of the trial was, for all practical purposes, the last gasp of the liberals as a group, and the efforts thereafter to maintain either a semblance of unity or a set of common goals were little more than ritualistic.

I have never been able to fully understand the issues that divided the liberals in the Hyde Park–Kenwood controversy. For years they had preached social and racial justice, and here was a situation in which at least the CIO and the NAACP thought that a major social injustice was being done. Egan, as a representative of the diocese, was joining the battle against the injustice. One would have thought the liberals would flock to his cause, but instead many of them turned upon him and denounced his intervention. There were several reasons given for this. One was that such intervention in civic and political problems was not the business of the church as a formal institution, but should be left to the laity.[13] Egan, of course, could have replied that in fact the Catholic laity had not become involved in the Hyde Park–Kenwood battle and that the Church, as a human institution, could not avoid being involved. It would either be against the program or it would be assumed to be for it.

Secondly, it was contended that the director of the Hyde Park–Kenwood Community Conference, Jim Cunningham, was a liberal of long standing and that Egan's campaign against the renewal plan was a personal attack on Cunningham. Cunningham himself in a public statement denied that

[13] The theoretical debate about whether the Church should be involved in community organization controversies such as the Hyde Park–Kenwood battle would rage on for several more years and has not yet been resolved. Interestingly enough, however, those who objected to Egan's involvement in Hyde Park–Kenwood did not object to his later involvement in the Rainbow Beach integration demonstration or in the march in Selma. Neither did they hesitate themselves to put in a highly slanted discussion outline of right-to-work laws in the CFM program.

the issue was religious or moral and stated that it was merely civic. Egan could have replied that in his judgment Cunningham was mistaken, but that he did not necessarily call into question the layman's sincerity. He also could have noted that Cunningham's denial of a moral issue in urban renewal was a curious thing to hear from a member of a group who could see all kinds of moral issues in other civic problems.

Thirdly, Egan was criticized for representing a conservative church apparently concerned with the large number of Negroes who would be forced to move into previously white neighborhoods of the southwest side against the great liberal University of Chicago. There was a great deal of status envy among the Chicago Catholic liberals with regard to the University of Chicago. The university was considered to be a great and glorious center of intellectualism and liberalism and one that the Church could do well to admire and imitate. Egan's opposition to its renewal program called to mind the denunciation of the university by pastors and even by bishops in years gone by, denunciations which the liberals bitterly resented. Egan could have easily replied that the university administration and business office were not liberal and that many members of the university faculty did not find it at all disloyal to criticize the Hyde Park–Kenwood plan. While Rossi remains objective and dispassionate in his book, it is not difficult to conclude that he had many grave reservations, both about the university's goals and methods.

There is reason to feel, therefore, that the final death throes of the liberal group were brought about by reasons other than those publicly discussed. Perhaps future historians will be able to discover what these reasons were. But for our present purposes, the reasons are not so terribly important. The Chicago liberal establishment had been slowly drifting apart for years and the Hyde Park–Kenwood controversy simply wrote a definite finis to its existence as a coherent group.

Although the liberal group existed as a community no more, its various projects continued to operate, some with more creativity and imagination than others. The liberals were, for the most part, very efficient administrators and their organizations continued usually with a great deal of vitality. What was lost was not so much existence but the intensive community enthusiasm and vision which brought them into being. The Vatican Council, which made many of the liberals' dreams come true, also compounded their own problems because its new theology demanded of them a new rhetoric and a new vision which they have not yet been able to acquire.

Egan's work in the Office of Urban Affairs (established by Cardinal Meyer shortly after his arrival in Chicago) was perhaps the most innovative. A network of community organizations (the Woodlawn Organization, the Organization for the Southwest Community, and the Northwest Community Organization were the most important) of the Alinsky variety appeared around the city. Egan became deeply involved with technical problems of housing, planning, renewal, and redevelopment. A small research and planning staff, headed by Michael Schiltz, with the assistance of Peter Beltemacchi, provided maps, population projections, and other social scientific information for the use of the chancery office.[14]

Egan realized that his major mistake in the Hyde Park–Kenwood battle was "going it alone" without prior consultation with the Protestant and Jewish groups. All three religious bodies agreed that such a mistake should never occur in the future; and after lengthy conversations, an Inter-religious Council on Urban Affairs was established which for all practical purposes was a beginning of an ecumenical effort in Chicago. Out of this conference and its joint activities several ecumenical discussion groups began to evolve. Such discussions and the activities of the inter-religious council and the local community organizations gave Chicago a brief head

[14] The research section of the Office of Urban Affairs, which survived only four years, would have had to be eliminated for budgetary reasons, a development which in my judgment was a first-rate tragedy. Schiltz and Beltemacchi, on a shoestring budget, had produced some extreme imaginative and helpful information —available in no other archdiocese in the country—that was easily worth ten times the price that it cost.

start on the rest of the country in preparing for the ecumenical explosion after the Vatican Council. It was a head start
that proved to be of decisive importance.

Shortly after the historic National Conference on Religion
and Race at the Edgewater Beach Hotel in 1963, a Chicago
Conference on Religion and Race was established, representing an ecumenical approach to the racial problems of the
city. Quinn's responsibilities for the migratory worker problem
were expanded to include substantial responsibilities in the
NCWC's Latin American office. Even though these responsibilities took him out of Chicago frequently, his base of operations was still in the city, and in combination with the
Cardinal's Committee for the Spanish-speaking (directed first
by Leo Mahon and later by Donald Hedley) provided a
strong impetus to Chicago Catholicism's involvement in
Latin American issues. Walter Imbiorski, Egan's successor at
the Cana Conference, used the office as a springboard for
developing programs of clerical education and a series of
population conferences in conjunction with the University of
Notre Dame. Although the obscurity on the birth control
issue which developed in the middle 1960s severely limited
the kind of statements that the Cana Conference could make
on the question, Imbiorski skillfully and imaginatively charted
a course for himself through extremely difficult territory.
Finally, in 1963 two recent graduates of Barat College of the
Sacred Heart, Grace Ann Carroll and Kathy Mulholland,
began an inner city volunteer project they most inappropri-
ately called CALM.[15] In an incredibly short time, with little
more than charm and nerve, they constructed a large and
elaborate organization with a substantial budget that was providing more than two thousand volunteer workers each week
for inner city projects. Egan and Imbiorski and some of the
liberals encouraged CALM, but others, particularly the older
liberal laity, have always viewed it with grave reserve, especially since the CALM leadership has consistently refused to
take the liberal predecessors very seriously. But whether

[15] The letters stand for Chicago Area Lay Movement but the
word CALM was invented before the title was thought up to fit it.

CALM represents the end of the old liberalism or the beginning of the new is a question that only the future can answer.

Another important work, again under Egan's inspiration and protection, was the Urban Apostolate of the Sisters, an organization of some five hundred nuns engaged in teaching in central city schools, which was formed as part of the Office of Urban Affairs in 1962.

While the Chicago Liberal Establishment has therefore, for all practical purposes, disintegrated, its work continues. Its success was immense if incomplete, and the successes are not necessarily over by any means. Even though many of the original group who clustered around Hillenbrand are weary and disillusioned, and even though the initial thrust is pretty well spent, the liberals did succeed in establishing a climate in Chicago which was extremely conducive to openness and experimentation. Many other things have come to be within the archdiocese which, while they may not have proceeded directly from the liberals' influence, would never have occurred if the liberals had not blazed the trail. Any evaluation on the success or failure must do more than look at the Christian Family Movement or the Young Christian Workers or the Cana Conference as they exist today. Innovative work in liturgy, race, ecumenism, education, and youth activities which has occurred in Chicago in the last two decades might have been possible even if it had not been for the work of the liberals. Yet these innovations would not have been nearly so successful nor attracted nearly so much enthusiastic support if the way had not been prepared for them by Hillenbrand and his followers. There is every reason to expect that in years to come the influence of the Liberal Establishment of the forties and fifties will continue to be felt.

There were many different reasons for the success of the Chicago liberals. They had three open-minded bishops in a row—Mundelein, Stritch, and Meyer—each in his own way permissive enough to permit experimentation and innovation, without demanding immediate or instantaneous success. If a project proved itself as time went on, they would lend it their enthusiastic support. If it failed, they would not hold the failure against those who had begun the experiment. In the absence of such toleration, the liberals could never have gotten their movements off the ground.

Second, the liberals, particularly Quinn and Egan, were extraordinarily skillful diplomats in their relations with their ecclesiastical superiors, with the pastors and clergy of the archdiocese, and eventually with their counterparts around the country. They were able, therefore, to create a much wider base of popular support and eventually to acquire far more power than if they had chosen to play the role of alienated rebels.

Third, the Chicago liberals were able to respond to actual issues—the social problems of the late thirties, the family problems of the postwar era, and once again the racial and social problems of the late fifties and the early sixties. They were able to persuade the decision makers in the diocese that their skills and experience could be valuable in the Church's attempts to cope with the issues of the day.

Fourth, in Monsignor Hillenbrand the liberals had a charismatic leader of immense abilities. If he had not been present and pulled the various strands together to synthesize them into an exciting and forceful vision, the liberal message would never have had very much vigor to it.

Fifth, around Hillenbrand there clustered, particularly in the early days, a cadre of loyal, enthusiastic, and extremely zealous clergy. Even though most of them were tempted to move from crisis to crisis, their common goals, their close personal friendships and their openness to new ideas and projects made them extraordinarily effective agents for innovation.

Sixth, the liberal clergy were able to appeal to a substantial number of action-oriented lay people, many of whom were successful and well-to-do. These laity in their turn could represent the liberal movements to the pastors and the chancery office as essentially respectable organizations. There was, of course, tension between the respectability and the somewhat revolutionary aims the liberals had, but surprisingly enough the tension wasn't very strong because most of the liberals were in truth quite respectable people and most of the respectable laity were in truth something of moderate revolutionaries.

It hardly needs to be emphasized that Chicago liberals represent in an extremely dramatic fashion the Americanizing tradition within the Church. Flexible, pragmatic, open-minded, experimental, curious, and efficient, they were able to seize upon the possibilities they saw in the contemporary situation and make the most of it. They were long on enthusiasm and oftentimes short on theory. They were skillful in obtaining consensus though on occasion uncertain as to what direction the consensus ought to go. They readily could balance all kinds of conflicting elements in the external environment, but were less than successful in balancing their own conflicts among themselves. They brought to Chicago even before the Ecumenical Council a number of the major themes of European theology and action which would substantially influence the council. Unfortunately when the council was over, they were not immediately able to integrate its advances into their own program, and at the present time, like most other Americans, they are wondering what in the world the future is going to bring.

There are also very definite limitations to the Chicago Liberal Establishment. When the tragic Texas automobile accident impaired the Hillenbrand charisma, there was no new leader on the scene capable of developing and expanding his vision. The liberal group's inability to resolve its succession problem was at the root of its ultimate disintegration.

The liberals were not able to develop anything in the way of deep theory. Their pragmatism and flexibility often smacked of anti-intellectualism.[16] Even though they read widely and ridiculed the anti-intellectualism of some of the clergy, the liberals themselves always seemed to assume that one did not really have to know very much or understand very much to launch a new program. They paid lip service to the develop-

[16] I remember remarking at one meeting that the programing for the Catholic action movements might benefit from a study of educational psychology; I was ridiculed for thinking that educational psychology was worth anything. It was pointed out to me that some of the best educational psychologists in the world were poor teachers. But it ought to be noted that most of the Catholic action programs for a number of years were extremely poor teachers.

ment of scholars who would enable them to deepen their own theoretical base. There was always talk about sending someone away to school for study. But even this talk was oriented in the practical direction; and very little serious pressure was ever brought in the chancery office to free people for scholarly pursuits. The liberals wanted the scholars, but they didn't place the need for scholarship very high on their agenda of priorities.

As the liberal works grew more complicated and extensive, communication among the various members broke down almost completely. There never was at any time and still is not now an effective organization for the Catholic action chaplains of the diocese. Occasional lip service was paid for the need for such an organization by study days for CFM, YCS, and YCW chaplains, but no chaplain's group had any role as consultants in the making of ecclesiastical policy for the Catholic action organizations.

Under such circumstances it is not at all surprising that the liberals were not able to attract young priests and young lay people. The younger clergy easily came to believe that the liberals were a clique that they could not penetrate but also came to view some of the liberal leaders as authoritarian and manipulative. While the very young clergy of the diocese even today still respect the work that the liberals did, the attitude is that at this point of the development of history there is nothing the liberals have which the young clergy would find any help at all. Some of the young lay people are even more bitter toward their lay counterparts in the Liberal Establishment, and most contacts between the two groups have been distinctly unpleasant, with the younger laity viewing the older ones as conservative, authoritarian, and frequently anticlerical.[17]

The liberals were never to really break out of a clericalist orientation. In crucial moments the main decisions were made by the clergy, either because they assumed the right to make the decisions or because the laity would run to them, seeking

[17] Some of the younger laity argue that the middle-aged liberals are still dealing with rhetoric and with questions that are preconciliar.

for solutions. Under such circumstances some of the laity who were attracted into the liberal group were strongly clerically oriented, which is to say that they were dependent on the clergy for decision-making and yet had a strong strain of anti-clericalism in their personality. By no means all the liberal laity are of this variety, but the system was unconsciously designed in such a fashion as would attract this type of personality. And some of those whose personalities were different eventually left the liberal organizations, either because they did not like the essentially clericalist orientation or because they found other and more exciting projects elsewhere.

The Vatican Council caught the liberals flat-footed. In the few years most of the items on their agenda for future hopes became realities and the liberals were faced with the postconciliar era not only without any particularly relevant theory but without any theorists. In the absence of theologians or trained social researchers, the liberals were at a distinct disadvantage in trying to adjust to a very different climate of the post-conciliar church.

For all the successes of the family and marriage educational orientation of the CFM and Cana respectively, they have not yet been able to produce substantial numbers of lay people with strong and realistic social action orientations. The family movements have thus far failed almost completely to have an impact on the social problems of the metropolis and particularly of the central city. This is not to say that the family movements were a mistake, but it is to say that perhaps too much effort and too many personnel were put into these involvements and other more critical areas were either understaffed or ignored. Many of the liberals resented Egan's involvement in urban problems in the late fifties and early sixties, but in retrospect, one would have hoped that the whole Liberal Establishment had turned to these problems in the early fifties. However, by then, it may well have been too late.

The first chairman of the Association of Chicago Priests was John Hill, who had been Hillenbrand's assistant as National Chaplain of CFM, YCW and YCS during the early

1960s and a curate at Egan's parish. The ACP quickly won the cooperation and generous praise of Archbishop Cody and the membership of most of the secular priests in the archdiocese. John Egan, James Kilgallen, Walter Imbiorski and Eugene Kennedy (a Maryknoll psychologist who had been close to the Chicago liberals) have served on the executive committee of the ACP. The election of nominees for a personnel board and a retirement board were major accomplishments of this professional association during its first year; and at its second plenary session, at the strong urging of Egan and Kennedy, among others, the ACP committed itself to a social action program which was in the finest tradition of bygone years.

In the meantime a group of laity, most of them products of the Catholic Action Movements (and some of them not a little disgruntled) organized the Chicago Conference of Laity to promote more active lay participation in the decision making of the Church. Some fifteen hundred people attended the first session of the CCL.

Finally a group of laity and clergy, most of them still in their twenties (and many of them affiliated with CALM), launched a new organization called The IV Dimension (hoping to put to rest forever "letter" names). It was their contention that, while the CCL had a role to play, it was too oriented to lay-clergy conflict and internal ecclesiastical problems for their taste. They hoped rather to direct their concerns towards question of "the quality of life" in the city and the Church's contribution to the search for urban community. Some of them assumed responsibility for the moribund liberal journal *New City* with the hope of making it a voice for their generation. Others laid plans for an experimental "Inner City" college.

It is too early to tell how these new structures will fare, though the ACP has attracted nationwide interest. But it would be a singularly ill-advised observer who would believe that the baton of leadership has passed from the hands of the Chicago liberals and their descendants.

As I noted in the beginning of this chapter, it is difficult to write objectively about something that has been very much a part of one's life for almost thirteen years. I will confess all kinds of ambivalences about the liberal movements in Chicago. They have not been a complete success. I would even go so far as to say that they could have readily been much more successful than they were if certain ill-advised decisions had not been made. But one cannot survey the history of the liberals from the late thirties to the mid-sixties without a sense of profound admiration for their accomplishments and even a feeling of pride that one has been able to be a small part of these accomplishments. Hence if the Chicago liberals did not succeed completely, it does not seem to be an exaggeration to say that they succeeded far more than anyone else who attempted to do the same things.

IX

JOHN FITZGERALD KENNEDY
Doctor of the Church?

Canonize John Kennedy? At first such a suggestion surely seems facetious, and unquestionably would bring laughter to the lips of the aloof, witty, ironic man who was the first Catholic President of the United States. Yet in another age, when the manner and purpose of canonization were different, John Kennedy would certainly be hailed as a saint. In the early years of Christianity, canonization was not a long and complicated process carried on under the careful supervision of ecclesiastical authority. It was rather the popular acclaim which the Christian community gave to someone who had become a hero. Great political leaders, especially those who died in the service of their country, were quite apt to become such heroes and be hailed as saints. England has its Edward, France has its Louis, Hungary has its Stephen. John Kennedy would certainly fit the qualifications because one wonders if any man who has ever lived has ever been so much of a hero to so many people in so many different nations of the world.

It may be argued that John F. Kennedy was not a pious man, and only pious people can be saints. In answer, it can be said that we do not know whether he was pious or not. He was surely a loyal Catholic, he most certainly was not an active Catholic in the sense of being one who was deeply involved in Catholic organizational activities. But neither loyalty nor activity by themselves constitute piety, for piety is ultimately the measure of man's relationship with God, and about this subject he was remarkably quiet. Even his alter ego, Ted Sorensen, has remarked that he never, in all the years he was with Kennedy, heard him discuss his notions of God. But if a man does not wear his piety on his sleeve it does not therefore follow that he is not pious, even if he himself does not realize his own piety. Should our purpose be to find the man who exemplifies the kind of virtues that appeal to an age and that are profoundly Christian in their origin, then John Fitzgerald Kennedy was certainly a virtuous man. He refused to be daunted by the massive physical obstacles of incredibly bad health. He was not afraid of the religious prejudice that stood between him and the presidency. He was, in his own words, "not satisfied" with the social and economic state of American society, and was restless for the elimination of injustice and poverty. He had an extraordinarily high sense of social dedication and pursued the presidency less for personal ambition, more for the desire of service. He underwent cheerfully the tremendous physical hardship of election campaigns and would not let the ordeal of the presidency interfere with his hope or his humor. To wrap the case up, he died in the line of duty, something which was reasonably close to martyrdom.

But of course, John Kennedy will not be canonized, since sainthood means something different today from what it did in the early Church. However, it is well to keep in mind that if he had lived fifteen hundred years ago his fellow Catholics would have hailed him as a saint. Perhaps what we need now is a new title. If John Kennedy is not to be hailed as a saint, then maybe we could acclaim him as "a hero of the Church." But one suspects that even this would be too much for him and that his laughter would not stop at that suggestion either. Further, it is not at all improbable that he would be amused by the mythical qualities that have been to cloak his real personality but a few years after his death. He has become everyone's hero and in the process turned into something of an ink blot into which everyone can project his own ideology of what the modern world ought to be. However, none is more hilarious than the notion of some Catholics that in one fashion or another John Kennedy is the operational equivalent of Harvey Cox's secular man. To think of one of the Kennedys as "detribalized" requires the sort of doctrinaire blindness that ought to be difficult even for Catholic liberals.

But if we Catholics are not to hail him as a saint and can hardly claim him as our own particular hero, what title is there we can bestow on John Fitzgerald Kennedy. Perhaps the most appropriate title would be "doctor of the universal church," though even here I feel we would run into canonical difficulties. Nevertheless, for two hundred years, American Catholics insisted that there was nothing in Catholic doctrine which conflicted with American democracy and they simply were not believed. Nevertheless, when John Kennedy stood before the ministerial association in Houston, Texas, to read his speech that bore on it the imprint of such distinguished Catholic liberals as John Cogley, John Wright, and John Courtney Murray, he spoke for the American Church with an effectiveness that had never been matched before. His words were not dissimilar to those John England had spoken to the Congress of the United States 135 years previously. (One wonders if Kennedy or any of his Catholic advisers had ever remembered John England's speech when they were putting together the text of the Houston talk.) But for the first time in the history of the American Church, a Catholic preaching the church's doctrine on the relationship between religion and society was believed, believed at least enough to be elected President of the United States and then in the three short years of his presidency to reinforce his words with deeds that probably for all time destroyed most of the hard core of anti-Catholic prejudice in the United States. If such a performance as this does not earn someone the title of "doctor of the Church," then one wonders what could.

The Houston performance was indeed a splendid one. Sorensen tells us that the air was thick with tension and hostility and that John Cogley whispered to him, "This is one time we need those guys that pray for Notre Dame before each football game." But as soon as he began, the tension vanished. The speech was in Sorensen's judgment (and he surely ought to know) the best speech in the campaign and one of the most important of Kennedy's life. Kennedy insisted that he should be elected or rejected on grounds of "not what kind of church I believe in for that should be important only to me but what kind of America I believe in." And he went on to say, "I believe in an America where the separation of Church and State is absolute, where no Catholic prelate would tell the President should he be Catholic how to act and no Protestant minister would tell his parishioners for whom to vote, where no church or church school is granted any public funds or political preference, an America which is officially neither Protestant, Catholic nor Jewish, where no public official either requests or accepts instructions on public policy from any ecclesiastical source, where there is no Catholic vote, no anti-Catholic vote, no bloc voting of any kind, and where religious liberty is so indivisible that an act against one church is treated as an act against all." Then he continued, "The religious views of the American president must be his own affair, neither imposed by him upon a nation nor imposed by a nation upon him as a condition for holding that office. I am not the Catholic candidate for president. I am the Democratic party's candidate for president who happens also to be a Catholic. I do not speak for my Church on public matters and the Church does not speak for me."

He did not hesitate to say that he would resign his office rather than violate the national interests in order to avoid violating his conscience. He did not "see any conflict could be even remotely possible" but still he insisted that if such a conflict should occur, he would of course resign and added, "I hope that any conscientious public servant would do the same." The questions were hostile. He was asked if he would intercede with Cardinal Cushing to obtain the Pope's approval of his position. He replied by saying the words which were merely an echo of John Carroll, that no ecclesiastical official should intervene in public policy and no public official in ecclesiastical policy. He was asked if he had the approval of the Vatican for this statement and he said he did not need such approval. He was asked what his response would be if the Church would attempt to influence his public duties and he said "that he would reply to them that it was an improper action on their part, one to which I could not subscribe, that I was opposed to it, as an interference in the American political system." One wonders what the Houston ministers expected Kennedy to say and one wonders why they were apparently so surprised by what he said, why they asked whether it was necessary to clear his position with the Vatican since he said nothing more than had been said by a long string of American leaders from John Carroll until the late Archbishop John T. McNicholas of Cincinnati. One wonders if the ministers were intelligent enough to squirm when Kennedy said in his speech, "Side by side with Bowie and Crockett died McCafferty and Bailey and Carey but no one knows whether they were Catholics or not for there was no religious test at the Alamo."

We do not know how many of the Houston ministers were won away from their irrational prejudices that autumn evening. But at least enough Americans were won away so that John Kennedy would be elected President. And with the election, nativism at last gave up the ghost. The Kennedy Administration put to rest forever the fear that Catholicism was an alien religion and that Catholic political leaders would use their positions to interfere with American freedoms. What the hierarchy and clergy could not sell to the American non-Catholic population for two hundred years, John Kennedy did sell. Catholicism was as American as any other religion and respected human freedom as much as any other religion.

But nativism's death was a reluctant one and in its last dying gasp it cost John Kennedy (according to the Survey Research Center at the University of Michigan) some five million votes. Catholic liberals may well rejoice that the Kennedy election represented the official end of anti-Catholic prejudice in the United States; it surely did. But not by a very great margin—somewhat under 120,000 votes. One wonders what it would have done to American Catholic morale if

Kennedy had been beaten on grounds much more obviously religious than those which defeated Al Smith. It is worth remembering, as Ted Sorensen reminds us, that even "including only the two party vote, a majority of the voters outside of Massachusetts had voted against him. A majority of the states, 27 out of 50, had voted against him. A majority of his own race had voted against him. So had a majority of his fellow college graduates and his fellow high incomers. Contrary to crowd impressions, so had a majority of women voters, so had a majority of Protestants, farmers, small town inhabitants, and business and professional men." No, nativism did not die easily.

Religion had haunted John Kennedy through most of his national political life. His defeat in the 1956 Democratic vice-presidential battle was in part due to his religion. It is conceded that it would have been even more decisive if Lyndon Johnson had not overcome the anti-Catholic prejudice of the Texas delegation including Sam Rayburn to swing its fifty-six votes to Kennedy. (Four years after the Houston speech, Rayburn was finally won over and commented with admiration, "He ate them blood raw." In Texas, one gathers, this is a compliment.) During the Wisconsin primaries, he was asked by a TV panelist whether he would attend the summit meeting even if ordered not to do so by his bishop. ("Of course, I would," he snapped back.) Protestants and Other Americans United for Separation of Church and State (POAU) pamphlets flooded the state of Wisconsin during the primaries and some Lutheran pulpits in the state were centers for anti-Kennedy campaigning. In West Virginia the Humphrey campaign song was sung to the tune of "Give Me That Old-time Religion," and as one Democratic leader said, "Protestants have nothing against Kennedy, they think he's intelligent, but they are going to vote against him. That's the way they've been reared." And another observed, "People here aren't against Kennedy. They're simply concerned about the domination of the Catholic Church." Of course Kennedy was quite capable of striking back. In West Virginia he commented, "Are we to say that a Jew can be elected Mayor of

Dublin, a Protestant can be named foreign minister of France, a Moslem can sit in the Israeli parliament, but a Catholic cannot be president of the United States?"

After the Episcopal bishop of West Virginia announced his opposition to Kennedy, the candidate replied, "If religion is a valid issue in the presidential campaign, I shouldn't have served in the House, I shouldn't now be serving in the Senate, I shouldn't have been accepted by the United States Navy." But some of the non-Catholic clergy of West Virginia continued to distribute the hoary fake called the "Knights of Columbus Oath" and the drumfire of bigotry did not stop. Finally, the Kennedys succeeded in turning bigotry to their own purposes to make the issue whether West Virginia was a state composed of bigots and this "swept him to a landslide victory." But before he won he had to say some fairly incredible things, such as, he "would not take orders from any Pope, Cardinal, Bishop or priest, nor would they try to give me orders. If any Pope attempted to influence me as president, I would have to tell him it was completely improper. If you took orders from the Pope, you would be breaking your oath of office and commit a sin against God. You would be subject to impeachment and should be impeached."

A fair number of Catholics grew weary of this sort of speech and wondered why it was necessary for a presidential candidate to go to such extremes to assume the obviously ridiculous possibility that an ecclesiastic would tell him how to run the country. But what the Catholic critics did not seem to understand is that only the strongest sort of language would break through the hard shell of nativist prejudice.

After the convention and as the election campaign itself roared on, the prejudice continued. The POAU predicted that if the United States ever became 51 per cent Catholic, Protestants would be treated as second-class citizens and damned souls. A Protestant minister in Boston would say, "Like Khrushchev Kennedy is a captive of the system." Norman Vincent Peale remarked, "Our American culture is at stake. I don't say it won't survive but it won't be what it was." To which Kennedy is said to have remarked, "I would like to think he was complimenting me but I'm not sure he was." The Republicans were handling the religion issue very shrewdly (which is what one expects politicians to do with all issues). They continually mentioned the issue by continually reaffirming that it was not an issue, but for most people it was indeed not *an* issue but *the* issue of the campaign. Dr. Ramsay Pollard, the president of the Southern Baptist Convention, pointed out, "No matter what Kennedy might say, he cannot separate from his Church if he is a true Catholic. All we ask is that Roman Catholicism lift its bloody hand from the throats of those that want to worship in the church of their choice. I am not a bigot." And this same believer in free American elections also said, "My church has enough members to beat Kennedy in this area if they all vote like I tell them to." One wonders what would have happened if a Catholic bishop had said the same thing. Sorensen describes the intensity of the anti-Catholic campaign: "Well over three hundred anti-Catholic tracts distributed to more than twenty million homes and countless mailings, chain letters, radio broadcasts, television attacks, and even anonymous telephone calls inflamed and assaulted the voters' senses at a cost to someone of at least several hundred thousands of dollars. One rightist publication could not decide whether Kennedy's election was a Popish plot or a Communist conspiracy but thought the two worked together anyway. Another said Kennedy stirred up the religion issue to conceal the fact that he was a Communist. One theme persisted—that the Pope would soon be governing America."[1]

The Reverend Harvey Springer, a "cowboy evangelist of the Rockies," offered a solution: "Let the Romanists move out of America. Did you see the coronation of Big John? Let's hope we never see the coronation of Little John. How many Catholics came over on the Mayflower—not one. The

[1] Sorensen goes on with the following addition to the Pope John legend: "Bishop Wright had told me that in 1959 Pope John who had been trying to learn English asked him about Kennedy's chances. 'Very good,' Bishop Wright replied. And the Pope fully aware of the 1928 stories jokingly added, 'Do not expect me to run the country with a language as difficult as yours.' "

Constitution is a Protestant Constitution." And Dr. George L. Ford of the National Association of Evangelicals observed that "religion definitely should not be an issue in politics and wouldn't be if the Catholic Church hadn't made it so." But this did not prevent Dr. Ford's association from trying to turn Reformation Sunday on October 30 into an excuse for anti-Catholic sermons and rallies.

Kennedy did win the election. He did triumph over nativism and put it more or less permanently out of business. But we must not forget a half decade later what a tough battle it was and how close was the decision. In those early morning hours of the day after the election, it was by no means obvious that nativism had not won again. John Kennedy triumphed over it and earned for his ability at last to make Catholic doctrine clear at least an unofficial title of "doctor of the Church." But he just barely won.

American Catholicism itself was not always altogether kind to John Kennedy and at times, if Sorensen is to be believed, he was irate with the pettiness and the fussiness of some of the criticisms. Thus the Catholic press was inclined to take strong exception to his March, 1959, interview in *Look* magazine when he said, "Whatever one's religion in his private life may be, to the officeholder nothing takes precedence over his oath to uphold the Constitution and all its parts." The statement was surely unexceptionable, especially in the context in which it was made, but the *Kansas City Register* compared his reasoning with that used by Nazi war criminals. And the *Catholic Review* of Baltimore observed, "He appears to have gone overboard in an effort to placate the bigots." He was termed a poor Catholic, a poor politician, a poor moralist, and a poor wordsmith. Cardinal Cushing was ready to rush to his defense with an article but Kennedy and his staff dissuaded the cardinal from the intervention. He was further upset the same year when the American Catholic bishops in their Washington meeting condemned the term "population explosion" as a "terror technique phrase." Kennedy suspected that this was deliberately aimed at him since he had used the term "population explosion" frequently in his speeches and he was confirmed in his belief that the hierarchy did not want him to be a candidate. Later in the Wisconsin campaign he thought that a ban on Catholics joining the YMCA issued in the midst of the campaign was aimed at him also. He commented once at a meeting of Catholics, "In my experience monsignors and bishops are all Republicans while sisters are all Democrats."

Nor did he feel that his chances in the primaries were particularly helped when the Vatican newspaper *Osservatore Romano* told Catholics that the Church has the duty and right to tell them how to vote and Vatican "sources" were reported as saying that the editorial applied to Americans as well as others although it was believed to be aimed at Communist candidates, particularly in Italy. Kennedy replied by issuing a statement in which he said that his support of "Church state separation is not subject to change under any conditions." Sorensen tells us that his private comment was, "Now I understand why Henry VIII set up his own Church." He was inclined once more to suspect that the statement had been deliberately timed to harm his prospects. It probably had not been so timed and was more than likely aimed at the Italian situation. The references to the United States were probably dug up by American newspapermen looking for a story. It is most unlikely that the people responsible for the *Osservatore* editorial had any notion that it could be applied to the American presidential campaign. In line with its great historic tradition, Rome simply did not understand what was going on in the United States and in all fairness could probably not be expected to understand.

The most serious blow to Kennedy's election, however, and one which if he had lost would have received the principal blame was the incredible Puerto Rican affair. Kennedy had been persuaded previously that Cardinal Spellman's public appearances with Eisenhower and Nixon were indicative of the hierarchy's basic opposition to him. When the Puerto Rican hierarchy instructed Catholics on the island not to vote for Governor Luis Muñoz Marin, Kennedy was absolutely convinced that the hierarchy was trying to defeat him. He could not believe that such an incident would be unplanned. And the headlines in Protestant denominational papers, "They said it couldn't happen in America," were a sufficient sign to him that he was in trouble. He noted, said Sorensen, "If enough voters realize that Puerto Rico is on American soil, the election is lost." In retrospect, it seems most improbable that the Puerto Rican bishops realized how their action would be interpreted. Kennedy was wrong in thinking that the clergy and the hierarchy were against him (as was Reinhold Niebuhr when that worthy divine remarked in the *New Leader* that he was sure that most priests voted against Kennedy. One wonders how many priests Dr. Niebuhr knew and what kind of public opinion poll he conducted to arrive at his conclusion). There is every reason to believe that the things Kennedy interpreted as organized opposition were merely passing incidents that were inevitable manifestations of the pluralism of the American Church. And in the secrecy of the ballot box, it seems, at least to this observer, that most clergy and probably most of the bishops remembered enough of their ancestral origins to vote for the Democratic and Catholic candidate.

Even after the election, Kennedy could not understand why he seemed to be selected for special treatment by the nation's bishops. Thus even though his school aid program was not substantially different from his predecessor's on the subject of aid to religious schools, his bill received a denunciation which the Eisenhower bill never received. The Catholic magazine *America,* losing its usual "cool," wrote a blistering editorial attacking Kennedy for not supporting aid to parochial schools. It is fairly difficult even from the perspective of the years to believe that *America* expected the first Catholic President to commit political suicide. But if he had supported aid for Catholic schools, it is first of all most unlikely that he would have gotten it; and second, it is most unlikely that there ever would be another American Catholic as President of the United States. Kennedy's support for aid to Catholic schools (whatever his personal view on the subject may have been) would have been interpreted by the battered but not yet totally liquidated nativists as a sign that the Catholic President was using his power to aid the Church.

One hesitates even to mention the critical comment about the personal lives of the President and his wife (and especially their churchgoing) that could be heard in all sections of the Catholic population during the Kennedy Administration, and that occasionally even found its way into the Catholic press. The comment of one Catholic columnist, the late outspoken Monsignor Conway, that the President and Mrs. Kennedy's personal religious life was no one's business but their own and that to even ask a question about it was probably mortally sinful did not, unfortunately, represent a widely shared attitude. The personal morality of a President is always the subject of speculation but that Catholics should speculate about the religious fervor of their first President was a disgrace and a sign that the American Church was still in a state of adolescence.

But Kennedy was elected despite the violent opposition of the nativists and the sniping from within the Church. He did win the election and he did serve with brilliance for three crisis-ridden years. And when his presidency was tragically cut short, his "witness bearing" about the harmony between Catholicism and American political beliefs had done its work well. Sorensen remarks that the one kind of anti-Catholic bigotry that he was least able to understand was that which preyed on the nativists' fear that with a Catholic President Mass would be said in the White House. The President's alter ego informs us that Mass was celebrated there only once, on November 23, 1963. On that day nativism was finished.

But if John Kennedy as a doctor of the universal church spoke to American non-Catholics about Catholic doctrine, he also spoke to the Church and warned it of a dramatic change in its own position in American society. This message was much less explicit than his message to non-Catholics and he may not himself even have realized that he was speaking it. Surely most American Catholics did seem to have understood it. But Kennedy also taught the Church. Much of the future

of American Catholicism depends on whether the Church
heard what he had to say.

On Inauguration Day, 1961, American Catholicism had
come full circle. For the first time since the death of Charles
Carroll of Carrollton, the most important, the most famous,
the most powerful American Catholic was not a member of
the hierarchy. In the eyes of Americans, Catholics and non-
Catholics alike, when John Fitzgerald Kennedy put his hand
on the Douay Bible to take the presidential oath, he, and none
of the cardinals or the archbishops, was leader of the American Church. American Catholicism would for three years
and perhaps many years thereafter be judged not on what a
cardinal or a bishop might say but on what John Kennedy
would do. The era when Catholicism would be identified with
the organized Church was over, as was the day when *the*
Catholic position would be that which was espoused by the
bishops and priests of the Church. With a clearly providential
coincidence, the theology of the Vatican Council was at the
same time describing the Church in terms which would provide theoretical justification for the American Catholicism of
the post-Kennedy era in which a layman could with great
ease become the leader of American Catholics without trying
to and probably even without wanting to.

The collapse of nativism during the Kennedy years has
been hailed as a great victory for American Catholicism. The
Church has at least become fully accepted in American society. No one could possibly deny the extent of the dimensions
of the victory. But it is a victory for which a price must be
paid. Internal loyalty as a response to external opposition
and prejudice was one of the cements that held together the
structure of the American Church. That structure itself was
organized principally to resist the threats of a hostile society
to the faith and religious practice of the immigrants. But
with the collapse of external opposition, and the dramatic
elimination of bigotry, unquestioning loyalty to existing structures no longer seems so terribly important. A whole generation of post-Kennedy Catholics are growing up who, while
not necessarily opposed to the ecclesiastical structure, do not
feel the need to affirm profound loyalty to every element

of it as a prerequisite for cultural and religious identity. A garrison approach becomes quite irrelevant when there is no longer an enemy outside attacking the fortress. John Kennedy said to the American Church in effect, "The garrison days are over, the enemy is no longer to be taken too seriously. But you must now develop an ecclesiastical style and an ecclesiastical organization which is appropriate for a religion that is thoroughly accepted in American society."

One hundred forty-five years had passed since the death of John Carroll, and American Catholicism had survived the violent trauma of the immigration experience. It was now once again a legitimately native American Church (even though half of its members were still immigrants or the children of immigrants, its young people in their twenties and thirties were as likely to have graduated from college and to be as economically successful as Protestant Americans of the same age). Mistakes may have been made in handling the immigrant crisis. The opportunities provided by John England and the Americanists may have largely been wasted but still the Church could grow and prosper and maintain internal unity because of the profound cultural loyalty of most of the immigrant groups. But the Kennedy election proved that immigrant loyalty to an ecclesiastical organization as a protector of its own identity was rapidly becoming obsolete. The Americanization argument, which had raged since the death of John Carroll, was now over. The Catholic was in fact thoroughly Americanized, and since in post-Vatican theology the people are the Church, there was no escaping the inevitable logic which said that the Catholic Church in America had become Americanized. The only question that remained was whether the structure of the organization and the style of American Catholicism would also become as Americanized as its population. If it could become thoroughly American as an ecclesiastical institution not only in theory but in practice, then the dream of Carroll, England, and Keane would have at last come true. If it could not (and this is the great peril of post-Kennedy Catholicism), then organized Catholicism in the United States will offer little in the way of relevance to the lives of the young Catholics who looked to John Kennedy as their hero and their saint and their doctor of the Church. They will not, for the most part, leave the Church. They will continue to receive the sacraments from it but they will not be able to take the organized ecclesiastical structure very seriously. Instead of obtaining from it the religious leadership and the wisdom that they have reason to expect and even to require, they will feel themselves increasingly embarrassed by its lack of understanding of the religious dimensions of modern life.

The best of the young Catholic laity today seem to be much like John Kennedy in their lack of interest in the internal affairs of the Church. They are not interested, as he was not, in belonging to Catholic organizations. They are not stirred up, as he was not, by the class-conflict rhetoric of the so-called laity-clergy struggle. They could not care less, as he could not, about how the ecclesiastical structure spends its funds, makes administrative decisions, governs its schools. The "non-issues" which bestir much of the Catholic press are of no more interest to them than they were to John Kennedy. They will be loyal to the Church as he was but they will be completely disinterested in the internal bickering going on among those, lay and clerical, whose principal concerns are the internal affairs of the Church. And they will think that those who ask the question, "Would Catholic schools have spoiled JFK?" are asking a totally silly and irrelevant question, just as one suspects that the late President himself would have thought it a silly and irrelevant question, since Catholic schools did not spoil either Eugene McCarthy or Richard J. Daley. The Kennedy posture of loyalty to the Church, and suspicion of the ecclesiastical structure blended with gentle fun-poking at it, will become the expected behavior for those Catholics of the post-Kennedy generation who are committed to the worlds of economics, politics, and social reconstruction. It is most unlikely that the social action in Catholic action organizations of the pre-conciliar Church will have any more attraction for them than it did for John Kennedy.

The harsh truth of the matter is that while John Kennedy was a loyal Catholic and, as we have suggested earlier, by ancient standards a saintly Catholic, he did not seem to perceive any connection between the teachings of his religion and his social and political commitment, nor much relationship between the morality of his Church and the problems he faced in the world's most important office. The Catholicism of the Irish parish in Boston was scarcely relevant (to use a much overworked word) to the President of the United States.

Perhaps some of the blame for this can be attributed to his own background. At no point in his life did he come in contact with a vital and imaginative nonparochial Catholicism of the sort which, for example, had a deep influence on Senator Eugene McCarthy or on some of the younger members of the Irish Mafia in Kennedy's own staff. But if enough examples of a thoroughly Americanized social Catholicism do exist in the country so that some of the national leaders of the Catholic faith can be influenced by it, it has by no means become so typical of American Catholic life that you cannot escape being influenced by it. If John Kennedy could not find much in his Church that was especially important to him as President of the United States, most of the explanation could be attributed to the fact the Church was still so concerned with its internal problems that it had not even begun to turn to those issues which would plague a President of the United States. Before Kennedy was elected, this was a failure that need not have been disastrous. But in the post-Kennedy age, the American Church must either change its narrow and predominantly parish-oriented focus or find that it is simply not speaking to the vast majority of its people, particularly its most important people.

The concern about maintaining the internal structure as the most important of all goals was certainly legitimate during the long immigration crisis but now that the immigration crisis is definitively over, the time has come for American Catholicism once again to speak openly and freely to an American society of which it is an integral part, both in its membership and in its organizational polity. Short of such a drastic change, American Catholicism will simply lose for all practical purposes the Kennedys of the future.

I sometimes think that what is needed is a Kennedy bishop or perhaps in our day and age even a Kennedy cardinal. For just as a Carroll bishop was required to give birth to American Catholicism, it could be that a relative of the most important Catholic layman since John Carroll could give American Catholicism some sort of rebirth. It is not terribly necessary that the leading figure in the American hierarchy who will emerge in the years to come be actually a member of the clan Kennedy (though one would be sadly mistaken to assume that none of the younger generation of Kennedys would be interested in the priesthood, and that they would not bring to the priesthood the same style that their elders have brought to political life). What is needed, no matter what his name, is an ecclesiastical leader who will speak to the United States and particularly to the young people of the United States with the same flair, the same vigor, the same vision that John Kennedy brought to the White House. Another and more sociological way of stating the matter would be to say that American Catholicism, if it is not to lose the post-Kennedy generation, must reorganize its internal structure in such a fashion that it is possible for a hierarchial leader of the Kennedy variety to emerge. Or at least it must be so reorganized that if an ecclesiastical Kennedy (real or symbolic) should arrive on the scene he would not be relegated as John England was to Charleston, South Carolina, nor would he, as John Ireland and John Keane were, be condemned at least implicitly for holding a heresy that never existed anywhere.

The Catholic population has become Americanized. The ecclesiastical structure has yet to follow suit. It missed the marvelous opportunities presented to it in its past, and the Americanizers, whatever their theoretical triumphs, were not always practically successful. The Catholic Church found itself in the early 1960s with a President to whom it could say little more except publicly, "Why don't you support Catholic schools?" and privately, "Why don't you receive communion more often?" For all its multitudinous organizational successes, for all the brilliance with which it protected the faith of the immigrants, American Catholicism's inability to respond to the phenomenon of John Kennedy in a more imaginative and creative way must be marked as a tragic failure. And by his relative indifference to what he presumably deemed the trivial internal concerns of Catholicism, JFK sat in judgment on this failure, probably without meaning to do so. John Kennedy spoke as a doctor of the Church, a teacher of the Church. What he said in effect to American Catholicism was, "Your people are changing, the world in which they are living is changing, and you are slowly but surely losing touch with them because they have become thoroughly American, and you, for all your patriotism and loyalty, have not yet become American in the methods with which you organize and govern your Church. You are committed to the attitudes, the techniques, the secrecy, the fears of the problems of another age and another world. You have not been true even to the best in your own traditions. You have not followed your flexible and pragmatic instincts nearly as far as you might. For all your devout Americanism, you have not had the nerve to become thoroughly American as an ecclesiastical institution. You have not had the courage to listen to the prophecy of Carroll, England, and Gibbons. You will either do so or in the long run my inauguration will not mark the beginning of a new era in American Catholicism but rather the beginning of the end. The young people who come after me will not drift away from the Church. They will remain, as I was, loyal Catholics but they will not find their Church very relevant. If history teaches you anything, it is that when you cease to become relevant to the needs and the problems and the opportunities and the expectations of your people then in the long run you will certainly lose them. You will either heed my warning or ultimately suffer the same fate as the Catholicism of North Africa after the death of Augustine."

We cannot imagine, of course, that John Kennedy ever thought those exact words, but nonetheless this is the lesson of the Kennedy years for the American Catholic Church. The Americanizers have finally won, belatedly but definitively. And the ecclesiastical structure will either catch up with them or over the years atrophy. The election of a Catholic President has provided the American Church with another opportunity of the sort that it experienced in 1820 with John England and in 1885 with the Americanists. But this opportunity could well be the last one.

X

IN CONCLUSION
The Continuing Crisis

In 1959, those of us who were to speak at the National Liturgical Conference at Notre Dame, Indiana, received a confidential letter several weeks before the meeting beseeching us not to discuss the possibility of vernacular in the liturgy. We were told that for the first time some of the members of the hierarchy would be present at the conference and might be offended if the vernacular liturgy was mentioned. The planners of the conference could have saved their money as far as I was concerned. Discreet and prudent young cleric that I was, I had absolutely no intention of mentioning the vernacular because I did not realistically think that there was any hope in the foreseeable future for substantial changes in the language of the Roman liturgy.

Within five years, the same hierarchy whom the liturgical planners feared would be offended by reference to the vernacular voted almost unanimously for a substantially vernacular Mass in the United States and two years later would, by a three-to-one vote, ask Rome for a completely English Mass. The nature of the change within American Catholicism is illustrated not only by the dramatic reversal of the position of the hierarchy on the subject of an English liturgy but also by the fact that large numbers of progressive Catholics would be far more critical of what they consider the bishops' slowness in matters liturgical now than they would have been ten

years ago. Those who would have been satisfied with just a
touch of English in 1959 now would not be satisfied short of
a drastic restructuring of the entire sacred liturgy. Changes
have taken place but expectations have changed far more
rapidly than reality. Or as one wise observer puts it, "It is
only when the cork is out, that the fizz froths up."[1]

The vernacular liturgy is perhaps more important symbol-
ically than substantively as a symbol of the pace of change in
American Catholicism. But the continuing crisis over liturgy
is symbolic of the problems of American Catholicism as it
approaches the two-hundredth anniversary of John Carroll's
return to Rock Creek. Change is taking place at what, by the
standards of even a decade ago, would have been considered
an astonishing pace. Yet change does not seem to alleviate the
continuing crisis. On the contrary, it often seems that the
more change that occurs the more serious the crisis becomes. The certainties that spanned the years from the clan
Carroll to the clan Kennedy are gone never to be recaptured,
and the quest for new certainties begun in a rather leisurely

[1] Another interesting sign of the change was the unhappy experience of the present writer at the 1959 Liturgical Week. The only
mid-August convention I'd ever been to was of the Hillenbrand
Catholic action variety where sport shirts were the required uniform. Naïvely assuming that this was to be the case at all meetings
when the temperature was ninety-five and never having been to a
liturgical conference before, I appeared in the ancient Drill Hall
at Notre Dame clad in a black and white sport shirt (it was not a
loud sport shirt, despite claims of the Catholic press to the contrary). Somewhat to my horror, I arrived on the platform to find
that one of my fellow panelists was attired in a cassock and the
other (a layman) in suit and tightly buttoned tie. It developed
very rapidly after the panel was over that few, if any, of the swel-
tering throng paid much attention to what I said and that my black
and white sport shirt had become a *cause célèbre*. I was hailed by
the liberal liturgists as a daring innovator and condemned by the
conservatives as having poor taste. I also gathered that at least
some of the handful of bishops present were far more concerned
about my black and white sport shirt than they were about the
possibility of vernacular liturgy. Alas, for the happy, bygone days
in the American Church when a sport shirt could create a crisis
and one could become a hero overnight by no more radical an act
than not wearing a Roman collar when the temperature in South
Bend, Indiana, was in the middle nineties.

fashion now seems to be almost frantic. One does not really need to read much of the past history of the Catholic Church in the United States to suspect that a crisis similar to that of the 1820s and of the 1890s has come upon the Church. One even senses that the present crisis makes the other two look mild by comparison.

The severity of the current transitional situation results from the fact that it is in reality the result of the intersection of two transitions. The American Church has finally and definitively left behind the immigrant ghetto and is wrestling with the problem of whether it can keep up with the Americanization of its population. In previous decades of the Church's history, one element of the hierarchical structure was ahead of part of the Catholic population in the process of Americanization and was pushing toward fuller adaptation to American society. But at the present time, most of the population seems to be somewhat ahead of most of the hierarchical structure in adjusting to American society. The fluidity of such a transition is aggravated by the fact that simultaneously the church universal is changing its stance and its style from that appropriate to the garrison church of the Counter Reformation to the open church of the ecumenical age. In leaving behind the values and methods of the post-Tridentine world and seeking values and methods appropriate for the post-Vatican world, the entire Church is struggling through an agonized period of growth and transition.

The combination of these two transitions from slum to suburb and from the Counter Reformation to the ecumenical age has produced a situation of great and at times critical instability; there are great hopes and easy disappointments, brilliant expectations and gnawing fears, generous impulses and stubborn last-ditch parochialism. To revert to the image quoted previously, the fizz is pouring out of the bottle and some of it may be spilled before the contents are transferred to a newer and more appropriate container.

The impact of the present transitions is different on different segments of the population. The most important group (which we can call the liberal elite) would include many clergy, most of the younger clergy and religious, significant portions of the well-educated adult laity, and those youthful laity who are most concerned about the Church. The exact size of the liberal elite is hard to fix but surely it could not be much above the eighty thousand circulation of the *National Catholic Reporter*. Such a relatively small group could be dismissed as quite unimportant if it did not include most of the potential leadership (and virtually all of the young potential leadership), whose dedication and enthusiasm are essential to see the Church through transitional crises. Some of the liberal elite are evolutionists who would be content with growth from the existing structures toward a substantially modified future ecclesiastical organism. Others, perhaps a smaller number, are revolutionaries who expect nothing from the present structure and feel that it must either be destroyed or permitted to wither so that a fresh and new start may be made. Within the liberal elite there are also to be found most Catholic intellectuals, journalists, social actionists, and ideological liberals. Some of them face the problems of transition in the Church with a dispassionate and long-range view which would be characteristic of a scholar or man of wisdom. But others of the liberal elite are restless, impatient, frustrated. They are swept along by fads and fashions and quickly fashion a rigid and inflexible party line. They have their heroes and their villains and their moods oscillate between great exultation and great depression. Papal and episcopal documents are analyzed with the same harsh fundamentalism of a right-wing Protestant Scripture scholar and the internal problems of the Church become such an obsession that they are unable to focus either on problems outside the Church or the progress of the very recent past. The members of the liberal elite are loyal, even passionately loyal to the ideals of the Church, but impatient, even passionately impatient with imperfections and what seems to them to be the agonizingly slow pace of renewal. The Pope, the bishops, the clergy, the lay masses, the ecclesiastical structure (particularly the Catholic schools) are seen as obstacles to the mission of the Church. The more volatile of the liberal elite are caught between a fear that the whole tottering structure will collapse and an eager hope that it will collapse. In their judgment the opportunities are great, the failings are immense, and the prospects for the future are generally rather bleak.

The second group we can dub the conservative elite. Although it is much harder to judge the size of this group, it does not seem to be nearly as articulate or well organized as the liberal elite. Some of its members make a calm and carefully reasoned case against change, arguing that the Catholic Church has no business trying to adjust to the modern world but rather must await eventual collapse of the modern world to build a new Christendom. Others would place the Church outside of culture and would permit it to sit in judgment on culture but not directly influence it.

The more numerous group of the conservative elite does not have such a well-thought-out position. Those members of the clergy and hierarchy who could be considered part of the conservative elite frequently are opposed to change because they are suspicious of or frightened about change or because they cannot accept it or integrate it into their personality systems. Their opposition to change marks them off from the conservative masses only because they are in a position of power and influence sufficiently strong to inhibit the pace of change.

By far the largest group within the American Church is what we could call the "liberal masses." These are the people who are sympathetic with some or most or all of the changes in the Church but take their position more out of instinct or convenience or prejudice without having fully understood or thought out the issues at stake. The size of the liberal masses is hard to estimate because many people are able to be liberal on one question and more conservative on another. Recent data would suggest that three-quarters of the population are in favor of liturgical change and more than half are in sympathy with changes on sexual morality, divorce, and clerical celibacy. While such items, of course, are only indicators of general attitudes and may not be in themselves of critical importance, they do suggest that there is a broad base of popular support for renewal and change within the Church. Curiously enough, it would seem that many of those who are in sympathy with liturgical change and sexual change were quite upset by the, from the theological view, relatively minor change in Friday abstinence. This would suggest that the liberal masses may be rather unpredictable and inconsistent. Changes which make life easier for them (birth control, for example) or improve the attractiveness of the Church's liturgy are relatively easy to accept. But changes which touch something which to them is at the core of Christianity (Friday abstinence) are more strongly resented than other modifications in Church policy or practice.

The final group are the conservative masses—that body of Catholics which are deeply and profoundly upset by the modifications of the post-conciliar age and feel that the whole structure of the religion is crumbling about them as elements of Christianity thought to be essential are discarded with reckless speed. Frequently it would appear that this group is the one that policy makers have the most in mind in setting the pace of change and formulating the public pronouncements. However, available statistical data would suggest that the hard-core conservative masses are relatively small in size. The opposition, for example to liturgical change, represents certainly no more than one-quarter of the Catholic adult population and perhaps considerably less than that. Even though other issues such as birth control or clerical celibacy produce larger conservative votes, there do not seem to be intense feelings on these issues among most people who take conservative stands. Therefore the image of a large group of relatively unsophisticated Catholics whose faith is being threatened by the post-Vatican renewal or who may be "scandalized" by the questioning of previously unquestioned elements within the Church seems to be largely a myth.

One of the strange ironies of contemporary Catholicism in the United States is that the overwhelming majority of the Catholic masses are far more sympathetic to modification (often, in the context of the present volume, this would mean Americanization) than the leadership groups within the Church are aware. It is possible, of course, that some leaders use the myth of the reluctant laity as a cover for their own fears and uncertainties, but it also seems quite apparent that many leaders are genuinely concerned about how the conservative masses will react. The available statistical data suggest that the conservative masses are a relatively small minority and that they are not inclined either to lose their faith or leave the Church because of the changes to which they do not subscribe. These data would suggest therefore that the critical problem for leadership is holding the allegiance of the liberal elites and clarifying in the minds of the undiscriminating liberal masses what elements in Catholicism admit of change and what ones do not. If this indeed is the principal problem with which the leadership groups must wrestle, it would seem a rather different leadership style is in order from the one presently exhibited.

A division of the Catholic population in the youthful age levels and particularly those currently in college might be somewhat different. There is a small group of rather surly and antagonistic rebels who would be willing to go much further than the left-wing members of the liberal elite in pulling down the ecclesiastical structure. There is a minuscule group of new conservatives who seem eager to recapture for themselves and their children post-Tridentine Catholicism. There is, thirdly, a large mass of generally bored and apathetic young people who resent the remnants of compulsory religion to be encountered on the Catholic campuses, are gravely skeptical of a number of traditional moral stances, and are more or less disinterested in the problems of ecclesiastical structure and the questions of renewal in the Church. Perhaps the most disturbing element of this phenomenon is the lack of interest. Catholic adults, whether they be for or against change, whether they be well informed or relatively uninformed, are at least interested. The apathy of college students is not such as to lead them out of the Church (though some of the liberal left will temporarily depart from the Church) but it does suggest that among this group there is a possibility of a very notable growth of religious indifferentism, which was quite unknown among their parents.

There is one last youthful group that ought to be mentioned, a group that I have dealt with elsewhere—"the new breed." Included in this element of the population are the "volunteers" and other young enthusiasts who have sublime faith that the Church is going *their* way and that eventually they will, either as laity or clergy, form the new shape of American Catholicism. This group is not particularly large but matches John Ireland in self-confidence if not in the absence of self-doubt. The members of the new breed, after they have progressed through their "crisis of faith" or their "identity crisis" experience, represent one of the more encouraging aspects of the contemporary Catholic scene in the United States. Even though they may know little or nothing of the Americanizing tradition, they are products of it and perhaps the best hope for its future development.

While the new-breed members of the clergy and religious are generally rather confident of the future, confusion and ambiguity still persist among most of the professional religious functionaries in the American Church. Anticlericalism is at its strongest in the clergy and religious and morale is perhaps lower than anywhere else in the Catholic population, a problem which is probably the basic reason for the drastic decline in vocations in recent years. Since the young priests and religious who are the ones most likely to attract new candidates for the religious life are themselves also the most likely to be confused and unhappy in the ambiguities of the present transitional situation, it would not be too much to suggest that at the present time the most serious crisis facing American Catholicism is the steady deterioration in the morale of its own professionals.

American Catholicism therefore approaches the future with a restless liberal elite, a vaguely dissatisfied liberal mass that wants more rapid change but does not understand either the theories or dynamics of change, a youthful population that is bored and apathetic about many religious questions, and a clergy and religious caught in a crisis of ambiguity for which it was not trained.

There are a number of characteristics of the present situation of continuing crisis that result from the situation described in the previous paragraphs.

1. There is more questioning going on than ever before in the history of the American Church. The most radical of the

Americanizers of the past would not have dreamed of questioning the dogmatic and moral tenets and organizational styles which are now under re-evaluation. While much of the questioning is based on the premise that the manner of explanation rather than essential belief is being re-examined, it is nonetheless true that until very recently many of the current re-evaluations would have been taken as direct assaults on the very nature of the Church itself. The re-examination of traditional moral, dogmatic, and organizational formulation unquestionably shakes the basic religious commitment of many of the people who are engaging in the re-evaluation, although the freedom to re-evaluate probably keeps in the Church a number of Catholic intellectuals who in a previous generation would have felt they had no choice but to leave. In the long run the freedom to re-evaluate basic formulations insofar as they are formulations will probably represent net gain for the Church. But at the present time it involves a considerable amount of anxiety and insecurity both for liberals who are doing the re-evaluating and the conservatives who are shocked by it.

2. At least among those over thirty, there is a great deal of interest and enthusiasm for the Church. Many of the old ethnically-linked loyalties are collapsing, but the result of the continuing re-evaluation has not been religious apathy but, rather, heightened religious interest. Nor has this interest been limited to Catholics, since the renewal of the Catholic Church has been front-cover and front-page news for the last five years. Vocations may be declining, the reception of the sacraments may have leveled off, and convert ranks may have gone down, but interest, controversy, and commitment to vigorous criticism have gone up. A good deal of anger suppressed in the past has been released and many basic religious attitudes of the past are being reoriented. But it would be difficult to describe the ferment that results from these drastic changes as being the last gasp of an organism which is about to expire. Many on both the liberal and conservative sides are persuaded that the decline in the indicators of religious activity as well as the greater freedom to question and challenge traditional formulations and traditional author-

ity represents the beginning of the death throes for Catholicism in the United States. But one could just as easily interpret
the available data as suggesting that a style of Catholicism
which was appropriate for an immigrant era might indeed
be in its death throes, but that a vastly different and more
thoroughly Americanized style is struggling to emerge. The
freedom of discussion, the conscious efforts to formulate
public opinion, the insistence on free speech and the rights
of appeal, and the need for consultation and consensus combined with an emphasis on flexibility and pragmatic evalu-
ations of hoary traditions can easily be viewed as simply a
new stage in the Americanization experience. It is possible
therefore to view the current situation as being merely the
logical result of the tradition of Carroll, England, Hecker,
Ireland, Spalding, and Keane—though one would have to
note that the Americanists of the present push the tradition
much further than any of the predecessors would have
thought possible.

3. The collapse of morale that we described earlier as
being characteristic of many clergy and religious is at its most
intense within Catholic education. While the persistent criticism of the Catholic schools from some of the liberal elite
has as yet had little effect on the general Catholic population,
it has badly shaken the confidence of many religious educators who are of course avid readers of the journals for
which the liberal critics write. Given the unhistorical and anti-
theoretical approach of the American Church in the past
century and a half, it was not at all surprising that the theoretical basis for a separate Catholic school system was relatively thin. The argument of John Hughes that the faith of
Catholics would be endangered in the public school system
along with very elevated statements from papal encyclicals
about developing the "whole man" have provided most of
the theory on which the separate Catholic school system has
rested. But recent empirical data have shown that the public
schools do not in fact threaten the faith of most Catholics
and that the education of the whole man includes more than
just the school and that indeed the school will be largely
unsuccessful in this activity if its efforts are not re-enforced

by the family. Thus when critics with precious little in the way of empirical evidence at their disposal begin to attack the separate Catholic school system, the educators themselves, very sensitive to the need for change in the Church and conscious of the weakness of the theory that has been traditionally offered, find themselves at a loss to provide new theoretical justification. They therefore assume very quickly that such a theoretical justification does not exist and that much of their life and work has been wasted. Such a collapse of morale and such a docile retreat in the face of criticism could only happen to a group whose theoretical and historical resources were weak. Whether Catholic education survives as a distinct entity in the next quarter century depends to a considerable extent on its own ability to develop a far higher level of historical and theoretical sophistication among its teachers and administrators.

4. The unhistorical and anti-theoretical approach is by no means limited to Catholic educators. Most of the leadership elite in the Catholic Church are effected at least to some extent by anti-intellectualism. Patient research and planning in preparation for change does not seem to be deemed necessary. Experts and consultants are used on an *ad hoc* basis and then only to provide detailed answers to specific questions. Almost all of the questions are posed in terms of techniques and methods and little or no attention is paid either to broad overarching goals or to even the possibility of re-examining the institutions which new methodology is expected to support. Research and scholarship are not rejected in themselves but neither are they conceded the respect which would enable them to provide any more than *ad hoc* answers to highly specific questions. The theoretical questioning of goals and a historical examination of existing institutions do not seem to be very purposeful to large sections of the leadership elite. Innovation and change are not rejected but frequently turned in the direction of eagerness to try new gimmicks instead of attempts for more profound understanding. The Catholic universities have contributed extremely little to basic research on the theoretical and practical problems that the Church faces in contemporary American society and hence

those looking to establish new institutions rarely if ever think of turning to the universities for help. The absence of theoretical concern in a university's graduate schools simply means that the universities have not progressed far beyond the Americanization level reached by the masses of the Catholic population. Unfortunately while a simple-minded and anti-theoretical pragmatism may be quite useful in times of relative stability, it becomes a distinct liability in times of extreme fluidity and change. In such a crisis, the untheoretical man grabs eagerly for new tricks not merely because he's afraid of striving for deeper understanding but also and more importantly because he simply does not know how to do so.

5. At the core of the continuing crisis in American Catholicism is the crisis of leadership—a crisis that is marked by great nervousness and anxiety in some elements of the leadership elite and by a loss of confidence in the credibility and courage of the leadership elite on the part of some other members of the Church. Curiously enough, the problem is rather more frequently a problem of style rather than substance. The pace of implementation of the Vatican Council in the United States surely cannot be said to lag behind the pace in most of the other countries of the Catholic world in terms of what is in fact being done. Indeed perhaps more has been done in American Catholicism to implement the council than has been done anywhere else in the world. The problem is not what is being done but rather with the way it is being done. The confidence of the liberals, both elite and mass, in the leadership is not threatened so much by the facts of renewal as it is by the rhetoric of renewal.

One comes away from contact with this rhetoric having the distinct impression that articulate and vocal elements within the leadership elite see the basic problem of Catholic progress in the United States to be the necessity of avoiding too much speed. Warnings are constantly issued about dangers of shocking or scandalizing the majority of the faithful who are ready for change. Reassurances are issued to this same presumed threatened majority of the faithful that they should not be afraid, because change and progress will be very gradual. Stern injunctions are proclaimed about the need for uniformity lest the faithful be shocked by the confusion of flexibility and experimentation. There is to be seen a considerable amount of hand-wringing about the dangers that too rapid change would mean for the future of the American Church, and grim forebodings are expressed about the future decline of Catholicism in the United States.

Many things can be said about the image of the reluctant lay majority described in the previous paragraph. First of all, while it is a useful myth for reassuring those elements of the leadership elite that are committed only to token changes, it has precious little relationship to reality. All the available empirical evidence suggests that on the contrary there is a broad and fairly general consensus that is not only sympathetic toward rapid change but positively eager for it. The myth of the reluctant laity simply does not accord with the facts. Second, those who fear that the faith of the lay masses is going to be shaken and perhaps destroyed by change demonstrate very little confidence in the strength and vigor of the faith of the people. The faith that is so delicate that it has to be preserved completely from ambiguity and confusion would not be much of a faith at all. If this were the best the American Church could boast of after almost two hundred years of existence, it would have to count itself a rather serious failure. Third, it is to be wondered whether the fear of change that it is claimed exists in the Catholic lay population is not in reality a projection of the personal fears and insecurity of those members of the leadership group who simply do not know how to contend with the ambiguities of the present moment.

By no means all or even a majority of leadership groups share such a nervous and pessimistic view of the possibilities of the present and the immediate future, but they have been perhaps frightened into silence by the anxieties of those whom Pope John called the prophets of doom. The more confident leadership elements continue to push their own plans for further growth, change, and Americanization but they do so silently, hedging their bets as it were, against the possibility that the prophets of disaster might after all be right.

If the assumptions of this chapter and indeed of this whole

book are correct, the rhetoric of caution, slowness, uniformity, and anxiety (coupled with occasional arbitrary actions
against vocal and articulate liberals), far from avoiding disaster, will actually in fact cause disaster. Given the sympathy
for change and the restlessness of substantial segments of the
Catholic population, the only sort of leadership rhetoric that
would be appropriate would be rhetoric that would emphasize
courage, confidence, and vision. A liberalizing rhetoric rather
than a restrictive one has ceased to be optional for a contemporary Catholicism in the United States, and such a
rhetoric would be particularly appropriate both because it
would probably reflect more accurately the personal feelings
of most of the leadership elite and would also be more in
keeping with the historical tradition of the Americanists and
the Americanizers within the Catholic Church in the United
States. If anyone wishes to learn what is the rhetorical style
that is most appropriate for leadership in the Church in the
United States in this continuing crisis of renewal, he should
perhaps reread the lives of Carroll, England, Hecker, Ireland,
and Keane. It is to be very much doubted that any of these
men would be frightened by the problems of the present time.
What is needed now perhaps more than anything else is the
self-confidence of the Americanists; or, not to put the matter
too weakly, what we need now is the almost arrogant self-
confidence of a John Ireland.

In conclusion, we may well ask what the prognosis is for
American Catholicism and particularly for the Americanizing
tradition within Catholicism, which has come to what is without a doubt its most serious crisis. The long-run outlook is
excellent. The similarity of viewpoint between the young
clergy and the young laity suggests that whenever the new
breed does succeed in taking over American Catholicism, it
will complete the work of Americanization begun by John
Carroll. Furthermore, the vigor and enthusiasm of the present
controversies would indicate that there is still an intense
commitment on the part of American Catholics to their
Church. One can only criticize as vigorously as the present
critics do when one is terribly concerned about the object of
criticism. The American Church has at its disposal awesome

resources of energy, talent, personnel, and finance. The principal problem, as we hinted before, may be more the rhetoric and style of its leadership than anything else. Under such circumstances, it would be very difficult to be pessimistic about the long-run prospects for the Americanizing element and its tradition.

However, the short-run situation is much more dubious. It is not evident how much is going to have to be lost in the short run before the pace of growth and change and renewal hits its stride, or to put the matter differently, how much has to be destroyed by revolution before the barriers to organic and evolutionary growth are removed. Ideally that growth is the most healthy which is able to salvage the maximum out of the past and the present (despite the enthusiasm of radicals for tearing away existing structures). It is still true that the more the existing structures are destroyed, the more difficult growth becomes. Far from being an asset, the blotting out of the past from the present is a frightful liability in attempting to develop the future. An optimism that does not believe that American Catholicism is going to have to pay a high price in present loss in order to produce future growth would be based on faith, perhaps, but on relatively little evidence that is observable at the present time. As we have hinted before, the most critical issue in the continuing crisis is the issue of the quality of leadership in the next few years. Much will depend on how imaginative, creative, sensitive, flexible, competent, and visionary the style and rhetoric of leadership can become. From this perspective, the most serious problem facing American Catholicism at the present time is the possible loss of nerve in the leadership elite.

In the midst of a nervous era when one set of certainties has been lost and a new set is still in formation, one can choose the posture of either fear or hope. The posture that one ultimately chooses needs of course to have some relationship with the evidence that reality offers. But it also transcends evidence and becomes a manifestation of who one is, out of what tradition one has come, and what one's basic orientations toward reality are. If anxiety, fear, insecurity, and nervousness represent the posture one ultimately chooses, then no evidence in the world can prove one absolutely wrong. But the basic conclusion of the present volume has to be that such a choice is at variance with both the tradition and the experience of the Catholic Church in the United States, and those who make such a choice will someday have to answer for it to Carroll, England, Hecker, Brownson, Keane, Spalding, Ireland, Gibbons, Ryan, and John Kennedy.

OTHER IMAGE BOOKS

A MARITAIN READER – Selected Writings of Jacques Maritain – Edited with an Introduction by Donald and Idella Gallagher (D210) – $1.45

JOY – Bertrand Weaver, C.P. A series of meditations on the concept of joy (D211) – 75¢

THE CHURCH TOMORROW – George H. Tavard (D212) – 85¢

POPE JOHN AND HIS REVOLUTION – E. E. Y. Hales (D213) – 85¢

THE TWO-EDGED SWORD – John L. McKenzie, S.J. Outstanding interpretation of the Old Testament (D215) – $1.35

THIS IS THE MASS, New and Revised Edition – Described by Henri Daniel-Rops. Celebrated by Fulton J. Sheen. Photographed by Karsh (D216) – $1.25

THE CHURCH IN AN AGE OF REVOLUTION: 1789–1870 (2 Volumes) – Henri Daniel-Rops (D217a, D217b) – $1.35 ea.

MORTE D'URBAN – J. F. Powers. A brilliant, poignantly satiric portrait of a worldly priest (D218) – 95¢

OUR CHILDREN GROW UP – Mary Reed Newland. A common-sense guide for Catholic parents (D219) – 85¢

THE INNER SEARCH – Dom Hubert van Zeller, O.S.B. Meditations with a refreshingly new approach (D220) – 95¢

STRANGERS IN THE HOUSE: Catholic Youth in America – Andrew M. Greeley (D221) – 95¢

THE DEPTHS OF THE SOUL: A Christian Approach to Psychoanalysis – Ignace Lepp (D222) – 95¢

COUNT BOHEMOND – Alfred Duggan. Preface by Evelyn Waugh. A novel of the First Crusade (D223) – 95¢

A FIGHT FOR GOD (2 Volumes) – Henri Daniel-Rops. This ninth volume of the *History of the Church of Christ* covers the period from 1870 to 1939 (D224a, D224b) – $1.45 ea.

THE LILIES OF THE FIELD – William E. Barrett (D225) – 75¢

LETTERS TO NANCY – from Andrew M. Greeley (D226) – 85¢

CHRIST AND THE CHRISTIAN – Robert W. Gleason, S.J. (D227) – 95¢

THE FAMILY AND THE BIBLE – Mary Reed Newland (D228) – $1.25

THE DIVIDING OF CHRISTENDOM – Christopher Dawson (D229) – 95¢

OUR CHANGING LITURGY – C. J. McNaspy, S.J. (D230) – 95¢

NO MAN IS AN ISLAND – Thomas Merton (D231) – 95¢

AND YOUNG MEN SHALL SEE VISIONS – Andrew M. Greeley. Letters to a young collegian on subjects of burning interest to young men today (D232) – 85¢

ROAD TO RENEWAL – Bernard Häring, C.SS.R. (D233) – 95¢

CONJECTURES OF A GUILTY BYSTANDER – Thomas Merton. A collection of notes, opinions, reflections (D234) – $1.25

OTHER IMAGE BOOKS

OTHER IMAGE BOOKS

ON THE LOVE OF GOD (2 Volumes) – St. Francis de Sales. Translated and with an Introduction by John K. Ryan (D164a, D164b) – 95¢ ea.

LIFE OF ST. DOMINIC – Bede Jarrett, O.P. (D165) – 75¢

IN SOFT GARMENTS – Ronald Knox. Treats the problems that face today's Catholics (D166) – 75¢

THE YEAR AND OUR CHILDREN: Planning the Family Activities for the Church Year – Mary Reed Newland (D167) – $1.25

THE CHURCH IN CRISIS: A History of the General Councils, 325–1870 – Philip Hughes (D168) – $1.25

ISRAEL AND THE ANCIENT WORLD – Henri Daniel-Rops (D169) – $1.55

THE SPIRITUAL EXERCISES OF ST. IGNATIUS – Translated by Anthony Mottola, Ph.D. Introduction by Robert W. Gleason, S.J. (D170) – 85¢

A NEWMAN READER: An Anthology of the Writings of John Henry Cardinal Newman – Edited with an Introduction by Francis X. Connolly (D171) – $1.45

WITH LOVE AND LAUGHTER – Sister Maryanna, O.P. (D172) – 95¢

THE GOLDEN STRING – Bede Griffiths, O.S.B. (D173) – 75¢

THESE ARE THE SACRAMENTS – Described by Fulton J. Sheen. Photos by Karsh (D174) – 95¢

FRANCIS: A Biography of the Saint of Assisi – Michael de la Bedoyere (D175) – 85¢

THE WAY OF PERFECTION – St. Teresa of Avila. Translated and edited by E. Allison Peers (D176) – 85¢

REFLECTIONS ON AMERICA – Jacques Maritain (D177) – 75¢

THE HIDDEN STREAM – Ronald Knox. Some fundamental precepts of the Catholic faith (D178) – 75¢

THE CATHOLIC REFORMATION (2 Volumes) – Henri Daniel-Rops (D179a, D179b) – $1.25 ea.

WE HOLD THESE TRUTHS: Catholic Reflections on the American Proposition – John Courtney Murray, S.J. (D181) – $1.25

LETTERS FROM VATICAN CITY – Xavier Rynne (D182) – 95¢

LIFE AND HOLINESS – Thomas Merton. Exposition of the principles of the spiritual life (D183) – 75¢

A MAN NAMED JOHN: The Life of Pope John XXIII – Alden Hatch (D184) – 95¢

MY LIFE WITH CHRIST – Anthony J. Paone, S.J. (D185) – 95¢

THE EMERGING LAYMAN: The Role of the Catholic Layman in America – Donald J. Thorman (D186) – 85¢

A FAMILY ON WHEELS: Further Adventures of the Trapp Family Singers – Maria Augusta Trapp with Ruth T. Murdoch (D187) – 85¢

OTHER IMAGE BOOKS

OTHER IMAGE BOOKS

A WOMAN CLOTHED WITH THE SUN – Edited by John J. Delaney (D118) – 85¢

INTERIOR CASTLE – St. Teresa of Avila. Translated with an Introduction and Notes by E. Allison Peers (D120) – 95¢

THE GREATEST STORY EVER TOLD – Fulton Oursler (D121) – $1.25

THE MEANING OF MAN – Jean Mouroux. The significance of man and his relation to God (D122) – $1.25

WE AND OUR CHILDREN – Mary Reed Newland. Counsels for molding the child in Christian virtues (D123) – 95¢

SOUL OF THE APOSTOLATE – Jean-Baptiste Chautard, O.C.S.D. (D124) – 85¢

THE SONG AT THE SCAFFOLD – Gertrud von Le Fort. A novel of faith during the French revolution (D126) – 65¢

THE CHURCH OF APOSTLES AND MARTYRS (2 Volumes) – Henri Daniel-Rops (D128a, D128b) – $1.35 ea.

LATE HAVE I LOVED THEE – Ethel Mannin. A deeply moving novel of spiritual regeneration (D130) – $1.25

ST. JOAN OF ARC – John Beevers (D131) – 75¢

A HISTORY OF PHILOSOPHY: VOLUME 1 – GREECE AND ROME (2 Volumes) – Frederick Copleston, S.J. (D134a, D134b) – $1.25 ea.

A HISTORY OF PHILOSOPHY: VOLUME 2 – MEDIAEVAL PHILOSOPHY (2 Volumes) – Frederick Copleston, S.J. Part I – Augustine to Bonaventure. Part II – Albert the Great to Duns Scotus (D135a, D135b) – $1.25 ea.

A HISTORY OF PHILOSOPHY: VOLUME 3 – LATE MEDIAEVAL AND RENAISSANCE PHILOSOPHY (2 Volumes) – Frederick Copleston, S.J. Part I – Ockham to the Speculative Mystics. Part II – The Revival of Platonism to Suárez (D136a, D136b) – $1.25 ea.

A HISTORY OF PHILOSOPHY: VOLUME 4 – MODERN PHILOSOPHY: Descartes to Leibniz – Frederick Copleston, S.J. (D137) – $1.45

A HISTORY OF PHILOSOPHY: VOLUME 5 – MODERN PHILOSOPHY: The British Philosophers, Hobbes to Hume (2 Volumes) – Frederick Copleston, S.J. Part I – Hobbes to Paley. Part II – Berkeley to Hume (D138a, D138b) – $1.25 ea.

A HISTORY OF PHILOSOPHY: VOLUME 6 – MODERN PHILOSOPHY (2 Volumes) – Frederick Copleston, S.J. Part I – The French Enlightenment to Kant (D139a) – 95¢. Part II – Kant (D139b) – $1.25

A HISTORY OF PHILOSOPHY: VOLUME 7 – MODERN PHILOSOPHY (2 Volumes) – Frederick Copleston, S.J. Part I – Fichte to Hegel. Part II – Schopenhauer to Nietzsche (D140a, D140b) – $1.25 ea.

OTHER IMAGE BOOKS